Perception and Illusion

Historical Perspectives

Library of the History of
Psychological Theories

Series Editor: Robert W. Rieber, *City University of New York, New York, NY*

PERCEPTION AND ILLUSION
Historical Perspectives

Nicholas J. Wade

A continuation Order Plan is available for this series. A continuation order will bring delivery of each new volume immediately upon publication. Volumes are billed only upon actual shipment. For further information please contact the publisher.

Perception and Illusion
Historical Perspectives

Nicholas J. Wade
University of Dundee
Dundee, United Kingdom

Springer
the language of science

Library of Congress Cataloging-in-Publication Data

A C.I.P. Catalogue record for this book is available from the Library of Congress.

ISBN 0-387-22722-9   e-ISBN 0-387-22723-7   Printed on acid-free paper.

Printed in the United States of America.

9 8 7 6 5 4 3 2 1

springeronline.com

To Daisy and Sam

Preface

Our contact with the world is through perception, and therefore the study of the process is of obvious importance and significance. For much of its long history, the study of perception has been confined to naturalistic observation. Nonetheless, the phenomena considered worthy of note have not been those that nurture our survival—the veridical features of perception—but the oddities or departures from the common and commonplace accuracies of perception. With the move from the natural world to the laboratory the oddities of perception multiplied, and they received ever more detailed scrutiny.

My general intention is to examine the interpretations of the perceptual process and its errors throughout history. The emphasis on errors of perception might appear to be a narrow approach, but in fact it encompasses virtually all perceptual research from the ancients until the present. The constancies of perception have been taken for granted whereas departures from constancies (errors or illusions) have fostered fascination. Philosophical approaches to perception have been based on observations, and it is the latter that are at the forefront of the present book. The methods of recording observations have become more refined, but this has not resulted in an increased concern with veridicality. Rather, the range of illusions that are studied has exploded. Illusions in this context refer to perceptual departures from veridicality, rather than the constrained variety of geometrical-optical illusions that sprang forth in the late nineteenth century. Any study of illusions is predicated on an assumption of a standard from which the errors can be assessed. The standards themselves have changed over the centuries, largely as a consequence of developments in the physical and life sciences. Accordingly, the nature of perceptual error will itself be examined before surveying the seen.

Thus, my intention is to treat perception, and principally vision, as an observational discipline. Recording the consequences of perception started long before written reports were kept, and so art will be encompassed within this purview. Writers have remarked on their own visual experiences since writing was invented, so that a large body of observations has accumulated. This body is dissected in the present volume. Descriptions of visual experience are likely to be anchored in a more solid environment than the theories proposed to account for them because the theories themselves have been dependent upon concepts derived from other disciplines. The function of vision is to guide our behavior, and in so far as this guidance is successful, there might seem to be little in the subject to warrant enquiry. Indeed, the eternally entertained theory of naive realism speaks to this issue—the world is as it is perceived. Nonetheless, there were circumstances in which the phenomena of vision were remarkable and remarked upon. Visual experiences in darkness (as a consequence of pressure or a blow applied to the eyeball) were not only remarked upon around 500 B.C., but they could have provided the phenomenal source for emission theories of vision—that light issues from the eye itself. Such theories might seem fanciful to us now, but the phenomena upon which they are based are as readily experienced today as they were two and a half thousand years ago, and descriptions of them have been repeatedly refined throughout that period. Afterimages provide a similar example; they can be seen following exposure to bright light, they take on the shape of the intense stimulus, and they linger for an appreciable time. They could have acted, together with the reflections seen in water and in the eye, as a basis for the belief that vision was mediated by images or copies of external objects. These phenomena and many others require an interpretation by any adequate theory of vision; the theories might be supplanted but the phenomena remain.

Science involves recording and interpreting natural phenomena. Nowadays, the records are the results of experiments and the many and varied phenomena are posited in well-defined compartments, like physics, physiology, and psychology. These compartments are a relatively recent convention, as are the specialists who labor under titles such as physicists, physiologists, and psychologists. Neither the phenomena nor the practitioners were so clearly defined in the distant past. In antiquity science, if such it should be called, was based upon describing and classifying observations of naturally occurring events. The sense of science was sight, and vision itself was an integral part of the development of science. What was seen could be described, cataloged, and even subjected to mathematical analysis. Plato's approach to natural phenomena, however, did not encourage the observational analysis of vision, because of his distrust of the evidence of the senses: the world of appearances was considered to be a world of illusions, and the essence of thought was to be sought in mathematics and ideal forms. Plato's idealism remained a dominant force in both science and philosophy. His preference for mathematics over matter influenced Euclid, who formulated a theory of vision in geometrical terms, with little concern for perceptual experience itself. These approaches to vision contrasted sharply with that of Aristotle, who placed more reliance on the evidence of his senses than on philosophical speculations.

The phenomena most intimately involved with vision were those of light. Indeed, the distinction between light and sight was not seriously entertained until Kepler described the optical properties of the eye, early in the seventeenth century. Before Kepler, vision was essential to optics, and disorders of vision provided materials for medicine. Accordingly, histories of optics and ophthalmology have focused on vision during their early phases, but have tended to subordinate it when either the physical nature of light was established or the dioptrics, anatomy, and physiology of the eye were better understood. Interpretations of the perceptual process continue to evolve and the present survey will consider developments in the twentieth century as well as those from earlier times.

The book reflects various strands of historical reseach in perception that have excited my interest. These interests have been shared with others, to whom thanks are due. Mike Swanston, Mike Cowles, Hiro Ono, Helen Ross, Stan Finger, Dieter Heller, Ben Tatler, Frans Verstraten, and Alan Wilkes have all helped to shape my thoughts regarding historical issues. The errors that survived their shaping should not, of course, be associated with them but must reflect my reluctance to follow more appropriate lines of enquiry. My greatest support has derived from my wife, Christine. However, it is not to her that the book is dedicated, but to our two new grandchildren born during its writing.

Contents

1

Recording Observations

The perceptual process commences with stimulation of the senses. The electrochemical activities initiated in the sensory receptors trigger nerve impulses in the sensory nerves which are relayed to the brain. Behavior can, and usually does, result from this sequence of events. Thus, these behaviors provide records of action of the senses. In one species, *homo sapiens*, the range of behaviors is broad and includes describing the experiences initiated by sensory stimulation and the links it might have with previous stimulations. We refer to these as observations and we associate them with verbal descriptions. Observations provide the bedrock of perception and of other actions of the brain. Records of observation precede records of their verbal descriptions, as will be discussed in the context of visual art. Verbal descriptions of observations were refined by Greek philosophers, who also introduced theories to account for the characteristics of perception. Both types of record will be described in this chapter—the artistic and the verbal. Relatively little is known about the origins of visual art; examples of marks made on tools and cave walls have been dated to many thousands of years ago. The adoption of experimental methods to record observations is a more recent development. An early example can be found in the work of Claudius Ptolemy (ca. 100–170) on optics, but it was more widely adopted after the investigations of Isaac Newton (1642–1727) on color phenomena.

The senses have evolved to make and maintain adaptive contact with the environment. Receptors for sources of environmental energy that have proved beneficial for survival have emerged and become more specialized for the needs of each species. Through the action of the senses an organism seeks sustenance, shelter, and sex in order to survive and reproduce. The process was described more poetically by that giant of evolution, Erasmus Darwin (1731–1802, the grandfather of Charles Darwin, 1809–1882). He wrote, in the first volume of *Zoonomia*: "The three great objects of desire, which changed the forms of many animals by their exertions to gratify them, are those of lust, hunger, and security" (E. Darwin, 1794, p. 506). Thus, there is sensitivity to the visual, auditory, aromatic, and tactile characteristics of a mate, the smell, taste, texture, and appearance of food would be sought, and the environmental features that afford protection from the elements will be selected and fought over. As Erasmus Darwin hinted at, and Charles Darwin clarified and amplified, individual members of species compete for these resources and adapt to changes in the environment. Charles also indicated that communication via the senses provides social intercourse that assists survival and accelerates the transmission of useful information. This occurred in species before humankind, but it is with human perception that we are principally concerned.

The senses of all species have become adapted to the demands of their survival and reproduction, and there is a great variety in the ways in which senses have evolved. The concern of this book is not on this variety but on the particular characteristics of human senses and the sources to which they are sensitive. In addition, the senses are linked to an intricately organized brain, which has evolved to extract more that the elements of material sustenance. It furnishes us with intellectual sustenance, too, and extracts from the patterns of sensory stimulation links to language and thought. Humans not only use their senses they muse about them, too.

Paradoxically, much of this musing has concerned minor errors of perception (often called illusions) rather than the constancies of what we perceive. For humans, experience of the world is generally stable, and the ability to perceive it is easily taken for granted. Objects have positions, shapes and colors that seem to be perceived instantly, and we can reach for them or move to where they are, without any apparent effort. We can recognize small differences between objects and we can categorize them despite small differences. Clearly, there must be some process that gives rise to visual experience, and it is not surprising that throughout history students of the senses have found it fascinating. A variety of questions arise from such considerations and have been asked since antiquity. If what we perceive is what we take to be true or factual about the world, are everyone's experiences the same? What is the perceptual world of infants like? What sorts of mistakes do we make in perceiving? Can perceptual experience be communicated to others? Artists, philosophers, physicians, and psychologists have tried to find answers to such questions, which can be considered among the most fundamental that can be posed about the human mind.

While we perceive the world around us with alacrity and ease, we have no direct knowledge of how this experience comes about. In fact, it can often be hard to believe that there is any mechanism involved in perception at all; for most people, most of the time, perceptions are simply 'given' as facts about the world that are obviously correct. Perception is not only a basic psychological process, but also a very remarkable one. Its success in providing us with accurate information about the characteristics of the world around us is an index of its power, because there are relatively few situations in which it is sufficiently in error to expose us to danger. A perceptual process that gave rise to subjective experiences grossly different from physical reality would make survival virtually impossible. The function of perception is not to furnish us with subjective impressions of our surroundings and the significant objects in the environment. Rather, it is to provide an effective platform for action.

In evolutionary terms the function of perception is to enable us to interact with the objects in the world surrounding us. Perceptions guide behavior. Vision is used to determine the location of objects with respect to the perceiver, so that they can be approached, grasped, cast aside, or avoided as appropriate for survival. Perceiving the location of objects and recognizing them is achieved when the body is stationary or moving, or if the objects themselves move. Accordingly, it is necessary to distinguish between static and moving objects whether the perceiver is static or moving.

Perception engages all the senses but the language in which our experiences are expressed tends to reflect the operation of particular senses. It might seem as though the senses work in isolation rather than in concert. The vocabulary of the senses is not evenly distributed either. Vision has the lion's share of words as well as work associated with our perceptual experiences. Moreover, within vision finer distinctions are made. Contour and color are often considered as separate features of the objects to be processed. This results in space and color being treated as independent aspects of vision, and students tend to pursue one or the other. This was not the case when the initial steps were made at recording perception. The early artists used their skills to decorate and depict with whatever means were at their disposal.

Humans enjoy contemplating the experiences provided by the senses, and much of our language is associated with describing them. In human cultures considerable effort is devoted to enhancing perceptual experiences by decorating our bodies and our surroundings and by producing artifacts (like pictures) to stimulate the senses and to channel our contemplations. With so much emphasis on extending our perceptual experiences it is tempting to think of their function as enabling us to enjoy and describe them. Paradoxically, it is in the area of representation that we have the earliest records of human perceptual experience. We have evidence of perception from the past because records have been kept. We associate these records with written texts, but earlier marks of human perception have been left in the art that was produced before writing was invented.

THE PRACTICE OF PERCEPTION

The distinguishing feature of humankind is generally taken as language. Humans can produce sequences of vocalizations that can communicate to others our subjective experiences, and we learn to understand the vocalizations made by others. Because sounds leave no trace, the origins of spoken language are shrouded in mystery. It probably arose from coordinating the cooperative activities of groups of individuals in the search for sustenance and shelter, and it enabled the transmission of ideas afforded by an enlarged cerebral cortex. We have more evidence regarding the origins of text because the marks were often made on surfaces that have been preserved, like clay tablets. Written scripts were invented independently in several different cultures and perhaps the oldest derived from Sumeria over 5000 years ago (see Carr, 1986; Gaur, 1984).

Early written records were mostly concerned with what we now consider mundane—the inventories of goods. These reflected the demands of larger social groupings of humans with increasing differentiation and specialization of skills. The settlements would have been relatively static, animals were domesticated, and ownership of land could be asserted. Nonetheless, long before these cataclysmic changes in human habitation took place, examples of sophisticated visual art had been produced in the caves as far afield as southern Europe and Australia.

These art works, and those that followed in the Egyptian, Greek, and Roman times, reflected the nonverbal records of perception (see Massironi, 2002). It would, however, be inaccurate to consider that these are records of vision unsullied by cognition. From the earliest examples of pictorial representation it is likely that the artificiality of the enterprise was appreciated, and accommodations to this artifice are the changes that have taken place in styles of art (see Wade, 1990). The records of art will be considered first with respect to space and then to color. As noted above, contour and color continue to be used as contrasting dimensions of visual perception.

ART

History is considered to have had its origin with the invention of text some 5000 years ago. Those whose recorded labors were left from earlier times are referred to as prehistoric. This survey of the seen will begin with some remarkable prehistoric signs of perception. Marks made on walls deep in caves located in Southern France and Northern Spain have fascinated historians of art for over a century—since their rediscovery in the late nineteenth century. They have been given less consideration by students of the senses. They were produced up to 30,000 years ago, and we can recognize the animals portrayed. Even some animals, now extinct, were recorded with sufficient accuracy on the cave walls for them to be identified in modern times.

The cave artists were representing objects, usually animals, in a way that could be recognized by themselves and by others who observed the works. They were capturing an aspect of visual space and representing it in a different manner. The objects depicted were solid and dynamic but the depictions themselves were not. They were lacking in the dimensions of depth and motion that the objects possessed. Accordingly, the artists were representing the objects (alluding to them) rather than presenting them. Cave paintings are remarkable sophisticated artistic productions. The artists could not have been painting what they were seeing but what they had seen. That is, the paintings were often found in relatively inaccessible parts of caves, and ones in which no animals, not even dead ones, could have been taken. The artists carried their subjects with them in their heads and painted them from viewpoints that render them recognizable to this day. The animals represented (usually in outline alone) were as if seen from the side—what I have called the stereotypical viewpoint (Wade, 1990). The major asymmetrical axis of the animal was minimally foreshortened. Whether this was the manner in which the mental images were stored or whether the most recognizable paintings were copied by other artists remains a matter of conjecture and controversy.

The aspect of allusion was elaborated further by Greek artists, who attempted to mimic nature more closely. The term 'illusion' is often applied to pictorial images, but 'allusion' would seem to be more appropriate. Pictures are allusions because they refer indirectly to the objects they represent; they are seen both as flat objects and as depicted surfaces apparently separated in depth. An illusion, on the other hand, provides a

unitary impression of size or orientation that happens to contradict physical measurements. I have introduced the distinction between allusions
and illusions to avoid the theoretical confusions attendent on the use of
the term illusion in the context of pictorial depth; there is no duality in the
perception of illusions, whereas it is inherent in figurative paintings and
photographs. Greek paintings have often been referred to as 'illusionistic'.

Gombrich (1960) has referred to the revolution in painting that took
place in early periods of Greek art, during the sixth and fifth centuries B.C.
when the desire to imitate nature was paramount. The artists strived to
make the pictorial representations as lifelike as possible, so that, ideally,
they would be confused with the real objects they represented. Thus, artists
attempted to make the pictorial image match the object so that it would
deceive the eye. In this endeavour Greek painters would have had access to
the developing science of optics, and basic aspects of optical projection, like
foreshortening, could have been incorporated in their pictures. Most of the
surviving examples are on pottery, although some mosaic compositions
still exist.

Thus, attempts at 'illusionistic' painting were produced by Greek
painters, although the term is most commonly applied to the style of linear perspective that was invented at the beginning of the fifteenth century
(see M. Kemp, 1990; Willats, 1997). Pliny the Elder (ca. 23–79), in his *Natural
history*, related the story of rivalry between two Greek painters, Zeuxis and
Parrhasius, in the fifth century B.C.:

> "This last, it is recorded, entered into a competition with Zeuxis, who produced
> a picture of grapes so successfully represented that birds flew to the stage-
> buildings; whereupon Parrhasius himself produced such a realistic picture of a
> curtain that Zeuxis, proud of the verdict of the birds, requested that the curtain
> should now be drawn and the picture displayed; and when he realized his
> mistake, with a modesty that did him honour he yielded up the prize, saying
> that whereas he had deceived birds Parrhasius had deceived him, an artist."
> (Pliny, 1952, pp. 309–311)

No examples of such works have survived, which makes it difficult to
assess their similarity to 'illusionistic' paintings after the Renaissance. The
birds might have been better arbiters of the illusion than were the artists.
Zeuxis, as a retort to Parrhasius, also painted a picture of grapes held
by a child: birds still flew to the painted grapes and were not frightened
away by the pictured boy. Thus, the apparent realism of the human was
not adequate to delude the birds, and the attraction might have been to
color rather than form. The artists, on the other hand, would have made
judgments with regard to their experience of earlier paintings. Prior to the
fifth century B.C. these tended to be outlines enclosing flat colors. Pliny
also stated that Parrhasius "was the first to give proportions to painting

and the first to give vivacity to the expression of the countenance, elegance of the hair and beauty of the mouth" (1952, p. 311).

Roman artists tended to draw considerably on the Greek predecessors, but one area in which they did introduce many points of perceptual interest was mosaics. They embodied within them the principles that were made explicit two thousand years later in Gestalt psychology. Wertheimer's (1923) principles of perceptual grouping found expression in Roman mosaics, as did many features of modern computer based design. Computers produce images made up from small elements or pixels. These vary in color and brightness, and when the myriad of elements are combined they produce a global impression that transcends the local features.

These principles have, however, been embraced by artists for more than two thousand years! Roman mosaics combined both pixelated images and Gestalt principles. The pixels were real rather than virtual, being tesserae, or small cubes of marble, stone, or glass. They were used to represent scenes and to display geometrical decorations. These were produced to formulae, and the same designs were produced throughout the Roman empire. It is in the geometrical motifs that the Gestalt principles were beautifully expressed (see Wade, 2004a). Mosaic designs display figure-ground segregation and reversal, good continuation, shape from shading, and ambiguity in depth. The mosaic artists did not need to provide written descriptions of their works to indicate knowledge of perceptual grouping—the mosaics spoke for them. The methods and designs were maintained over several centuries, and were remarkably similar over the whole Roman empire (see Dunbabin, 1999).

The movement in art thought to have the most intimate contact with perception is linear perspective. It emerged in Florence in the early fifteenth century, and it represented a novel way of capturing visual space on a flat surface. Gombrich (1960) referred to the different modes of representing space as "the riddle of style". He posed the question: "Why is it that different ages and different nations have represented the visible world in such different ways?" (p. 3). This was so despite the acceptance that there can have been little genetic change in humankind over the last few thousand years: the cave dwellers would have seen their world in much the same way as we do ours, although the contents of those worlds differed greatly. Objects would have been seen as having specific sizes and locations; they could be approached and grasped or avoided; some, like other animals, moved and their motion through space could be predicted. Survival would not be possible if we did not see the objects in the environment as constant despite changes in our positions with respect to them. One of the aspects that has not remained constant over time is how the objects are represented pictorially. Radical changes of style took place in the ways objects were depicted over the last 30,000 years of recorded art.

The ancient texts on optics, when they were reintroduced to the West from the thirteenth century, were called *Perspectiva* and they treated direct vision. The term perspective was derived from such texts, which often described aspects of pictorial representation and theatrical scene painting. However, linear perspective had a particular significance in the Renaissance because it reflected a return to the Greek pictorial ideal of attempting to imitate nature. The rules of perspective were devised in the intellectual cauldron of early fifteenth century Florence. Linear perspective was demonstrated by architect and painter Filippo Brunelleschi (1377–1446) and formalised by a contemporary mathematician, Leon Battista Alberti (1404–1472). Basically it was derived from the optics of Euclid (ca. 323–283 B.C.). He analyzed vision in terms of a cone emanating from the eye. Perspective is the application of Euclid's visual cone to a glass plane intersecting it, and this device is now known as Alberti's window. Thus, the principles of reducing a three-dimensional scene to a two-dimensional picture were formulated before the image forming properties of the eye had been described (see Chapter 4).

Science and art meet in perspective. Perhaps it should more accurately be said that the optics of antiquity met the art of the Renaissance in the context of linear perspective. The technique of perspective painting was rapidly adopted by artists from that time onwards, and many textbooks described its rules. There are some excellent treatments of the history of perspective, but that by Kemp (1990) is especially instructive because it deals with the emergence of linear perspective in the fifteenth century, and its subsequent development. Greek artists also applied some form of perspective, as Edgerton (1975) argued elegantly.

Linear perspective involves specifying a station point, picture plane, ground plane, and vanishing point enabling depiction of a single image of a scene. Alberti described the rules for capturing the image, and a number of techniques for representing it. Some of these were mathematical, others involved a grid through which the scene is observed and a similar grid onto which the lines can be drawn. A famous woodcut by Albrecht Dürer (1471–1528) shows an artist painting a model using such a system. A gnomon or sighting vane was used in order to define a station point, and the figure was viewed with the eye as close to it as possible. Perhaps the simplest means of drawing in perspective was the application of Alberti's window. If a single eye is maintained at a fixed position with respect to a window then the objects in the scene beyond the window can be represented in accurate perspective simply by tracing their outlines on the surface of the window. Another device, which combined the science and art of optics, was

marshalled by some artists to form images in accurate central perspective—
the *camera obscura* (a dark chamber or what is now called a pinhole camera).
Representations of solid objects on two-dimensional surfaces, following
the rules of linear perspective, were assisted by using the *camera obscura*.
A rudimentary form of the instrument was described by Ibn al-Haytham
(ca. 965–1039); he was known as Alhazen after his book on *Optics* was
translated into Latin and he will be referred to as such throughout this book.
Leonardo da Vinci (1472–1519) also likened the eye to a camera and carried
out some simple experiments on image formation (see Wade and Finger,
2001). Despite these fertile suggestions, the *camera obscura* was used more
extensively by artists rather than by scientists. This was the case mainly
because the optics and anatomy of the eye were only dimly discerned before
the seventeenth century, and so its relevance to vision was not appreciated.

Although Leonardo did see the significance of the functioning of the
camera to that of the eye, the contemporary knowledge of optics did not
enable him to represent the manner in which light was brought to a focus
in the eye (see Strong, 1979). Rather than use his model of the eye, he used
his eyes themselves to probe the nature of the physical world and our perception of it. Leonardo's observational skills were without equal, and he
was acutely aware of the distinction between viewing a scene and a pictorial representation if it: "A Painting, though conducted with the greatest
Art and finished to the last Perfection, both with regard to its Contours,
its Lights, its Shadows and its Colours, can never show a *Relievo* equal to
that of Natural Objects, unless these be view'd at a Distance and with a
single Eye" (1721, p. 178). That is, the perception of depth is incomplete in
a painting unlike that for a scene viewed with two eyes.

Leonardo acknowledged that the distinction involved seeing with one
or two eyes, and he struggled long and hard with the contrast between
monocular and binocular vision. As noted above, Alberti described how a
painting could be constructed in perspective by interposing a transparent
surface through which the scene was viewed:

> "When they [painters] fill the circumscribed places with colours, they should
> only seek to present the forms of things seen on this plane as if it were of
> transparent glass. Thus the visual pyramid could pass through it, placed at a
> definite distance with definite lights and a definite position of the centre in space
> and in a definite place in respect to the observer." (Alberti, 1435/1966, p. 51)

Accordingly, Leonardo was able to utilize the concept of Alberti's window, which provided a monocular match between a picture and a view of
a scene from a single point. The question remained concerning what happens when two viewpoints are adopted. Leonardo examined this many
times in the context of a small object lying in front of a background. He

returned to the issue repeatedly as indicated by the many diagrams he made of it. In each instance, vision with two eyes was optically and phenomenally different from that with one. The example he used, of viewing a sphere with a diameter less than the distance separating the eyes, reflected one condition Euclid analyzed, but Leonardo added the characteristic of seeing the whole background (see Wade, Ono, and Lillakas, 2001).

Every time Leonardo returned to the problem, he came to the same conclusion that he could not depict correctly on canvas everything he saw with two eyes. In short, he was unable to simulate what he saw with two eyes. Alberti's procedures simulate the monocular visual world on a canvas, but not that of the binocular visual world. Leonardo produced many drawings which represented both binocular and monocular observation of a small sphere. The accompanying texts emphasize the differences between viewing a scene and a painting of it in terms of perceived depth and the amount of the background that is visible. In his *Optics* Euclid described the consequences of viewing spheres that were smaller than, the same size, and larger than the separation between the eyes (see Burton, 1945). Euclid's discussion was restricted to the amount of the sphere that was visible in each case, with no reference to what was visible beyond the spheres. When the sphere was smaller than the interocular separation then more than a hemisphere was seen.

Leonardo saw not only the benefits that could derive from the application of the rules of linear perspective but he also made the first systematic distortions of these rules. Soon after central perspective had been widely adopted in art, it was distorted in the form of accelerated and decelerated perspective architectures and anamorphic paintings. Descriptions of reversals of apparent depth were recorded long before the formalization of rules for linear perspective (see Wade, 1998a), although most attention was paid to reverse perspective in the nineteenth century; Wallin (1905) described these studies in detail. In anamorphic art the appropriate viewpoint differs from normal or perpendicular to the picture plane, so that the pictorial content can only be seen when the picture is viewed awry or through some appropriate optical device like a cylindrical mirror (see Baltrusaitis, 1976). However, one of the most pervasive forms of manipulation has been the many and varied attempts to fool the eye *(trompe l'oeil)* with flat paintings. Successful examples of *trompe l'oeil* are rare, and those that do succeed usually place constraints on the viewer. For example, Samuel van Hoogstraten's (1627–1678) perspective cabinet in the National Gallery (London) has a single viewing aperture on either side, and Andrea Pozzo's (1642–1709) ceiling painting "Apotheosis of St Ignatius" in the church of St Ignatius (Rome) defines a viewing position on the floor (see Pirenne, 1970). These have been referred to as visual illusions rather than visual allusions to depth that are seen with conventional perspective pictorial images. That is, they produce a unified and compelling percept of a depth that is not present on the painted surface; the conflicting cues provided by binocular vision and pictorial framing are either not operating (as in van Hoogstraten's cabinet) or are not applicable due to the dimensions and structure of the pictorial image (as with Pozzo's ceiling).

The first anamorphoses probably came to the West from China. These were analysed mathematically and optically by Jean-François Nicéron (1613–1646; 1646) in his book on curious perspectives. He produced linear, conical and cylindrical anamorphoses. The principles behind these anamorphoses are those that Adelbert Ames (1880–1955) applied in his famous perceptual demonstrations (see Ittelson, 1952).

COLOR

Artists were faced with the practicalities of mixing different colored pigments long before color mixing became a scientific concern. The rules for their combination were rough and ready, but they served the purposes of the artists, and were commented upon by philosophers. Plato (427–347 B.C.) provided some basic examples of mixing pigments, but he despaired of any exact rules of combination being achieved; he considered that rules for the separation and mixing of colors would never be determined by "a child of man sufficient for either of these tasks". Aristotle (ca. 384–322 B.C.), on the other hand, made the astute observation that some colors could not be derived from mixing, and that these corresponded to those visible in the rainbow: "There are colours which they [painters] create by mixing, but no mixing will give red, green, or purple. These are the colours of the rainbow, though between the red and the green an orange colour is often seen" (Ross, 1931, p. 372a).

As we shall note for the perception of space, it was Ptolemy who added the experimental dimension to color mixing. He was able to show that a disc with different colors painted on it will combine the colors when rotated:

> "A similar phenomenon [of color mixing] occurs from very fast motion: for example, from the motion of a rotating disk of many colors, because one and the same visual ray does not linger upon one and the same color, since the color recedes from it [the visual ray] on account of the speed of rotation. And thus the same ray, falling on all colors, cannot distinguish between the first and the most recent, nor between those that are in diverse locations. For all the colors appear throughout the whole disk at the same time as though they were one color—which would be a similar color to the one that would actually occur from color mixtures. For the same reason, if points that are on the disk, although not

on the center of rotation, were marked in a different color from that of the disk, they would appear like circles of uniform color when in rapid rotation. But if they were marked out on a line set on the disk and going through its axis, the surface of the disk will appear to have a uniform color throughout the whole rotation. For when color rotates about a distance perceptible to sight in the same perceived temporal moment, it is deemed to spread itself over all places through which it travels. For the phenomenon that occurs in the first rotation is always followed later by repetitions of the same sort." (Translated from Lejeune, 1956, pp. 60–61)

Within Greek science, color was considered in terms of an analogy with the four elements, and of these fire and water were predominant. The numeration of four basic colors was clearly stated by Democritus (ca. 460–370 B.C.); they were white, black, red, and green: "each of these colours is the purer the less the admixture of other figures. The other colours are derived from these by mixture" (Stratton, 1917, p. 135). Moreover, he adapted the concept of pores in the eye to account for color vision: only when the geometrical shapes associated with particular colors corresponded to those of the pores would color be experienced. Both Plato and Aristotle considered that color was of paramount importance in perception, and that it could be dissociated from light. They appreciated that pigments could be extracted from certain substances, and they were well aware of the ways in which they could be mixed by artists. However, they stressed the importance of black and white: Plato treated them as opposites, and Aristotle considered that all colors could be made up from these two. Consequently, despite the equation of colors with the four elements, black and white tended to dominate the analyses of color until the time of Leonardo da Vinci.

The rainbow was an obvious and remarkable natural phenomenon in which a range of colors could be experienced. Aristotle discussed the rainbow in his *Meteorology* and was aware of the limited range of atmospheric circumstances accompanying its visibility (see Pendergrast, 2003; Zemplen, 2004). A variety of theories for the rainbow was advanced, but the situation changed with experimental investigations of prismatic colors. Although the occurrence of colors, due to light passing through or reflected from glass or crystals, had been known of since antiquity their experimental examination had not been undertaken. A preliminary study of the prismatic spectrum was conducted by Thomas Harriot (ca. 1560–1621) at the beginning of the seventeenth century, and it was subjected to more detailed scrutiny later in the century. René Descartes (1596–1650; 1637) treated the analysis of colors visible in the rainbow in his discourses on *Meteorology*. His mechanistic interpretation of visible colors was in harmony with his concept of light generally: colors corresponded to different rates of rotation of bodies in the medium.

Newton demonstrated experimentally that sunlight (white light) is made up of rays that can be bent or refracted by different amounts when passing through a prism, so forming the visible spectrum. He conducted experiments with a prism from 1666, reporting the results in a paper to a meeting of the Royal Society on 6 February 1672; it was published in the *Philosophical Transactions* later that year. The paper stimulated widespread interest as well as opposition, particularly from Robert Hooke (1635–1703) and Christiaan Huygens (1629–1695), who argued that there were only two basic colors. Hooke and Huygens represented the traditional position, in which the spectral colors were considered to be modifications of white light rather than white light consisting of separate components.

The controversy stirred by the theory so perturbed Newton that he did not publish his full account of it until his *Opticks* appeared in 1704. By this time, he was President of the Royal Society, and Hooke had died so that he was no longer a threat. Newton was aware that the range of refractions from a prism was continuous and yet the colors seen were restricted in number. He reported seven colors—red, orange, yellow, green, blue, indigo, and violet—and he arranged them in a particular circular sequence, after the manner of the musical scale. Colored lights could be combined in such a way that their compounds were defined with respect to the color circle. Combinations of primary colors that were opposite one another on the circle produced a whitish compound that was positioned near the center.

Much of the subsequent debate focused on the nature and number of primary colors. For Newton, who introduced the term in 1672, they were the discrete colors that could be seen in the prismatic spectrum, despite his appreciation of continuity across the spectrum. With the formulation of the color circle they also became the colors from which compounds could be derived. Thomas Young (1773–1829) proposed that red, green, and blue were primaries, and that the vast range of colors that could be produced by appropriate combinations of a small number of primaries led to speculations regarding the physiological basis of color vision. This was the basis for the trichromatic theory of color vision. Young (1802a) also speculated that color vision could be mediated by retinal mechanisms that responded selectively to each of the three primaries.

Newton had shifted the analysis of color towards the physical dimension, while not excluding the subjectivity of color perception. He also used the analysis of white light into its spectral components to synthesize new colors. For Greek scholars color seemed to be a property of objects: it could be extracted from some plants and ores, in order to produce pigments that could be mixed with one another. Nonetheless, the belief in the purity of white was retained by some long after Newton's experiments on the prismatic spectrum. The most notable instance of this was Johann Wolfgang von Goethe (1749–1832), who sought to shift the study of vision away from physics and towards phenomenology. In phenomenological terms white was pure and indivisible.

Newton's approach to the analysis of color was based on mixing lights from different parts of the spectrum. The alternative approach, based on color experience, was championed by Goethe (1810/1840). Newton had stated that "the Rays to speak properly are not coloured", thus accepting the subjective dimension in color vision, but he did not subordinate the physics of light to the philosophy of sight in the manner of Goethe. One of Goethe's greatest difficulties was reconciling the purity of the perception of white light with the conception of its compound nature. However, he was able to enlist a variety of phenomena (like color contrasts, color shadows, accidental colors, and aspects of color blindness) which posed severe difficulties for the trichromatic theory. Despite the wealth of observations contained in his *Theory of colours* few students of vision saw Goethe's theory as other than evidence of the distance that separated art from science. In a lecture surveying Goethe's scientific researches, Hermann Ludwig Ferdinand von Helmholtz (1821–1894) attempted to take a sympathetic view by stating that he was primarily a poet, and that he was not disposed to support experimental enquiries into natural phenomena: "Thus, in the theory of colour, Goethe remains faithful to his principle, that Nature must reveal her secrets of her own free will; that she is but the transparent representation of the ideal world" (Helmholtz, 1895, p. 45).

OPTICS

Art is the application of vision, following certain procedural rules, of which linear perspective is the most familiar. Pictorial art is faced with the problem of representing solid objects on a flat surface. Visual principles are involved in this compression, and insights into the visual process were derived from the many experiments that artists made in plying their trade. Nonetheless, the principles of linear perspective were not influenced by theories of light and sight; it mattered not whether the light was emitted from the eye or received by it. As long as the rays traveled in straight lines, the rules of perspective could be applied. The scope of visual art and visual science was extended by the application of many novel devices, particularly those invented in the early nineteenth century, which were referred to as philosophical toys (see Chapter 5).

When Johannes Kepler (1571–1630; 1604) provided an account of how light passed through the transparent structures of the eye to form a focused image on the retina, the analogy of the eye with a camera (containing a lens) could be exploited fully. It also resulted in an acceptance of reception theories of light. If light was focused by the lens onto the retina then there was no need for emission of light from the eye. Optics was being displaced to the domain of physics rather than remaining in the province of perception. However, Kepler did not have available to him an adequate account of the anatomy of the eye. This was provided by Christoph Scheiner (1571–1650) in 1619. Thereafter, speculations about functions of the eye (like accommodation) could be guided by the operation of a camera, and artificial eyes could be constructed which followed similar laws of optics. For example, Scheiner (1630) illustrated corrections that could be applied to eyes and cameras for errors of refraction. Thus, the camera was probably the first philosophical toy, as it could be applied to art and science. Less than two decades later, Athanasius Kircher (1602–1680; 1646) illustrated the manner in which an image is formed in the eye, and employed similar optical principles to project images in dark room. He also provided an illustration the magic lantern, which was to entertain and astound the wider public until the photographic camera supplanted it.

In the late 1830s, when the camera was wedded to light sensitive metal plates by Louis Jaques Mandé Daguerre (1789–1851) or to chemically coated paper by William Henry Fox Talbot (1800–1877) its influence on art was immense. Although the camera had long been known, fixing images formed within it was a novelty. This period was also noted for the invention of a variety of instruments that could assist both artists and scientists. The camera enabled artists to capture scenes in perspective with comparative ease, whereas scientists could consider the eye as a similar optical instrument.

GREEK SCIENCE AND PERCEPTION

For two thousand years, prior to the scientific enlightenment, the interpretation of mental processes in the western world was dominated by the wisdom of Greek philosophers. They brought some degree of order to the study of mind, although the ideas they expressed were widely divergent. Much the same applied to the study of perception. The principal contrast that existed was between those who sought to observe and try to account for those observations and those who considered that thought was above perception. The observational tradition has grappled with the vagaries of perception—the differences that occur over time and the contrasts that can take place in an instant. The representatives of this approach are taken as Aristotle and his pupil, Theophrastus (ca. 370–286 B.C.). The rational tradition searched for constancies beyond the moment of perception. For some, like Plato, these were to be found in ideal forms that were not expressed via perception but by thought. For others, like Euclid, recourse to mathematics and optics was the way in which the vagaries of vision could be transcended. The contrast between observation and optics will run through this book, and it can be found in contemporary approaches to vision.

THE IDEAL AND THE OBSERVABLE

Greek philosophers, like Greek physicians, had absorbed many ideas from previous cultures, and thus it is a gross oversimplification to commence as though the ideas were generated by them. Nonetheless, they did present their views with relative clarity and many of their writings have survived, so that their observations remain accessible to us. The contrast of convenience is that between the near contemporaries Plato and Aristotle, because the concepts they embraced continue to be argued over and incorporated in theories of perception to this day. Plato distrusted the senses and sought truth through abstract reasoning whereas Aristotle viewed the senses as an important source of knowledge about the external world. These distinctions are at the heart of rationalism and empiricism.

Plato believed that the world of appearances was one of illusion, as opposed to the world of thought in which ideal forms existed. The forms reflected universal qualities of objects rather than features which could be sensed. The abstract forms could be investigated by reasoning rather than observation, and this resulted in a preference for rational rather than empirical enquiry. Plato's position demonstrates the influence that language has had on philosophical thought: particular members of a category that are given a single name (e.g., horse) do not reflect their universal characteristics. The senses are concerned with particulars rather than universals and so were not considered to furnish useful knowledge.

Plato distinguished between the body and the soul: the body was part of the material world whereas the soul was immaterial. He likened the rational soul to a charioteer steering the competing horses of emotion and appetite; the rational soul was considered to be morally superior to the others and should guide their actions. These distinctions were to have considerable significance because they later permeated both philosophy and theology. Mind-body dualism provides the foundation of Descartes' philosophy as well as a constant current in Christian theology. The latter also placed great emphasis on the moral superiority of reason over irrational feelings and passions. Nonetheless, Plato's awe of the eye and vision was stated thus:

> "Vision, in my view, is the cause of the greatest benefit to us, inasmuch as none of the accounts now given concerning the Universe would ever have been given

if men had not seen the stars or the sun or the heaven. But as it is, the vision of day and night and of months and circling years has created the art of number and has given us not only the notion of Time but also a means of research into the nature of the Universe." (1946, p. 107)

Plato was a philosopher and a poet whereas Aristotle was a scientist and a systematic teacher. Aristotle was one of Plato's students but displayed detachment from his mentor in developing his own philosophy. Aristotle adopted more naturalistic explanations of phenomena which did not denigrate the senses. He was interested in universals but believed that they could best be understood by the study of particulars. Therefore he preferred an empirical approach to a rational one. He is often considered to be the first psychologist because of his emphasis on observation and because he tried to order phenomena in a systematic manner. Many of his classifications of natural phenomena are still used, and he studied a broad range, from botany to behavior. He placed humans at one end of a continuum of living things that extended to plants. The distinguishing feature was the possession of mind—the ability to reason.

Aristotle's studies of the senses were extensive and he suggested that sensations were brought together to form a common sense, which he located in the heart. He added to the phenomena of vision by describing afterimages, aftereffects, and binocular double vision. He argued that light was received by the eyes rather than emitted from them; the latter view was held by most of his contemporaries. He discussed many other psychological phenomena including remembering, thinking, dreaming, and development.

THE FIVE SENSES

The origins of sciences are based on taxonomies, and many of these are rooted in Greek philosophy. Description and classification precede more detailed analysis. Most of the Greek taxonomies have been replaced as science has developed more sophisticated methods and has adopted an experimental approach to its subject matter. The elements of Greek natural science—earth, air, fire, and water—have been replaced by those of the periodic table. The humoral basis for Greek medicine—black bile, yellow bile, phlegm, and blood—has been replaced by the cell doctrine, and cells themselves are now known for their many specializations. It seems that only in psychology are the ancient taxonomies still alive and well!

Aristotle's five senses of sight, hearing, smell, taste, and touch are rooted in our culture. No matter what science might divine to the contrary, they are so defined in the popular imagination. The prominence of eyes, ears, nose, and tongue on the head, and the specific experiences associated with them, have acted in the past, as well as in the present, to fix these four senses. Touch presents more problems because its sensitivity is not localized to a particular sense organ, and the experiences derived from the skin are many and varied. Aristotle confronted these aspects of anatomy and experience and reached similar conclusions:

> "In dealing with each of the senses we shall have first to speak of the objects which are perceptible by each. . . . I call by the name of special object of this or that sense that which cannot be perceived by any other sense than that one and in respect of which no error is possible; in this sense colour is the special object of sight, sound of hearing, flavour of taste. Touch, indeed, discriminates more than one set of different qualities. Each sense has one kind of object which it discerns, and never errs in reporting that what is before it is colour or sound (though it may err as to what it is that is coloured or where that is, or what is sounding or where that is). Such objects are what we propose to call special objects of this or that sense. 'Common sensibles' are movement, rest, number, figure, magnitude; these are not peculiar to any one sense, but are common to all." (Ross, 1931, p. 418b)

Later in *De anima* Aristotle distinguished between experience and organ: "By a 'sense' is meant what has the power of receiving into itself the sensible forms of things without the matter. . . . By 'an organ of sense' is meant that in which ultimately such a power is seated" (p. 424a). This, again, provided problems for the experience of touch, because there was no specific organ associated with it. Once more, the issue was voiced by Aristotle: "If touch is not a single sense but a group of senses, there must be several kinds of what is tangible. It is a problem whether touch is a single sense or a group of senses. It is also a problem, what is the organ of touch" (p. 422b).

Touch, requiring contact in order to experience it, was often taken as the most important sense, and the one relative to which others could be related. According to Aristotle: "The primary form of sense is touch, which belongs to all animals" (Ross, 1931, p. 413b). It is perhaps for this reason that he maintained that touch is a single sense, that the number of senses is restricted to five, and that: "there cannot be a special sense-organ for the common sensibles either" (p. 425a). Boring's (1942) conclusion about this dogma was clear: "It was certainly Aristotle who so long delayed the recognition of a sixth sense by his doctrine that there are but five senses" (p. 525).

Aristotle's survey of the senses was more extensive than those of his predecessors (see Beare, 1906). Most of the knowledge we have of the earlier Greek commentators derives from the writing of his pupil, Theophrastus. He categorized writers on the senses into two groups: those who considered that the senses were stimulated by similarities or by opposites. Thus, taste and touch could be treated as similar, since both involve contact. The means of sensing by sight, hearing, smell, and taste was speculated upon by most writers, but less was said about touch. For example, with regard to Alcmaeon (fl. 500 B.C.), Theophrastus wrote: "All the senses are connected in some way with the brain; consequently they are incapable of action if <the brain> is disturbed or shifts its position, for <this organ> stops up the passages through which the senses act. Of touch he tells us neither the manner nor the means of its operation" (Stratton, 1917, pp. 89–91).

Alcmaeon located the center of sensation in the brain, although Aristotle did not adopt this view, referring the processes of perception to the heart. In the context of touch, Anaxagoras (ca. 500–438 B.C.) discussed sensing warmth and cold, and Democritus contrasted heavy with light, and hard with soft. Plato wrote that touch distinguished between hot and cold, hard and soft, heavy and light, as well as rough and smooth. Theophrastus himself said relatively little about touch. His theory of the senses in general involved some intermediary between the object and the sense organ; for vision, hearing, and smell this could be more readily maintained than for touch.

Theophrastus did, however, discuss vertigo or dizziness (as when looking down from a great height or after rotating the body) and the visual motion that accompanies it. According to the Roman commentator, Diogenes Laertius (fl. 3rd C), Theophrastus wrote a book on vertigo but it has not survived. Aristotle referred to the visual vertigo that follows drinking too much wine, and later Lucretius (ca. 98–55 B.C.) gave a graphic description of vertigo following rotation of the body: "The room seems to children to be turning round and the columns revolving when they themselves have ceased to turn, so much so that they can hardly believe all the building is not threatening to fall in upon them" (1975, pp. 307–309). Ptolemy was able to induce vertigo by visual means alone: "A continuous revolution of the visual field results in objects appearing to move. Movement of this kind is produced in visual vertigo" (Lejeune, 1956, p. 73).

The approach by Galen (ca. 130–200) to the senses displayed the advantages of anatomical dissection. He berated Aristotle for denying that all the senses do not have connections with the brain: "Hence all the instruments of the senses—if we are to believe our eyes that see and our hands that touch them—communicate with the encephalon" (May, 1968, p. 391). Galen's theory of the senses was physiological, and it was based on the concept of pneuma advocated by Empedocles (ca. 493–433 B.C.): "Unless the alteration in each sense instrument comes from the encephalon and returns to it, the animal will still remain without sense perception" (May, 1968, p. 403). Galen restricted his discussion to the "four sense instruments in the head, namely, the eyes, ears, nose, and tongue, all of which take the source of their sensation from the encephalon" (p. 400). He did refer to vertigo caused by observing whirling patterns as well as by body rotation. These were described in the context of diseases which lead to dizziness:

> "All these affections start obviously in the head and especially the affection which is called *skotoma* (vertigo), the name of which indicates its nature. People who are subject to this ailment are affected by *skotoma* of their vision on account of the smallest causes, so that they often fall, especially when they turn round. Then, what happens to other people only after having turned round a great many times, that will overcome these people after one single turn. They can even be affected by vertigo, when they see another person or a wheel turning or anything else which whirls, even when their head had been overheated for any other reason . . . There is general agreement upon the fact that such frequent turning movements provoke an unequal, tumultuous and disorderly flow of humors and pneuma. Therefore it is only natural that people subject to skotoma are on guard against any motion of this kind." (Siegel, 1970, p. 138)

The situation remained relatively unchanged through the medieval period: "Aristotle's account of sensation and perception was held in great esteem in the Middle Ages, and his systematic approach and many of his specific doctrines were widely copied" (S. Kemp, 1990, p. 35). Attention was directed principally at interpretations of vision, with much less heed paid to the other senses. Developments did occur in fusing Aristotle's account of the senses with Galen's pneumatic physiology, and the medical tradition of describing diseases of the senses became more refined.

The Introduction of Observation

Theophrastus has provided a surviving record of Greek thought about the senses, and he himself added a stricter dimension of observation. The historian George Stratton (1865–1957) remarked that: "An understanding of Greek physiological psychology before Plato and after Aristotle requires that one know his Theophrastus" (1917, p. 5). Stratton's book *Theophrastus and the Greek physiological psychology before Aristotle* consists of a translation from Greek into English of "Theophrastus's work *On the senses*" because it "is the most important source of our knowledge of the earlier Greek physiological psychology" (p. 15). Without it the knowledge of early theories of perception would be even more meager. Indeed, Stratton went so far as to say that "we are indebted to Theophrastus for more than to all the other ancient authorities combined" (p. 16) for a knowledge of Greek psychology before Plato. Not only did Theophrastus outline earlier theories of perception, but the descriptions were often accompanied by fulsome criticisms. For example, Democritus' atomic theory of colors is described thus:

"The simple colors, he says, are four. What is smooth is white; since what neither is rough nor casts shadows nor is hard to penetrate,—all such substances are brilliant.... Black is composed of figures the very opposite <to those of white>,—figures rough, irregular, and differing from one another.... Red is composed of figures such as enter into heat, save that those of red are larger.... Green is composed of both the solid and the void.... The other colors are derived from these by mixture." (Stratton, 1917, pp. 133–135)

Theophrastus points to the contrast between this theory involving four primaries and others which proposed only two (black and white). He then concludes that Democritus:

"should have given some distinctive <figure> to green, as he has to the other colors. And if he holds <green> to be the opposite of red, as black is of white, it ought to have an opposite shape; but if in his view it is not the opposite, this itself would surprise us that he does not regard his first principles as opposites, for that is the universally accepted doctrine. Most of all, though, he should have determined with accuracy which colors are simple, and why some colors are compound and others not." (p. 141)

As Stratton noted:

"Theophrastus's work is more than a report of what his predecessors observed and thought. After a passionless and undistorted account of another's theories, there comes in almost every case a criticism, with a severity of logic that permits one better to know the kind of scrutiny to which these early psychological doctrines were subjected in the later Athenian universities. 'Absurd' or 'childish', Theophrastus does not hesitate to call them, with marshalled evidence for his condemnation." (1917, p. 16)

Theophrastus was a favored pupil of Aristotle: he was bequeathed Aristotle's library and manuscripts, and after Aristotle's departure from Athens he directed the Lyceum for the remainder of his long life. Through his teaching and writing Theophrastus sought successfully to make the Aristotelian system more widely accessible. Indeed, the ideas of the two philosophers are generally so similar that attributions of distinctions between them have often proved difficult to determine. Both ranged widely in their writing about natural phenomena, although only a few fragments of Theophrastus' have survived. Most of these have concerned the classification of plants, and he has been called the 'father of botany' (Bodenheimer, 1958). He mentioned and tried to classify over 500 species of plants, often describing how they reproduce and the diseases to which they are prone. In all his enquiries he was noted for basing his conclusions on observations rather than theory.

While Theophrastus echoed the views of Aristotle in most matters, he did adopt a more thorough going empiricism that his teacher. He tried to avoid any appeal to final causes and to restrict his accounts to observations of natural phenomena (see Watson, 1968). Perception was said to accord with nature so that it is veridical, and objects are sensed indirectly through some medium. Theophrastus did posit the processes of perception and thought in the brain rather than in the heart, as Aristotle had contended. Prior to Stratton's (1917) translation attention had been directed principally to the descriptions Theophrastus had given about the ideas of others; Stratton brought the thoughts of Theophrastus himself into sharper relief.

THE INTRODUCTION OF OPTICS

Of the Greek philosophers and mathematicians, Euclid assembled and systematized the phenomena of optics most lucidly; he followed Plato's lead and defined optics mathematically, thus equating light with sight. Euclid based his optics on the then well-known fact that light travels in straight lines, and pursued the consequences of this with commendable persistence. Vision was restricted to the cone of rays emanating from the eye and meeting the objects within it. The geometrical projections to these objects were lawful, and this lawfulness was applied to vision, too. Those objects subtending a larger angle were perceived as larger. Thus, Euclid provided not only an account of optical transmission through space, but also a geometrical theory of space perception itself. The perceived dimensions of objects corresponded precisely to the angles they subtended at the eye, and illumination of those objects had its source in the eye. The theory neither mentioned nor could account for any aspects of vision that involved color.

Euclid commenced his *Optics* with seven definitions:

1. Let it be assumed that lines drawn directly from the eye pass through a space of great extent;
2. and that the form of the space included within our vision is a cone, with its apex in the eye and its base at the limits of our vision;
3. and that those things upon which the vision falls are seen, and those upon which the vision does not fall are not seen;
4. and that those things seen within a larger angle appear larger, and those seen within a smaller angle appear smaller, and those seen within equal angles appear to be of the same size;
5. and that things seen within the higher visual range appear higher, while those within the lower range appear lower;
6. and, similarly, that those seen within the visual range on the right appear on the right, while those within that on the left appear on the left;
7. but that things seen within several angles appear to be more clear. (Burton, 1945, p. 357)

From the foundation of these definitions, Euclid was able to erect a geometrical theory of space perception. Vision was determined by visual angle, and the angle had its origin in the eye. That is, light was emitted from they eye rather than received by it (see Chapter 3), and the optical lines drawn from the eye were visual lines, too.

Euclid's theory of vision was not the only one that was entertained in Greek science, but it was the most elegant. Vision was generally considered to involve some process of contact between the eye and objects (see Lindberg, 1978), and other means of achieving this contact were advanced. Democritus proposed that all nature was composed of atoms in motion; these atoms were continually emitted from objects to compress the air and carry impressions to the eye. These impressions were like a copy or image of the object that could be received by the eye, and this theory was amplified by Epicurus (ca. 342–270 B.C.). Democritus set in train a materialist philosophy that was to resurface with the scientific revolution of the seventeenth century, though its impact on Greek science was more limited. The concept of some copy of objects, carried through the air to the eye, was to have widespread and longlasting appeal, and it was itself transformed into eidola, simulacra, species, images, etc. Indeed, by the end of the thirteenth century, Roger Bacon (ca. 1220–1292) was able to list the terms image, species, idol, simulacrum, phantasm, form, intention, passion, impression, similitude of the agent, and shadow of the philosophers, used by authors of works on vision (Lindberg, 1983), to which could be added the effigies, figures, and membranes of Lucretius. According to Epicurus, the copies were received by the eye, and so this theory was one of intromission or reception, in contrast to Euclid's projection or extramission theory.

THE INTRODUCTION OF EXPERIMENT

Ptolemy is usually cast in the theoretical mold of Euclid (see Crombie, 1967), but he leavened Euclid's geometrical optics with some facts of both physical optics and visual perception (Delambre, 1812). In particular, he appreciated: that light should be thought of as continuous rather than discrete; that color was an integral component of light; that visual size cannot be equated with visual angle; that vision is not equal throughout the visual pyramid (rather than cone); that two pyramids of vision (one for each eye) need to be combined; and that experiments could be performed to study this binocular combination (see Lejeune, 1948, 1956, 1989; Smith, 1996, 1998). He set in train a reconciliation between physical and psychological analyses of vision which was amplified by Alhazen. We know relatively little about Ptolemy's theory of light, because the first book of his *Optics* has not survived. What is clear is that his approach was more experimental, and that he introduced measurements of both reflected and refracted light.

Space perception represents an arena in which optics and observation were often in conflict. Euclid provided geometrical analyses of almost all visual phenomena. Thus, for example, size perception was equated with visual angles, so that the same object would have a different apparent size according to its distance from the eye. Ptolemy's interpretation of the phenomena were more subtle, since he realized that visual angles alone did not accord with the characteristics of observation. By adding distance and orientation to visual angles, he was able to give accounts of size and shape constancies.

Euclid's geometrical analysis of size perception did have the virtue of precision, and so it is not unexpected that it should reappear centuries later in the context of artistic representation. In many ways, perspective was a formalization of Euclid's optics, as it is concerned with capturing visual angles of objects at different distances. Both Ptolemy and Alhazen listed the properties available to vision. In his *Optics* Alhazen enumerated eight conditions for perceiving objects accurately, but there were other properties, too. In a later manuscript he took issue with Ptolemy, suggesting that there were twenty two "things perceived by sight" (Sabra, 1966, p. 147). The additional ones were concerned with features such as texture (roughness and smoothness), light and shade, similarity, and beauty.

The contrast between Euclid and Ptolemy can be readily appreciated in their analyses of size perception. Euclid equated visual size with visual angle. He wrote: *"Objects of equal size unequally distant appear unequal and the one lying nearer to the eye always appears larger"* (Burton, 1945, p. 358). Ptolemy, on the other hand, realized the limitation of this optical approach to space perception, and added the dimensions of distance and orientation to that of visual angle: "Vision knows the true size of objects from the base of the visual pyramid and the distance the object is from us" (Lejeune, 1956, p. 35). Ptolemy also proposed that the judgment of size was learned, and that it was based on inference. These distinctions were amplified by Alhazen:

> "Sight cannot perceive the magnitudes of visible objects by an estimation based on the angles which the objects subtend at the centre of the eye. For the same object does not look different in magnitude when its distance is moderately varied.... The magnitude of objects is therefore perceived only by judgement and inference. And the inference through which the object's magnitude is perceived consists in estimating the base of the radial cone, i.e. the object's surface, by the angle of the cone and by its length, namely the distance of the object from the eye." (Sabra, 1989, pp. 174 and 176)

The analysis derived by Ptolemy and adopted by Alhazen was absorbed into the medieval accounts of optics and incorporated into both rationalist and empiricist theories of vision. Ptolemy provided one of the most penetrating accounts of vision in antiquity. Book II of his *Optics* classified visual phenomena into those of color, body, position, size, form, movement, and rest, and he went on to consider illusions that occur under each of these headings. Binocular vision was addressed in the context of the perception of position in Book II, and it was returned to at length in Book III. Books I–III of Alhazen's *Optics*, written in the eleventh century, employed similar but more extensive divisions to those of Ptolemy, and also assessed the errors of sight in each of them. Descartes, in his *Dioptrics*, considered that all the qualities of sight could be reduced to light, color, location, distance, size, and shape.

SUMMARY

The early history of perception is based on the descriptions of phenomena, often observed in the natural environment. It is a natural history which reflects the differential emphasis placed on one of two principles: optics and observation. Both of these principles were clearly enunciated in Greek science: optics was the province of Euclid and observation that of Aristotle. By assuming that light was emitted from the eye, Euclid reduced vision to rays drawn from the eye to objects. Thus, visual size was equated with visual angle, although his descriptions became less constrained in the context of motion perception. Aristotle adopted a receptive theory of light, and so he was not bound by the logical requirement of defining perception in projective terms. Accordingly, he placed more reliance on the evidence of his senses than on projective geometry: he described and classified phenomena. Thus, we find that the early history of spatial vision was based upon Aristotle's observations which were often interpreted in terms of Euclid's optics, even though the two views were usually incompatible. Advances were made by those who recognized the incompatability between optics and observation and attempted to resolve it.

Aristotle lived during the declining years of the golden age of Greece and of the Greek city states. Both Platonic and Aristotelian ideas were elaborated in the next centuries and Greek science and medicine were retained throughout most of the classical Roman period. While there were great technological and legal advances in the Roman empire, there was relatively little innovation in philosophy and science. Philosophy and monotheistic Christian theology became enmeshed in the fourth century A.D., prior to the sacking of Rome and the descent into what are called the Dark Ages. Greek writings were preserved and advanced in the eastern Mediterranean and in North Africa, where Islamic scholars translated them; many were housed in the vast library at Alexandria. Certain areas, notably mathematics and optics, were developed considerably, but much of the ancient Greek thought was no longer available to medieval Christian philosophers. It returned to southern Europe gradually from the thirteenth century onwards when the works were translated from Arabic into Latin, and it was one of the principal factors leading to the Renaissance. There were many other factors that fashioned the Renaissance during the fifteenth and sixteenth centuries. These included the decline in the power of Roman Catholic Church, as evidenced by the Reformation and the establishment of Protestantism; the invention of printing machines; and the Copernican revolution that placed earth as a peripheral part of a larger universe.

During the Renaissance nature was examined again with a human rather than a divine eye. Art was one of the first areas in which this rediscovery of human potential was expressed. The invention of linear perspective in the early fifteenth century was influenced by translations into Latin of medieval *Perspectiva*, which described both physical and physiological optics. Theories of image formation on a surface in front of the eye resulted in paintings that mirrored more precisely the optics of the real world, and actual as well as allegorical scenes were portrayed. It took two more centuries before the link between linear perspective and image formation in the eye was appreciated. Much of the delay was occasioned by the absence of an accurate anatomy of the eye. Medieval medicine was practiced according to the tenets of Greco-Roman authorities. Even anatomical dissections rigidly followed the structures described by Galen. It remained to Andreas Vesalius (1514–1564) to observe human anatomy through his own eyes rather than Galen's. With the newly found knowledge of ocular anatomy Kepler elucidated the workings of the eye as an optical instrument, describing the formation of an inverted and reversed image on the retina.

The principal issues involved in the spatial constancies were formulated over 2000 years ago, and a possible resolution was provided about 1000 years later. Euclid posed the problem and presented a solution in terms of visual projections. That is, visual size was defined by visual angle, or perception corresponded to the projected size of the stimulus. This remarkably simple equivalence did not, however, match the characteristics of everyday perception, and this was appreciated by Alhazen who suggested a novel resolution. He adopted a distinctly cognitive interpretation of size constancy, and this position was extended to shape constancy by Descartes:

> "As to the manner in which we see the size and shape of objects... their size is estimated according to the knowledge, or the opinion, we have of their distance, compared with the size of the images that they imprint on the back of the eye... And it is also obvious that shape is judged by the knowledge, or opinion, that we have of the position of various parts of the objects, and not

by the resemblance of the pictures in the eye; for these pictures usually contain only ovals and diamond shapes, yet they cause us to see circles and squares." (1637/1902, 1965, p. 107)

Although both these historical interpretations were based on cognitive processes, their importance lies in distinguishing between projection and perception. That is, the general problem of space constancy could be described as one of transforming signals that are initially mapped in terms of projected values into signals that correspond to the physical dimensions of objects. The perceptual constancies received formal definition early in the twentieth century, with the development of equations for measuring them by relating perceived, projected, and physical indices of stimulus dimensions (Brunswik, 1928; Thouless, 1931).

2

Nature of Perceptual Error

The term perceptual error is a very strange one. There can only be perceptions. Errors are associated with some deviation from a reference or standard. Thus, an error of measurement refers to some deviation from a reading that can be shown (either by another instrument or by other observers) to be in discrepancy. By the same token, the term misperception is a misnomer. However, there is some utility in the term if the dimensions of time and space are incorporated. A discrepancy in the perception of the same object can occur over time, as Aristotle noted in the context of the motion aftereffect. In like manner, the color of a surface can be modified by surrounding it by one of a different color. In these cases, perceived object properties are variable. It is in this sense that perceptual errors were initially described.

Errors in perception were remarked upon before the basic perceptual processes were either described or appreciated. This was so because it was possible to compare observations of the same objects over time and to note any discrepancies between them. The modern definition of illusions applies to differences between the perception of figures and their physical characteristics. Consensus concerning an external reality did not exist in antiquity, and so attention was directed to those instances in which changes in perception occurred. That is, when the same object appeared to have different properties under different conditions. According to this observational definition of illusions, all that is required is an assumption of object permanence; thereafter, and changes in the appearance of the same object will be classified as illusions.

An abiding example of this is the variation in the apparent sizes of celestial bodies. The moon illusion—its larger appearance near the horizon than high in the sky—is, of course, a size illusion, but it has also been interpreted as a distance illusion. The moon illusion presented an enigma in the past and it is one that still persists. Modern attempts at explaining it remain problematical (see Ross and Plug, 2002). It provides a quintessential example of illusion because the observations have been consistent but the interpretations have shown a progressive change: it was analyzed initially as a problem of physics, then physiology, and finally psychology.

The celestial illusion was known long before Aristotle. Plug and Ross (1989) describe a seventh century B.C. cuneiform inscription on a clay tablet from Nineveh that could be interpreted as describing the phenomenon. Aristotle's account was clear, and he related the variations in size to the effects of mist: "the sun and the stars seem bigger when rising and setting than on the meridian" (Ross, 1931, p. 373b). This was essentially the explanation given by Ptolemy in the *Almagest*, despite his appreciation that objects in a rarer medium appear smaller: "It is true that their true sizes [of the celestial bodies] appear greater at the horizon; however, this is caused not by their shorter distance, but by the moist atmosphere surrounding the earth, which intervenes between them and our sight. It is just like the apparent enlargement of objects in water, which increases with the depth of immersion" (Ross and Ross, 1976, p. 378). However Ptolemy wrote the *Almagest* before his *Optics*, in Book III of which a psychological account of the phenomenon, in terms of apparent distance, is given:

> "For generally, just as the visual ray, when it strikes visible objects in [circumstances] other than what is natural and familiar to it, senses all their differences less, so also its sensation of the distances it perceives [in those circumstances] is less. And this is seen to be the reason why, of the celestial objects that subtend equal angles between the visual rays, those near the point above our head look smaller, whereas those near the horizon are seen in a different manner and in accordance with what is customary. But objects high above are as seen small because of the extraordinary circumstances and the difficulty [involved] in the act [of seeing]." (Sabra, 1987, p. 225)

There has been some dispute concerning the relationship between the two passages from Ptolemy (see Ross and Ross, 1976; Sabra, 1987). Alhazen absorbed both interpretations, and acknowledged that both can apply, but that differences in apparent distance were the principal cause of the illusion:

"What sight perceives regarding the difference in the size of the stars at different positions in the sky is one of the errors of sight. It is one of the constant and permanent errors because its cause is constant and permanent. The explanation of this is [as follows]: Sight perceives the surface of the heavens that faces the eye as flat, and thus fails to perceive its concavity and the equality of the distances [of points on it] from the eye ... Now sight perceives those parts of the sky near the horizon to be farther away than parts near the middle of the sky; and there is no great discrepancy between the angles subtended at the eye-center by a given star from any region of the sky; and sight perceives the size of an object by comparing the angle subtended by the object at the eye-center to the distance of that object from the eye; therefore, it perceives the size of the star (or interval between two stars) at or near the horizon from comparing its angle to a large distance, and perceives the size of that star (or interval) at or near the middle of the sky from comparing its angle (which is equal or close to the former angle) to a small distance." (Sabra, 1987, p. 241)

Alhazen's account is in Book VII of his *Optics*, which was transcribed at a later date than Books I–III. His explanation was absorbed into the medieval texts on optics where it was repeated virtually unchanged.

Ptolemy and Alhazen were concerned with more general features of perception than the moon illusion, and Alhazen was more explicit in categorizing the three modes of vision in which illusions can occur. Illusions were to be understood in terms of the breakdown of the process of inference. Nonetheless, the categories Alhazen gave for the errors of sight were fewer than the visible properties he listed. Errors of inference were confined to distance, position, illumination, size, opacity, transparency, duration, and condition of the eye.

After the Renaissance, linear perspective was one of the techniques of visual illusion that could be manipulated, as is evident from the remarks of Francis Bacon (1561–1626). The mythical House of Salomon, described by Bacon in his *New Atlantis*, displayed "all delusions and deceipts of sight" as evidence of the advancement of science. Size and distance played a prominent role in such deceipts.

COMPARISONS OF PERCEPTS

While emphasizing the veridicality of sensing in general, Aristotle did entertain the possibility of errors (illusions) entering into a particular sense. The examples he mentioned were those of color or sound confusion and errors in spatial localization of colors or sounds. Illusions are often considered to be a modern preoccupation, based on specific theories of perception, but their origins are ancient and illusions can be investigated with little in the way of theory. As noted above, if there is an assumption of object permanence, then an illusion occurs when the same object appears to have different properties (of color, position, size, shape, motion, etc.) under different circumstances. Aristotle's description of the motion aftereffect was based on a comparison of percepts: "when persons turn away from looking at objects in motion, e.g., rivers, and especially those which flow very rapidly, they find that the visual stimulations still present themselves, for the things really at rest are then seen moving" (Ross, 1931, p. 459b). The phenomenon was presumably considered worthy of note because the stones at the side of the river appeared stationary prior to peering at the flowing water but not afterwards (see Wade and Verstraten, 1998). The changing perception of objects was the source of Aristotle's interest in phenomena like afterimages, aftereffects, color contrasts, and diplopia. It was precisely such variation in perception that led to the Platonic distrust of the senses.

Ptolemy drew a distinction between subjective and objective aspects of visual phenomena, and devoted considerable space to errors of perception. Indeed, he was one of the first writers to provide a detailed account of illusions; they are classified, and then considered under the headings of color, position, size, shape, and movement. Alhazen adopted a similar analysis of the errors of direct vision although he extended the range of phenomena for which they occur.

Many commentators have argued that illusions are a modern preoccupation in the study of perception. This statement, when restricted to geometrical optical illusions is certainly correct because they only received this name in the mid-nineteenth century. Moreover, the phenomena so called are often associated with a particular theoretical outlook. Empiricist philosophers, and those students of perception who followed them, set out from an ambiguous starting point. They assumed that the retinal image was static and impoverished, and that something had to be added from past experience to remove the equivocality. Illusions could intrude during this amplification of the retinal information (see Gregory, 2003). However, the studies of illusions (as errors of perception) have a much longer history, and it is one that is not tied to particular theoretical approaches. The benchmark applied is perception itself, bound with an assumption of object permanence.

COMPARISONS WITH PHYSICS

An illusion requires a yardstick or reference relative to which it can be assessed. In fact, underlying virtually all illusions are the mismatches of observation described above. However, in terms of interpretations the interest is directed to the source of the mismatch. The classical example is the apparent bending of a stick when immersed in water. There is a compelling contrast between the appearance of the stick in air and partially immersed, but does the stick change its characteristics? This provided a challenge to the assumption of object permanence, and alternative explanations were sought.

The investigation of aspects of optics derived from precisely such observations. Ptolemy examined instances of refraction, and formulated some general properties of it. However, it was the appreciation that the retinal image could be described in geometrical terms that provided the physical yardstick. In 1604, Kepler wrote:

> "Thus vision is brought about by a picture of the thing seen being formed on the concave surface of the retina. That which is to the right outside is depicted on the left on the retina, that to the left on the right, that above below, and that below above. Green is depicted green, and in general things are depicted by whatever colour they have. . . . the greater the acuity of vision of a given person, the finer will be the picture formed in his eye." (Crombie, 1964, p. 150)

Kepler formulated the problem that generations of students of vision have since attempted to resolve: how do we perceive the world as three-dimensional on the basis of a two-dimensional retinal image? Indeed, this 'legacy of Kepler' can be considered as having defined the problem in terms of single, static retinal images rather than considering the starting point as binocular and dynamic. Kepler himself was cautious regarding the conclusions that could be deduced from the inverted and reversed retinal image: "I leave it to the natural philosophers to discuss the way in which this image or picture is put together by the spiritual principles of vision" (Crombie, 1964, p. 147). Philosophers have not been united in their opinions, but they have appreciated that physical optics was not the solution to vision. Nonetheless, the measurement of the physical properties of a stimulus remains at the heart of analyses of perception, veridical or otherwise.

COMPARISONS WITH PHYSIOLOGY

The situation regarding the senses was radically revised in the nineteenth century, with developments in physics, anatomy, and physiology. Sources of stimulation could be specified and controlled more precisely. This had already occurred in the context of color, with Newton's methods of spectral separation of white light and mixing components of it (Newton, 1704). Young (1802a) proposed that all colors could be produced by appropriately compounding three primaries; he suggested that the eye was selectively sensitive to each. Young (1807/2002) also introduced the term 'energy' in the context of weight, and this concept was related by others to different dimensions of sensitivity, like light and sound.

The link between energy and sense organs was forged soon thereafter. Charles Bell (1774–1842) is noted for discovering that the anterior spinal nerve roots are motor (see Cranefield, 1974). His principal concern, however, was in specifying the senses and their nerve pathways to the brain. His experiments were described in a privately published pamphlet which also related stimulation to specific senses:

> "In this inquiry it is most essential to observe, that while each organ of sense is provided with a capacity for receiving certain changes to be played upon it, as it were, yet each is utterly incapable of receiving the impression destined for another organ of sensation. It is also very remarkable that an impression made on two different nerves of sense, though with the same instrument, will produce two distinct sensations; and the ideas resulting will only have relation to the organ affected." (Bell, 1811/2000, pp. 8–9)

In the context of vision, the demonstration of this fact had been known to Alcmaeon: pressure to the eye, even in darkness, produced the experience of light (see Grüsser and Hagner, 1990). Bell was able to bolster this observation with the application of electricity to the eye: "If light, pressure, galvanism, or electricity produce vision, we must conclude that the idea in the mind is the result of an action excited in the eye or in the brain, not any thing received, though caused by an impression from without. The operations of the mind are confined not by the limited nature of things created, but by the limited number of our organs of sense" (1811/2000, p. 12). Bell's attempts to link perception with physiological processes in the visual system reflected the growing body of physiological evidence that was accruing in the nineteenth century. The pace quickened with the developments in anatomy and physiology. Achromatic microscopes enabled cells to be seen, and electrical stimulation of nerve fibers led to the neuron doctrine.

Cells were described soon after the first microscopes were focused on organic matter in the seventeenth century (see Harris, 1999). Hooke (1665) gave them this name when he observed the structure of sections of cork. Antonius van Leeuwenhoek (1632–1723) gave accounts of several animal cells, including nerve fibres, when he directed his simple magnifier to animal tissue. Leeuwenhoek had neither the benefit of achromatic lenses nor staining methods when he observed the structure of optic nerves; he did, however, have a sharp knife to cut sections of the nerve. He was attempting to discover whether the nerves were hollow:

> "Some Anatomists affirm'd the *Optic* Nerve to be hol'ow, and that themselves had seen that hollowness, through which they would have the Animal spirits,

that convey the visible species, represented in the eye, pass into the Brain; I thereupon concluded with my self, that, if there were such a cavity visible in that Nerve, that it might also be seen by me, especially since, if it be so it must be pretty bigg, and the body pretty stiff, or else the circumjacent parts would press it together. And in order to this discovery, I sollicitously view'd three Optic Nerves of Cows; but I could find no hollowness in them; I only took notice, that they were made up of many filamentous particles, of a very soft substance, as if they only consisted of corpuscles of the Brain joined together, the threds were so very soft and loose: They were composed of conjoined globuls, and wound about again with particles consisting of other transparent globuls."
(1674, pp. 179–180)

The existence of small thread-like structures in the nerve bundles was also evident in the diagrams of nerves serving the senses. For example, Descartes (1637) indicated that the two optic nerves consisted of many thin filaments, and those arising from similar regions of each retina projected to the same parts of the pineal body (see Wade, 2004c). This was another instance of function (binocular single vision) defining the structure (the single pineal body) that could determine it. Relatively little attention was paid to these observations because the resolving power of the microscopes was poor, due to the aberrations introduced by their optical components. The microscopic world was transformed by the introduction of powerful achromatic instruments in the 1820s, and rapid advances were made thereafter. The cell doctrine was most clearly articulated at the end of the next decade by Theodor Schwann (1810–1882).

Nerves were thought to consist of bundles of fibrils, filaments, capillaments, threads, or villi (as they were variously called), the dimensions of which were exceedingly small, but beyond the resolution of the early microscopes. Nonetheless, estimates of their dimensions were made on the basis of the limits of vision rather than those of microscopes. Moreover, it was a growing concern with vision and its functions that led to the estimates of nerve fiber diameters. What is, perhaps, more remarkable is that the speculations were made before the cell doctrine had been proposed and before the structure of nerve cells was established.

With the growth of knowledge about cells and neurons they were used increasingly to interpret perceptual phenomena. That is, structure was used to define function. This was epitomized in the writing of Helmholtz. He gave an account of the structure of the retina in his *Handbuch der physiologischen Optik* (Helmholtz, 1867), and he applied it to the interpretation of visual resolution in terms of the size of retinal elements. The views he expressed were bolstered by the then recent microscopic revelations:

"Acuity of visual perception is also connected with the size of the retinal element stimulated by light. The light that falls on a single sensitive element can produce nothing but a single light sensation. In such a sensation there is no way of telling whether some parts of the element are highly illuminated as compared with other parts. A luminous point can be perceived when its image on the retina is very much smaller than a single retina element, provided the amount of light from it that falls on the eye is sufficient to affect the sensitive element appreciably." (Helmholtz, 1925/2000, p. 32)

Helmholtz also integrated this material with studies by Tobias Mayer (1723–1762; 1755) of visual resolution using gratings as stimuli, and with Jan Evangelista Purkyně or Purkinje's (1787–1869; 1823) descriptions of the wavy distortions that can be seen when viewing very fine gratings. Purkinje noted that: "During intense viewing of the parallel lines of an engraving one observes an oscillation of the lines which on closer inspection involves some being closer together and others farther apart, so that the lines appear in the form of waves" (1823, p. 122). Helmholtz illustrated the waviness that is apparent in fine gratings, and interpreted it in terms of the lines falling over a honeycomb of retinal elements.

Alfred Wilhelm Volkmann (1800–1877; 1862) argued that human visual acuity could not be reduced to the sizes of retinal cones, because the resolution was finer than their dimensions—what would now be called hyperacuity. However, in his Supplement to the first edition of his *Handbuch*, Helmholtz (1867) dismissed this possibility because he believed that it questioned the involvement of the retinal cones in visual acuity:

"The author does not believe, therefore, that we are forced to abandon the view that the retinal cones are the perceptive elements. But it is possible, judging from the most recent observations of M. Schultze, that the rod-like ends of the cones in the yellow spot, turned towards the choroid and separated from each other by black pigment, which measure only 0.00066 mm, may be the only sensory elements, and not the entire cones." (Helmholtz, 1925/2000, p. 37)

That is, the terminations of the cones in the fovea are smaller than the cell bodies of the cones and could serve to resolve such small separations. Helmholtz (1896) was able to draw on considerably more evidence about retinal microstructure in the second edition of his *Handbuch*, particularly that of Max Schultze (1825–1874; 1866). Schultze's findings were mentioned briefly in the Supplement to the first complete edition (Helmholtz, 1867), and they were given more prominence in the second edition.

Visual resolution provides a good example of the manner in which structure and function have been related. In the eighteenth century, when little about detailed anatomical structure was known, function (in terms of measures of visual resolution) determined structure (the dimensions of retinal elements). With increasing microscopic knowledge about sense organs, structure was used to define function.

DISTAL AND PROXIMAL COMPARISONS

The importance of function over structure was re-emphasized by the Gestalt psychologists in the early twentieth century. They drew a distinction between the distal and the proximal stimulus, and this was used to assess perception and its veridicality. As has been noted, in order for an illusion to be so considered two measurements of the stimulus are required. The most common are the physical characteristics of the stimulus and some suitable index of its perception. What is the physical description of a stick that is partially immersed in water? It is straight if the stick itself is measured, but not if a photograph is taken of it partially immersed. For this reason Gestalt psychologists made a distinction between the distal and proximal stimuli (the physical stimulus and its projection to the eye). If we understand something about the transmission of light through different media then we should incorporate it in our definition of perception and of illusions. If the light striking the retina (the proximal stimulus) has been transformed in some way, it would be remiss not to incorporate that knowledge in the analysis of its perception. Therefore, Gestalt psychologists would say that an illusion occurs when there is a mismatch between the proximal stimulus and perception.

The Gestalt movement had its origins, as did behaviorism, in the rejection of the New Psychology of Wilhelm Maximilian Wundt (1832–1920). The reasons, however, were quite different. Behaviorists rejected Wundt's methods whereas Gestaltists rejected Wundt's atomism. In redefining psychology as the study of behavior, John Watson (1878–1936) turned his back on its short history as the study of conscious experience. He avoided working with human subjects because he considered that introspection was unreliable and an unsuitable method on which to base any science, and so established the rat and the maze as the subjects for psychology. His views were both radical and initially unpopular, but they were propagated with a religious fervor. Watson launched the behaviorist attack on structuralism in 1913. His dissatisfaction was with the method rather than the theory; in fact behaviorist theory was also empiricist and associationist. The method of analytic introspection was rejected because it was subjective. Sensations and perceptions were inferences based upon introspections, and were not open to public scrutiny as would be expected of a science. His manifesto was clearly stated: "Psychology as the behaviorist views it is a purely objective experimental branch of natural science. Its theoretical goal is the prediction and control of behavior. Introspection forms no essential part of its methods, nor is the scientific value of its data dependent upon the readiness with which they lend themselves to interpretation in terms of consciousness" (Watson, 1913, p. 158).

Watson argued that the only aspects of psychology that could be measured reliably were the stimuli (S) presented to subjects and the responses (R) they made. Hence, behaviorism was often referred to as S-R theory; the organism was likened to a black box about which nothing could be known directly, but only by inference. Watson and the growing band of behaviorists in America distrusted the study of perception generally, because it could evidently take place without any obvious response. When it was studied, it was in the context of discrimination learning, where the emphasis was more on the process of learning than on perception. Those behaviorists interested in human perception tended to measure overt aspects of it like eye movements. Thus, in the early twentieth century, the Gestaltists became the heirs to perceptual research almost by default.

The Gestalt psychologists opposed Wundt's atomism, considering that complex percepts could not be reduced to simple sensory elements. Max Wertheimer (1880–1943) redefined psychology as the study of configurations or *Gestalten*. Gestalt psychology had its origins in perception but its ambit extended throughout the whole of psychology (see Ash, 1995). Its precursors were to be found in the innate categories of space and time proposed by Immanuel Kant (1724–1804), and in Goethe's phenomenology. Wertheimer conducted a series of experiments on apparent movement—motion seen between two stationary and separated stimuli when presented in rapid succession. The inability to distinguish between real and apparent motion was taken as damning any approach that explained perception in terms its sensations. Perception was considered to be holistic rather than atomistic: "There are wholes, the behaviour of which is not determined by that of their individual elements, but where the part-processes are themselves determined by the intrinsic nature of the whole. It is the hope of Gestalt theory to determine the nature of such wholes" (Wertheimer, 1938, p. 2). Not only was it said that the whole is more than the sum of its parts, but the perception of the whole is prior to that of its parts. Publication of Wertheimer's thesis on the phi-phenomenon, in 1912, is taken as the origin of Gestalt psychology; it was principally concerned with perception, and a range of robust demonstrations was devised to support its holistic nature. Much of its attraction lay in the power of the perceptual demonstrations.

Kurt Koffka (1886–1941) was the second member of the Gestalt triumvirate. He served as a subject in Wertheimer's experiments on the phi-phenomenon, which were conducted in Frankfurt in 1910. After being apprised of their significance Koffka became the leading advocate of the Gestalt approach. He used Gestalt concepts in studies of development and thinking, and he made American psychologists aware of the new movement in his writings and lectures on Gestalt psychology in the United States (see Koffka, 1922). Koffka did pose the fundamental question of "Why do things look as they do?". He also emphasised that visual perception is three-dimensional and that our perception is in terms of the object properties (the distal stimulus) rather than those at the receptor surface (the proximal stimulus).

Wolfgang Köhler (1887–1967) introduced the concept of field forces operating in both perception and in its underlying neurophysiology. Moreover, the brain processes were considered to be isomorphic (having the same form) with the percept, so that principles of brain function could be inferred from perceptual phenomena (see Köhler, 1930). He went on to develop a speculative neurophysiology based mainly on the principles of perceptual grouping and on his experiments with figural aftereffects. It could be said that these speculations did more to hasten the demise of Gestalt theory than any other factor: neurophysiologists failed to find any evidence for such fields of electrical activity in the brain, and so tended to dismiss Gestalt theory in general rather than Köhler's unsuccessful attempt at neuroreductionism in particular. The robust visual phenomena at the heart of Gestalt psychology remained an enigma.

Wertheimer (1923) formulated some descriptive rules for perceptual organization and produced a wide range of demonstrations that could be used to support them. The principles were described by Wertheimer in two papers published in the journal *Psychologische Forschung* (now *Psychological Research*) which the Gestalt psychologists founded to propagate their theory. The figures used by Wertheimer consisted mainly of open and closed circles. The initial and fundamental perceptual process was considered to be the separation of a figure from its background, because all the other grouping principles can only operate with segregated figures. Normally, a figure is defined by contours that surround it completely, whereas the ground is larger or lacking a defined boundary. Under certain circumstances neither of these conditions are met, and perceptual instability ensues—first one part and then the other is seen as figure, and this perceptual alternation continues.

Most of the remaining demonstrations of Gestalt grouping principles have clearly segregated figures; they are usually outline drawings, and these are shown to observers who are asked to describe what they see. The main grouping principles were said to be proximity, similarity, symmetry, good continuation, goodness of figure, and closure. Many more organizing principles have been described by Gestalt psychologists, although these are the main ones. Their intention initially was to provide an alternative theory of active, innately organized perception to counter the passive, structuralist views of Wundt and his adherents. The theory was supported by these demonstrations, which drew upon phenomenology. However, it should be noted that the demonstrations themselves were not representative of normal object perception because they were based upon line drawings. That is, the evidence for the principles of organization is based upon the manner in which two-dimensional pictures are perceived rather than three-dimensional objects.

The work of the Gestalt psychologists was originally in German, and many of the source articles are available in a collection of translations edited by Ellis (1938). Here one can find articles by Wertheimer, Köhler, and Koffka on Gestalt psychology generally, as well as on specific issues like the laws of organization in perception. Gordon (1997) presents a comprehensive account of Gestalt theory, together with an assessment of its impact on modern perceptual research.

PHANTOMS

Illusions are sometimes called phantoms because they have the characteristic of defying belief. However, there are some more immediate phantoms that afflict those who have had a limb amputated. They are compelling sensations that come from the severed part, and they have been a concern of students of perception since they were clearly described in the seventeenth century. The experiences of sensations arising from the amputated part are generally referred to as phantom limbs because the full knowledge of the missing part has little influence on the experiences deriving from the non-existent member.

The term 'phantom limb' was coined by Silas Weir Mitchell (1829–1914). Mitchell (1871) treated injuries received by soldiers during the American Civil War, and he described the sensations that amputees experienced in their lost limbs. Many such cases have since been reported, and phantom limbs pose some perplexing problems for theories of perception (see Ramachandran and Blakeslee, 1998). Damage or loss of other senses results in the absence of experiences formerly associated with their function. Blindness and deafness are particularly clear examples. But the sense organs for seeing and hearing—the eyes and ears—are localized in the head, and specialized receptors for light and sound are not found in other regions of the body. The skin senses are necessarily diffuse, and the consequences of loss are quite unlike those for the localized senses.

Although Mitchell gave the phenomenon its name, reports of phantom limbs were made long before the American Civil War. Reporting experiences from amputated parts has a much longer history, but it remains remarkably short considering the incidence of the condition. That is, amputations have a much longer history than reports of the perceptual consequences of them. The experience of sensations in lost limbs also provides an example of the ways in which novel phenomena can be interpreted. In this instance, the first phase is a description of the phenomenon. This is followed by attempts to incorporate it into the body of extant theory. Finally, the phenomenon is accepted and utilized to gain more insights into the functioning of the senses.

The first phase of understanding any phenomenon is an adequate description of it. In this sense, Ambroise Paré (1510–1590) initiated medical interest in this intriguing phenomenon. Evidence of loss of limbs, through disease, accident, warfare, or ritual has been commented upon since records began. With this legacy, it is remarkable that reports of phantom limbs entered so late into medical records. Perhaps this was because few of those who had limbs amputated survived to describe their experiences. Paré made great strides in the surgical treatment for amputation; he applied ligatures to the large vessels in the limbs to staunch the bleeding following amputation and he applied tourniquets above the site of severance. As a consequence of his improved surgical techniques, more of Paré's amputees survived. He described many such operations and the procedures that can be adopted in order to increase the likelihood of postoperative survival. Indeed, Paré described and illustrated a wide range of prostheses that could be used after amputation. These included mechanical hands, arms, and legs, all with moveable parts. He not only performed the operations, but followed the progress of patients following amputation. To Paré's great surprise, some of his patients reported sensations in the lost limb. In his *Apologie*, he devoted a chapter to amputations, indicating the signs necessitating it, and the procedures for conducting the operation. The most common cause for the operation was gangrene. Paré noted that the gangrenous extremity was bereft of sensitivity, and yet might still respond to pricking. He realized that this could indicate a false sensitivity in the affected part, and might retard operation. He then related the feelings to those of phantom limbs:

"You should certainly know that a Grangreene is turned into a Sphacell, or mortification, and that the part is wholly and thoroughly dead, if it looke of a blacke colour, and bee colder than stone to your touch, the cause of which coldnesse is not occasioned by the frigiditie of the aire; if there bee a great softnesse of the part, so that if you presse it with your finger it rises not againe, but retaines the print of the impression. If the skinne come from the flesh lying under it; if so great and strong a smell exhale (especially in the ulcerated Sphacell) that the standers by cannot endure or suffer it; if a sanious moisture, viscide, greene or blackish flow from thence; if it bee quite destitute of sense and motion, whether it be pulled, beaten, crushed, pricked, burnt or cut off. Here I admonish the young Chirurgion, that hee be not deceived concerning the losse or privation of the sense of the part. For I know very many deceived as thus; the patients pricked on that part would say they felt much paine there. But the feeling is

oft deceiptfull, as that which proceeds rather from the strong apprehension of
great paine which formerly reigned in the part, than from any facultie of feeling
as yet remaining. A most cleare and manifest argument of this false and de-
ceiptful sense appears after the amputation of a member; for a long while after
they will complaine of the part which is cut away. Verily it is a thing wondrous
strange and prodigious, and which will scarce be credited, unlesse by such as
have seen with their eyes, and heard with their ears the Patients who have many
months after the cutting away of the Leg, grievously complained that they yet
felt exceeding great pain of that leg so cut off." (Paré, 1649, p. 338)

Once attention had been drawn to the phenomenon then its phenomenology was examined in more detail; it can also be integrated into
prevailing theories. This second phase is found in the speculations of
Descartes. In his book on optics, Descartes (1637/1965) argued that all
sensation is located in the brain. Objections to this view were expressed by
some of Descartes' correspondents, and he responded by commenting on
reports of sensations in amputated limbs; they were used as evidence that
all sensations take place in the brain. In subsequent letters concerning such
sensations, Descartes attributed them to activity in the brain normally associated with the missing limb. He stated that this was a condition familiar
to doctors and surgeons of the day:

"for they know that those whose limbs have recently been amputated often think
they still feel pain in the parts they no longer possess. I once knew a girl who
had a serious wound in her hands and had her whole arm amputated because of
creeping gangrene. Whenever the surgeon approached her they blindfolded her
eyes so that she would be more tractable, and the place where her arm had been
was so covered with bandages that for some weeks she did not know that she
had lost it. Meanwhile she complained of feeling various pains in her fingers,
wrist and forearm; and this was obviously due to the condition of the nerves
in her arm which had formerly led from her brain to those parts of her body.
This would certainly not have happened if the feeling or, as he says, sensation
of pain occurred outside the brain." (Descartes, 1991, p. 64)

In addition, Descartes considered that the phenomenon indicated the
unreliability of the senses. In his sixth meditation on *The existence of material things, and the real distinction between mind and body* he wished to "see
whether the things which are perceived by that mode of thinking which
I call 'sensory perception' provide me with any sure argument for the existence of corporeal things" (1984, p. 51). The first aspect he considered
was the perception of his own body parts, but doubt was cast upon this
from examples of sensations in amputated limbs: "And yet I had heard
that those who had a leg or an arm amputated sometimes still seemed to
feel pain intermittently in the missing part of the body" (p. 53). Finally,
Descartes also used the phenomenon to support the unity of the mind in
comparison to the fragmented nature of the body: "Although the whole

mind seems to be united to the whole body, I recognize that if a foot or arm or any other part of the body is cut off, nothing has thereby been taken away from the mind" (1984, p. 59).

Early reports of phantom limbs were second-hand (so to speak); they relied on the amputees relating their experiences to physicians or surgeons. Other writers used the distilled medical descriptions as the sources of their own analyses. Most of the amputees had little prior medical experience, and the accuracy of their account was often dependent upon the literary skill of the surgeon (see Finger, 1994; Finger and Hustwit, 2003; Wade and Finger, 2003). This was not the case for William Porterfield (ca. 1696–1771), who was able to give a first-hand account of his own phantom leg. Porterfield was a Scottish physician of some prominence and an authority on the senses. In his *Treatise on the eye, the manner and phænomena of vision*, published in 1759, he described his experiences following amputation of his own leg. In the *Treatise* he used his experiences of a phantom limb to support the projective features of perception generally. He was attacking the theory that a pictorial image existed on the retina, and that this was perceived by the mind. He described his own experiences of a phantom limb in this same general context:

"Tho' there was a Picture in the *Retina* in that vulgar gross Sense that so many imagine, yet it is impossible that the Mind could perceive it there; because all the Sensations or Perceptions of the Mind are present within it and in the *Sensorium*: I appeal to every one's Experience, if he ever sees or observes any Pictures or any Thing else in the *Retina*. And to say we see, observe or perceive Pictures there, without being sensible or conscious of it is absurd and ridiculous. The Mind or sentient Principle does not at all perceive in the *Retina*, but in the *Sensorium* where it is present; for when, thro' any Defect or *Paralysis* of the Nerve, the Motions or Vibrations impressed on the *Retina* by the Rays forming the Picture are not propogated to the *Sensorium*, or that the place in the Brain in which the Mind resides, the Mind perceives nothing; nor is it indeed possible it can perceive any thing; for whether the Mind be thought active or passive in its Perceptions, it is certain, that it can perceive nothing but what is present with it; for it can no more perceive *where it is not*, than *when it is not*; and it may as well be or exist *where it is not*, as act, suffer, or perceive *where it is not*. All Things perceived must therefore be present with the Mind and in the *Sensorium*, where the Mind resides; and that not only virtually, but substantially...

It is therefore evident, that, did the Mind perceive Pictures in the *Retina*, it behoved to be there present: And for the same Reason, did it perceive in the other Organs of Sense, it behoved also to be present to all the Parts of the Body; because the Sense of Feeling is diffused thro' all the Body: Nay, in some Cases it behoved to be extended beyond the Body itself, as in the Case of Amputations, where the Person, after Loss of his Limb, has the same Perception of Pain, Itching, &c. as before, and feels them as if they were in some Part of his Limb, tho' it has long been amputated, and removed from the Place where the Mind places the Sensation. Having had this Misfortune myself, I can the better vouch the Truth of this Fact from my own Experience; for I sometimes still feel Pains and Itchings, as if in my Toes, Heel or Ancle, &c. tho' it be several Years since my Leg was taken off. Nay, these Itchings have sometimes been so strong and lively, that, in spite of all my Reason and Philosophy, I could scarce forbear attempting to scratch the Part, tho' I well knew there was nothing there in the Place where I felt the Itching. And however strange this may appear to some, it is nevertheless no way miraculous or extraordinary, but very agreeable to the usual Course and Tenor of Nature; for, tho' all our Sensations are Passions or Perceptions produced in the Mind itself, yet the Mind never considers them as such, but, by an irresistible Law of our Nature, it is always made to refer them to something external, and at a Distance from the Mind; for it always considers them as belonging either to the Object, the Organs, or both, but never as belonging to the Mind itself, in which they truely are; and therefore, when the nervous Fibres in the Stump are affected in the same Manner as they used to be by Objects acting on their Extremities in the Toes, Heel or Ancle, the same Notice or Information must be carried to the Mind, and the Mind must have the same Sensation, and form the same Judgment concerning it, viz, that it is at a Distance from it, as if in the Toes, Heel or Ancle, tho' these have long ago been taken off and removed from that Place where the Mind places the Sensation.

If this should prove hard to be conceived, it may be illustrated by what happens in the Sensation of Colours; for tho' the Colours we perceive are present with the Mind, and in the Sensorium, yet we judge them at a Distance from us, and in the Objects we look at; and it is not more difficult to conceive how Pain may be felt at a Distance from us, than how Colours are seen at a Distance from us." (1759a, pp. 362–365)

Porterfield displayed considerable sophistication in the analysis of his phantom limb, by associating the projective features of the experience with other aspects of perception. He was well-versed in Newtonian color theory, and cited Newton many times. Indeed, he gave a quotation from Newton's *Opticks* on the title page of his *Treatise*. The reference to color in the quotation above relates to Newton's statement that the rays are not colored, but that the experience of color is subjective. Porterfield was extending this subjectivity of sensation to phantom limbs, and incorporating the sensations into the body of perceptual theory. A similar relationship is drawn for the visual perception of direction, an aspect of spatial vision that exercised Porterfield considerably. He wrote:

"Now, as Objects seen by Reflection or Refraction appear and are seen, not in their true Place, but in some other Place from which they are absent, and that because the Rays fall upon the Eyes, and make a Picture on their Bottom, in the very same Manner as if they had come from the Object really placed there, without the Interposition of the Glass; so, when the Impression made upon the nervous Fibres of the Stump is the same as if it had come from the Object acting on their Extremities, the Sensation must also be the same, and the Mind, by forming the same Judgment concerning it, must feel it as in the Toes, Heel or Ancle &c. in which those nervous Fibres terminated before the Leg was taken off." (Porterfield, 1759a, pp. 366–367)

Porterfield does not regard the experiences of the lost limb as phantoms, but as a natural consequence of stimulating the brain in a manner similar to that which existed prior to amputation. He integrated the phantom limb experiences with a general theory of perception.

This position was generally accepted by physicians in the eighteenth century. For example, George Fordyce (1736–1802) in his text on medicine related phantom sensations to the normal functioning of the nervous system:

> "The sensibility depends entirely on a part's being connected with the brain by the nerves; for, If the nerves be going to any part be cut through, the sensibility is lost. If the nerves going to any part be moderately comprest, the sensibility is diminished. If the nerves be comprest strongly, the sensibility is lost. If the pressure be soon removed, the sensibility recurs. If the pressure be continued for a long time before it is removed, the sensibility returns more slowly, or not at all. Pressure on the brain, diminishes the sensibility of the whole body. If a small branch of nerve be cut through, so as to take off the sensibility of a part of the skin, it may be restored in time. The sensibility may be impaired, or lost, without any sensible pressure on the nerve, or alteration of its structure. When there is no wound in the body, the sensations appear to be in the place where the application exciting them is made. If an extremity be cut off, an application made to the stump, may produce sensations which appear to be in the part amputated." (1771, pp. 93–95)

A similar sentiment, voiced again with primary reference to the nerves and their pathways, was written in the next decade by John Hunter (1728–1793): In his book *Observations on certain parts of the animal œconomy* he described two cases of phantom sensations in the missing penis:

> "I knew a gentleman who had the nerves which go to the glans penis completely destroyed by mortification, almost as high as the union of the penis with the pubes; and at the edge of the old skin, at the root of the penis, where the nerves terminated, was the peculiar sensation of the glans penis; and the sensation of the glans itself was now only common sensation; therefore the glans has, probably, different nerves, and those for common sensation may come through the body of the penis to the glans. A serjeant of marines who had lost the glans, and the greater body of the penis, upon being asked, if he ever felt those sensations which are peculiar to the glans, declared, that upon rubbing the end of the stump, it gave him exactly the sensation which friction upon the glans produced, and was followed by an emission of the semen." (Hunter, 1786, pp. 216–217)

These examples were of particular significance as both Fordyce and Hunter considered that all senses responded to touch and pain, in addition to their specific sensations. In his papers, which were not published during his lifetime, Hunter (1861) expressed it thus: "Touch is probably the only sense that is cognizable by another sense besides the immediate sensation" (p. 7). That is, if touch alone was experienced as a phantom sensation, then it might reflect the central operation of common sensitivity. If the specific sensations associated with a particular body part could be experienced after amputation then that was stronger evidence for the localization of sensation in the brain.

Others were able to corroborate the reports gathered by Hunter. One was by his adversary, Andrew Marshal (1742–1813); Hunter and Marshal were both Scottish doctors working in London. Despite this, they came to fisticuffs over the possible link between brain pathology and madness (see Wade, 2004d). Marshal also noted the effects of loss of the penis, and related it to the other senses:

> "When we compare the different senses together, two or three observations occur to us; one is, that the first four senses take place only when certain due degrees of impression are made on the extremities of the nerves distributed to that organ: if the impression is too slight, no peculiar sensation arises; if it exceeds in measure, instead of the sense of seeing, hearing, &c. there is merely a sense of pain. Thus the first four senses, when their organs are injured, agree with the sense of feeling. Another observation is, that as the sense of feeling arises from impressions made in those parts of the body, so it is more difficult to destroy than the other senses. When the extremities of the nerves of the other senses are destroyed, peculiar sensations connected with them also cease, as was mentioned above: but the remaining body of nerves retains a sense of feeling; and the extremities of the nerves appropriated to feeling only, being destroyed, the extremities of the portion left resume the peculiar susceptibility of the original extremities. In the case of W. Scott, whose penis was carried off by a gun-shot, the stump of it, which was even with the skin of the pubis, resumed the peculiar sensibility of the glans penis; also the cicatrix of sores in other parts of the body is susceptible to impressions of touch." (Marshal, 1815, pp. 222–223)

Yet further fuel for this philosophical fire was provided a few decades later by Charles Bell who referred to sensations in a lost penis obliquely in his *Idea of a new anatomy of the brain* (Bell, 1811/2000). Bell made recourse to phantom limb sensation to support his view that the seat of sensation is in the brain; however, his sensibilities led him to express the report of sensations in the missing penis in Latin:

> "It may be said, that there is here no proof of the sensation being in the brain more than in the external organ of sense. But when the nerve of a stump is touched, the pain is as if in the amputated extremity. If it be still said that this is no proper example of a peculiar sense existing without its external organ, I offer the following example: Qŭando penis glandem exedat ŭlcŭs, et nihil nisi granulatio maneat, ad extremam tamen nervi pudicæ partem ubi terminatur sensus supersunt, et exquisitissima sensus gratificatio." (Bell, 1811/2000, pp. 11–12)

The Latin text translates as "When an ulcer consumes the glans penis so that nothing remains but granulation, the most exquisite sensory gratification still survives at the end of the pudic nerve where the sensation terminates."

Both Bell and Johannes Müller (1801–1858) employed phantom limb phenomena as supports for the doctrine of specific nerve energies. Müller provided descriptions of thirteen cases of sensations following amputation. His summary of the effects of amputation is astute:

> "*When a limb has been removed by amputation, the remaining portion of the nerve which ramified in it may still be the seat of sensations, which are referred to the lost part.*—This is a fact known to all surgeons, and is subject to no exception. It is usually said that the illusion continues for some time, namely, as long as the patient is under the care of the surgeon; but the truth is, that in most cases it persists throughout life: of this it is easy to convince oneself by questioning a person whose limb has been amputated, at any period after the operation. The sensations are most vivid while the surface of the stump and the divided nerves are the seat of inflammation, and the patient complains of severe pains felt, as if in the whole limb which has been removed. When the stump is healed, the sensations which we are accustomed to have in a sound limb are still felt; and frequently throughout life tingling, often pains, are felt, which are referred to the parts that are lost. These sensations are not of an undefined character; the pains and tingling are distinctly referred to single toes, to the sole of the foot, to the dorsum of the foot, to the skin, &c. These important phenomena have been absurdly attributed to the action of the imagination, &c. They have been treated merely as a curiosity; but I have convinced myself of their constancy, and of their continuance throughout life,—although patients become so accustomed to the sensations that they cease to remark them." (Müller, 2003, pp. 745–746, original italics)

Müller's claim that the experience of phantom limb sensations in amputees was universal needs to be modified slightly: Mitchell found that eighty-six of ninety cases he examined reported sensations in the missing limb (Finger and Hustwit 2003). These features make the absence of reports before Paré even more surprising. Limbs have been amputated because of damage or disease for millenia, and some must have survived the trauma of amputation to experience these enigmatic feelings. Moreover, the common feature of all reports is the existence of localised pain in the severed part; other sensations associated with the skin and muscles (like being touched, temperature sensitivity or movement) have not been so commonly reported.

The phenomena associated with phantom limbs continue to intrigue and excite. They could have been described in the section on the comparison between percepts; in this case the comparison involves a longer component of memory. A current pattern of stimulation in the brain is associated with ones from the past, and similarities are experienced. In his treatise on monsters and marvels, Paré described a case of a man who was born without arms, and could perform remarkable feats nonetheless; Paré did not comment on any aspect of phantom sensations reported by the man. Despite the puzzles they still pose, these phantoms have provided perception with some potent concepts.

SUMMARY

Students of vision have been more intrigued by illusions of the senses than by the veridical perception of object properties. Since most of perception is veridical, it is the occasional departures from veridicality that have provided fascination. Illusions, or errors of perception, have been gauged by many means. The most venerable method has involved the comparison of percepts: when object properties appear to differ under different circumstances, then an illusion is said to have occurred. The only assumption that needs to be made is that the objects have not themselves changed between the two events. Physical benchmarks were introduced with an increasing understanding of the physical world. Thus, perplexing percepts like the apparent bending of sticks when immersed in water could be given a more mundane interpretation when the laws of refraction were specified. However, the reference that has proved most attractive to many students of the senses is comparison between percept and underlying physiology. This lies at the heart of Gestalt approaches to perception which emphasized the distinction between distal and proximal stimulation.

Phantom limbs provided an intriguing contrast between the manner in which phenomena have been interpreted by philosophers and physicians. The speculative approach of the former is countered by the pragmatic progress of the latter. It seems more than likely that both philosophers and physicians of the distant past encountered anecdotes of phantom experiences, but it was a physician (Paré) who considered that it warranted description. He was closer to his patients and his procedures to be able to make the link. The veneer of myth and mystery, that clearly cloaks many of Paré's marvels and monsters, had not had time to settle.

Indeed, this contrast can be applied to errors of perception in general. It will be encountered in the next chapter, when the nature of veridicality is addressed.

3

Nature of Veridicality

In antiquity, sight was essential to the study of optics, and disorders of sight influenced theories of vision. Ophthalmology has a longer recorded history than optics: several surviving papyri dating from the second millenium B.C. describe disorders and treatments of the eye. For example, the Ebers papyrus describes dimness of sight and strabismus (see Bryan, 1930). A millenium later, there were specialists in diseases of the eye practicing in Egypt. An illustration of a cataract operation of the type that was probably performed almost two thousand years ago was redrawn by Thorwald (1962), and written records indicate that such operations had been conducted a thousand years earlier (see Magnus, 1901). Greek medicine profited greatly from these earlier endeavors, and added to them. Neither Egyptian nor Greek ophthalmology was free from the mystical and metaphysical, and observation was frequently subservient to philosophical doctrine.

The eyes were not only windows to the world, they were also the window through which the world was thought to be illuminated! That is, light itself was considered to have its origin in the eye. This view survived for thousands of years throughout which time light and sight were inextricably intertwined. The separation of the physics of light from the physiology and psychology of sight was one of the major developments in the study of visual perception, and it is the first aspect of veridicality that will be discussed here. Resolving the nature of light, and the way it is refracted through the eye to form an image on the retina, was thought by some to solve the problem of vision. However, with increasing knowledge of the anatomy of the eye, and the pathways from the eyes to the brain, the problem of vision took on new dimensions. Practical issues could be addressed, too. For many centuries, the aged were unable to inspect objects in any detail because of the deteriorating eyesight and the absence of any means for correcting for it. Pragmatic solutions were applied from the late thirteenth century—long before they could be supported theoretically. When the dioptric properties of the eyes were clarified, more precise corrections could be applied, not only for the aged eye but for short-sighted younger eyes, too.

NATURE OF LIGHT

Ideas about the nature of light in Greek science were inseparable from those of the eye with which it was experienced. Accordingly, Greek theories of light incorporated the visual apparatus to varying degrees, thereby confounding light with sight. Two aspects of sight initially fuelled speculations about light: the experience of light following pressure or a blow to the eye, and the visibility of a reflected image in the eye. The idea of light being emitted from the eye was founded on the first of these, and the notion of an image being carried back to the eye was the source of the second. A third feature of sight, which distinguished it from the other senses, was that the experience could be terminated by closing the eyelids during daytime.

For around two thousand years, most theories struggled, with varying degrees of success, to account for these phenomena. In fact, the major advances in optics have involved differentiating physical from psychological phenomena. For the dioptrical properties of the eye it was achieved in 1604 by Kepler, who portrayed the manner in which images are formed on the retina; for color it was Newton who, in 1672, published the results of his prismatic experiments which indicated that the spectrum is a property of light rather than glass. Exactly a century after Kepler, Newton (1704) published his mature theory of light and colors in his *Opticks*. Light and sight were conflated in a variety of ways by Greek thinkers, and their ideas were transmitted and extended by Arabic writers like Ibn al-Haytham (Alhazen), to be reabsorbed into European thought from the thirteenth century onwards to form the medieval *Perspectiva* (see Crombie, 1952; Lindberg, 1976; Park, 1997; Sabra, 1989).

Sight aided optics and ophthalmology in the early stages of their developments, but it has not generally been accorded the same attention for the periods following the separation of seeing into physical, physiological, and psychological domains. For example, it has been said that Kepler's dioptrical analysis of the retinal image represented a "successful solution of the problem of vision" (Lindberg, 1976, p. x). It certainly did provide a secure platform from which the analysis of vision could proceed, but from the psychological point of view, Lindberg's statement is at best an oversimplification. Kepler formulated the problem that subsequent generations of students of vision have attempted to resolve: how do we perceive the world as three-dimensional on the basis of a two-dimensional retinal image? Indeed, Gibson (1966) took this to be a pseudoproblem, and I have referred to this 'legacy of Kepler' as having reduced the problem to the analysis of single, static retinal images rather than considering the starting point as binocular and dynamic (Wade, 1990). The relationship between the inverted and reversed retinal image and perception was treated circumspectly by Kepler himself; he did not wish to enter into this domain of philosophy. Natural philosophers have not subsequently spoken with a single voice, but they have appreciated that physical optics is not the solution to vision. The policy I will adopt is to restrict consideration of the physical dimensions of light mainly to the period in which it was confounded with the psychological. The disputes between corpuscular and wave theorists will only be touched upon here; detailed appraisals can be found in Ronchi (1970) and Ziggelaar (1993).

GREEK OPTICS

Most speculations about sight, advanced by Greek thinkers over many centuries, incorporated elemental philosophy—fire, earth, water, and air permeated perception. Touch was often taken as the most important sense, and the one relative to which others could be related; qualities associated with it, like hot, cold, moist, and dry were thought to be common to all the senses, and were in turn linked to the four elements. Thus, vision was generally considered to involve some process of contact between the eye and objects, and several means of achieving this contact were advanced. These included various versions of emission (or extramission) theories, in which light originated in the eye and was projected from it. Reception (or intromission) theories, in which light traveled from objects to the eye, were also advanced, as were speculations incorporating aspects of both emission and reception. Emission theories could have been founded on the experience of light when pressure is applied to the eye (see Beare, 1906; Grüsser and Hagner, 1990), and they are consistent with the cessation of sight when the eyes are closed.

In the sixth century B.C., Alcmaeon observed the first phenomenon and noted that "the eye obviously has fire within, for when one is struck [this fire] flashes out" (Stratton, 1917, p. 89). This speculation was extended by Empedocles, who believed that the eye consisted of an internal fire send-ing out light like a lantern. He proposed that all the senses contained pores or passages into which something could fit. The passages of the eye were arranged alternately of fire and water, and white was perceived through "fiery pores" whereas black objects were perceived through the "watery" (see Stratton, 1917; Siegel, 1959). Dimness of sight derived from clogging the passages. Species and individual differences in day and night vision were attributed to the amount of fire in the eye, and the location from which it originated. Alcmaeon made a distinction between perception and thinking on the basis of species differences; he considered that all animals perceive in a similar way, but only humans have the capacity to under-stand. Empedocles, on the other hand, argued that the two processes are identical.

Theories based on light passing to the eye were proposed by Leucippus (fl. 450 B.C.) and supported by his pupil, Democritus and others (see Ronchi, 1970). They could account readily for the absence of sight with eye closure but not for the experience of light when pressure was applied to the eye. What was received by the eye was often more than light, but some image of the object itself. Leucippus, in advancing the equation of touch with all perception, suggested that images were carried from objects to make contact in the eye:

> "Now we do not actually see the objects coming nearer to us when we perceive them, therefore, they must send to our soul 'something' which represents them, some image, eidola, some kind of shadow or some material simulacrum which envelops bodies, quivers on the surface and can detach itself from them in order to bring to our soul the shape, the colors and all the other qualities of the bodies from which they emanate." (Ronchi, 1970, p. 7)

According to Democritus all nature was composed of atoms in mo-tion, and they were continually emitted from objects to compress the air and carry impressions to the eye. The impression was like a copy of the object that could be received by the eye. Thus, the solution to many of the problems of perception that taxed subsequent students of sight was pro-vided prior to any physiological process. The images carried with them the constant features of the objects, and for Democritus these included their three-dimensionality. This theory was amplified by Epicurus who also believed that the images retained the shape and color of the objects themselves. The concept of some copy of objects, carried through the air to the eye, appealed to many students of vision. Moreover, it received support from the observation that the image of an object could be seen reflected from the eye of an observer. Epicurus believed that the copies were received by the eye, and so this theory was one of reception.

A combination of emission and reception was proposed by Plato, although his theory of vision was always subservient to his philosophy of ideal forms. Plato suggested that light was emitted from both the eye and objects, and vision took place externally where these two streams united. According to Theophrastus: "His view, consequently, may be said to lie midway between the theories of those who say that vision falls upon [its object] and of those who hold that something is borne from visible objects to the [organ of sight]" (Stratton, 1917, p. 71). One of the difficulties with this theory was that light continued to be emitted from the open eye at night. Plato suggested that we cannot see at night because light is extinguished in darkness, just as heat and dryness are extinguished by cold and dampness. Aristotle was scornful of this speculation stating that neither heat nor dryness were attributes of light. For Plato, as for Aristotle, it was not light but color that was the principal source of interest in vision. Plato distinguished between light and color, considering that light had its ultimate source in the sun, but color was a property of objects themselves.

Aristotle's theory is more in line with modern conceptions of light, and accounts of it can be found in his books on the soul and on the senses (see Beare, 1906; Smith and Ross, 1910; Ross, 1913, 1927, 1931). As noted in Chapter 1, his concern was with observation, and the phenomena he experienced directed the interpretations he proposed. Thus, he queried the emission theory of Empedocles by the simple expedient of testing a prediction that would follow from it: if light was emitted from the eye then vision should be possible at any time the eyes were open, including night time. The fact that the prediction was not supported led him to suggest an alternative theory of the nature of light. Similarly, he distinguished between vision and touch by noting that an object in physical contact with the eye could not be seen. His alternative interpretation was that vision is the result of some movement in the medium separating the eye from the objects perceived. Aristotle denied that the image visible in the eye of another observer was the source of vision: "The image is visible [in the eye] because the eye is smooth [like a mirror]. It exists, however, not in the eye but in the observer; for this phenomenon is only a reflection" (Siegel, 1970, p. 27). Ronchi (1970) remarked that Aristotle's criticisms of emission and contact theories were concise but his alternatives were not as clearly formulated.

Aristotle's theory was extended by Theophrastus. He attacked the idea proposed by Anaxagoras that "seeing is occasioned by the reflection in the eyes" (Stratton, 1917, p. 97) by noting that perceived size was not related to the size of the reflected image; he also remarked that "motion, distance, and size are visual objects and yet produce no image" (Stratton, 1917, p. 99). Theophrastus accepted Aristotle's contention that vision acts via the transmission of light through some medium. According to this view, light, generated by the sun, was reflected from objects but required a medium (air) through which to travel before it could be received by the eye. The emphasis on the medium, variously called the transparent or the diaphanous, reflected Aristotle's distinction between light as a substance, and light as a motion of the medium. Such motions could be instantaneous and they could be perceived by many observers simultaneously. Aristotle's conception of light was not, however, widely adopted.

It was noted in Chapter 1 that Euclid followed Plato's lead and defined optics mathematically, thus equating light and sight. For Euclid, vision was restricted to the cone of rays emanating from the eye and meeting the objects within it. The geometrical projections to these objects were lawful, and this lawfulness was applied to vision, too. Thus, Euclid provided not only an account of optical transmission through space, but also a geometrical theory of space perception itself. The perceived dimensions of objects corresponded precisely to the angles they subtended at the eye, and illumination of those objects had its source in the eye. The emissions from Euclid's eyes were referred to as visual rays, and their properties were conflated with a number of phenomenal features. The visual rays were discrete, and so small objects could fall between them, and remain unseen; that is, there is a limit to the dimensions of objects that can be detected, namely, a threshold for visual acuity. Moreover, those objects seen by rays in the center of the visual cone will be seen more clearly than those towards the edge; that is, direct (foveal) vision has better acuity than indirect (peripheral) vision. It followed, as Euclid stated, that nothing could be seen at once in its entirety, implying that the visual rays would move over an object (by moving the eyes) in order to see all its features. The theory was entirely concerned with spatial vision and neither mentioned nor could account for any aspects of sight that involved color.

Greek theories of light were transmitted through the Roman period mostly by Graeco-Roman writers, although the transmission was modulated by a growing desire to integrate optical theories with the practicalities of observation. Lucretius made many references to vision in his poem *De Rerum Natura*; he believed that light (lumen) was emitted from the sun, and when it struck objects it carried images (eidola) of them to the perceiver. Lucretius appreciated that images in themselves would not be useful to perception unless they carried with them some index of the distance the objects were away from the observer, so that its dimensions could be determined. The mechanism that he proposed for this—of the image brushing aside the intervening air—was exceedingly vague, but he was addressing a general problem that exists in all accounts of spatial vision. Lucretius followed in the line of the Epicureans, but the relative merits of such reception theories were still in conflict with emission theories, as supported by Hero of Alexandria (ca. 60). He divided the science of vision into three parts: optics, dioptrics, and catoptrics (see Cohen and Drabkin, 1958). He considered that the velocity of light was infinite, because of the immediate visibility of heavenly bodies upon opening the eyes.

We know relatively little about Ptolemy's theory of light, because the first book of his *Optics* has not survived, but it can be partially reconstructed. What is clear is that his approach was more experimental than his predecessors, and that he introduced measurements of both reflected and refracted light. Ptolemy extended Euclid's geometrical optics by incorporating facts of both physical optics and visual perception, and by studying them experimentally (see Chapter 1). In particular, he appreciated that light rays should be thought of as continuous rather than discrete in the way Euclid had stated. He proposed that color was an integral component of light, and he conducted experiments on color mixing using a rotating color wheel. He argued that visual size cannot be equated with visual angle, and introduced the concept that perceived size was derived from visual angle and distance; that is, he addressed the issue of perceptual constancy. He was in agreement with Euclid about the variations in visual acuity throughout the visual pyramid (rather than cone). The two pyramids of vision (one for each eye) needed to be integrated and he conducted experiments with a board in order to study this binocular combination (see Crone, 1992; Howard and Wade, 1996; Smith, 1996). Ptolemy also realized that illusions occur in vision: "For there are some errors that are caused in all the senses and others that are confined to things seen, of which some are visual and others are in the mind" (Lejeune, 1956, p. 56). He was one of the first writers to provide a detailed account of illusions. Indeed, he devoted over one third of Book II of his *Optics* to errors of sight; they were classified, and then considered under the headings of color, position, size, shape, and movement. In short, Ptolemy initiated a reconciliation between physical and psychological analyses of vision which was amplified by Alhazen (see Sabra, 1989).

Galen was a near contemporary of Ptolemy; both were active in Alexandria and Galen was likely to have been aware of and to have benefited from knowledge of Ptolemy's optical investigations (Siegel, 1970). Galen addressed matters of sight in the context of anatomy and speculative physiology, though he made many astute observations, particularly in the context of binocular vision. He also ventured, with some misgivings, into the arena of optics. In his book *On the usefulness of the parts of the body* (May, 1968), Galen expressed regret for introducing optical concepts in a medical text, since they were at that time deeply unfashionable. His theory of vision was physiological, and it was based on the pneumatic concepts advocated by Empedocles: pneuma, or visual spirit, passed along the hollow tubes of the optic nerves to interact with returning images of external objects in the crystalline lens: "The lens is the primary organ of vision. It is one of the constituents of the eye and is composed of uniform parts. It is altered by something pertaining to the colors of the outside object which the animal perceives" (Siegel, 1970, p. 58). Here we find another enduring notion, that the 'seat of vision' resides in the lens of the eye. Indeed, Galen himself supported this proposal by virtue of the blindness that results from cataracts and the sight that is restored when they are surgically removed. By adopting an anatomical and physiological analysis of vision, Galen was confronted with the existence of two eyes and the observation by them of a single visual world. He was able to draw from Ptolemy's analysis of certain aspects of binocular single vision, and to suggest his own physiological theory for its occurrence. The pneuma were unified from a single site in the anatomical process—the optic chiasm—where the two optic nerves were thought to be united.

Little was added to optical theory in the late Roman period, and the Greek texts were retained and copied initially in Byzantium and later in Persia and North Africa. Translations of Greek works into Arabic reached their peak in the ninth and tenth centuries, and they in turn were translated into Latin from the twelfth century. Because of strictures against dissection, Galen's anatomy and physiology of the eye were generally accepted by Islamic scholars, but they did extend knowledge of optics. Al-Kindi (ca. 860) summarized the principal theories of optics proposed by Greek philosophers. Vision could follow from intromission, as the atomists like Democritus had argued, by extramission after the manner of Euclid's theory, by some form of Platonic interaction, or via some medium. Al-Kindi rejected three of the four possibilities, adopting a Euclidean extramission theory. His rejection of the others was largely a negation of any form of intromission in the process of vision. The difficulty with theories incorporating intromission was conceived in terms of the contrast between optical projection to a point (the eye) and perceptual constancy: the former underwent many variations that were not evident in the latter. This apparent conflict between perspective and perception was to influence medieval scholars, too.

Both Avicenna (980–1037) and Alhazen accepted that the crystalline lens was the receptive organ for vision, although Alhazen did hint at times that the retina was involved, too. However, he adopted a theory of light similar to that of Aristotle, in which the medium was of prime importance. Alhazen's book on optics had virtually no impact on his contemporaries, but it was rediscovered almost two centuries later, and translated into Latin in the thirteenth century as either *Perspectiva* or *De Aspectibus* (Smith, 2001).

NATURE OF VERIDICALITY   57

MEDIEVAL OPTICS

The translation into Latin of the book on optics by Alhazen awakened Western scholars like Roger Bacon (Burke, 1928), Vitellonis (or Witelo, ca. 1230–1275; Smith, 1983), and John Pecham (ca. 1230–1292; Lindberg, 1970), to the physics of light, its mathematical treatment, and its application to vision. Later still, in 1572, Alhazen's *Opticae thesaurus* was published, together with Witelo's *Perspectiva*, in a single volume, edited by Friedrich Risner. It was in Kepler's (1604) reaction to the latter that among the things omitted by Witelo was the optical analysis of the retinal image. The medieval *Perspectiva* were principally about direct vision, that is visual optics rather than catoptrics or dioptrics. They shared a common assumption that vision should be analyzed in terms of a pyramid with its base on external objects and its apex located on the surface of or in the eye. This perspective pyramid carried with it the problems posed by Al-Kindi, namely the conflict between optical projection and visual perception. One consequence of this was to treat perception with great suspicion, while accepting the validity of perspective projections. Thus, through much of the late medieval period considerably more attention was directed to physical than to psychological dimensions of optics (Ronchi, 1970; Meyering, 1989).

Robert Grosseteste (ca. 1168–153) is not considered to have had access to Alhazen's *De Aspectibus*, and his analysis of light and vision was Platonic, with light emitted from the eye interacting with that reflected from objects. In the fifth century, Plato's distinction between the material, sensual body and the rational soul had been incorporated into Christian theology by St. Augustine (354–430), and it even permeated the nature of light: spiritual light was the internal illuminant of ideal forms, and physical light was considered to be analogous to this (Crombie, 1953). The ideal forms were rarely encountered in perspective projections; they were present in the mind and could be illuminated by divine light. Hence we find the emergence of distinctions between different forms of light—lux and lumen— which were maintained from the time of Albertus Magnus (ca. 1198–1280, see Dewan, 1980) to Reisch (1503). Lumen was external light, as from the sun or fire, whereas lux was perceived light.

The impact of absorbing the optics of Ptolemy (which had been translated into Latin in the twelfth century) and of Alhazen is clear in the contrast between Grosseteste and Roger Bacon. For Bacon, pyramids of light strike the eye but the physiological dimension remained Galenic. The crystalline lens was still taken to be the 'seat of vision' and 'species' remained a part of the process. Binocular combination was achieved at the optic chiasm: "We are to understand, moreover, that from the common nerve an imaginary straight line is directed between the two eyes and the object seen, meeting the axes of the eyes in the same part of the object seen, and this is the common axis" (Burke, 1928, p. 511). Objects peripheral to the common axis were not seen as distinctly.

The science of optics remained relatively unchanged in the late medieval period. In the sixteenth century both Franciscus Maurolico (1494–1575) and Giovanni Battista della Porta (1535–1615) continued the tradition of the early medieval perspectivists, and also described the refraction of light through lenses. Porta likened the *camera obscura* to the eye in the second edition of his popular treatise *Magiae naturalis* (1589), and he wrote a more serious book on vision, *De refractione*, four years later. The work of Maurolico contains strands that were to be amplified by Kepler (1604), although his work was unlikely to have been available to the latter. It was written in manuscript form between about 1520 and 1555 but it was not published until 1611, after Kepler's (1604) critique of Witelo's *Perspectiva*. Witelo's work was widely circulated towards the end of the sixteenth century: as noted above, it had been edited and published by Risner in 1572, together with Alhazen's *Opticae thesaurus*, and it was these analyses of optics that stimulated Kepler's interests.

The confusions about the nature of light at the end of the sixteenth century were crystallized by Andreas Laurentius (1558–1609; 1599/1938). He compared and contrasted the emission and reception theories of Plato and Aristotle. Among the nine "Reasons to proue that we see, by sending foorth something" were:

> "Wherefore should the eye grow weake with looking, but because there commeth out of it too much light, and that all the spirits vanish and fade away? Whence commeth it that such as would see a very little thing a far off, do claspe their eyes, & halfe close their eyelids? Is it not that so they may vnite the beames, and joyne together the spirits, to the end that afterwards they may cast them out more forcibly and directly?" (pp. 38–39)

While Plato suggested that there was fire or light in the eye, Aristotle's eye was filled with water, and Laurentius found the demonstrable support for the latter to be ample proof of Aristotle's theory. Nonetheless, he did provide "Reasons prouing that we see by taking in something"; in the main these were repetitions of Aristotle's observations about the passivity of sensation generally, responses to intense lights, and dimness of sight in old age.

EARLY MODERN OPTICS

Physical optics came of age in the seventeenth century (see Mach, 1926; Ronchi, 1970; Sabra, 1967). In addition to his *Ad Vitellionem paralipomena* of 1604, Kepler wrote *Dioptrice* in 1611. In the first of these he added many things to Witelo's perspective, both experimentally and theoretically. Amongst them was the formulation of the basic principle of photometry that the intensity of light diminishes with the square of the distance from the source. The classical arrangement for demonstrating this principle was illustrated by Rubens in the frontispiece to Book V of Franciscus Aguilonius (1567–1617; 1613). The light from candles passes through two circular apertures on to a screen; a septum ensures that each aperture receives light from one source only. In Rubens' engraving the light from a single candle at one distance is equal to that from two at about twice the distance. It is probable that Aguilonius was neither aware of nor subscribed to Kepler's inverse-square formulation (see Ziggelaar, 1983), but he did provide the experimental basis on which photometry would be built in the next century by Bouguer (1729, 1760, 1961) and Lambert (1760). Kepler devoted considerable attention to refraction in *Dioptrice*, but he did not determine the general sine law. Willebrord Snell (ca. 1581–1626), in an unpublished manuscript written around 1621, described the relationship between angles of incidence and refraction, upon which the subsequent technical advances in optical instrument manufacture were based. He did not use sines in his formulation, but the dimensions that he described are equivalent (Vollgraff, 1936).

Snell's law, as it became known, was elaborated by Descartes (1637/1965) in his *Dioptrique*, and he treated the analysis of the rainbow in his discourses on meteorology. His experimental approach to displaying the prismatic spectrum was somewhat different to that adopted later by Newton (1704): sunlight fell normally on one face of the prism, and was refracted at the second face, upon which the aperture was placed; he noted that the distinctness of the spectrum was dependent on the size of the aperture. His mechanistic interpretation of visible colors was in harmony with his concept of light generally: colors corresponded to different rates of rotation of bodies in the medium.

Had Huygens not been aware of Snell's manuscript and made reference to it in his *Dioptrique* (1653), the relation between sines of the angles of incidence and refraction might have been called Descartes' law. In his *Traité de la lumiere* (1690/1912) Huygens made analogies between mechanical events like projectiles bouncing from surfaces, and applied these to reflections and refractions of light. Light, according to Descartes, acted like a mechanical force which is transmitted through transparent media. His theory of light attracted much criticism in his day because of the inconsistencies it embraced. On the one hand he argued that light was propagated instantly, and on the other that it varied its velocity according to the density of the medium through which it traveled.

The phenomenon of diffraction was demonstrated by Franciscus Maria Grimaldi (1613–1663; 1665), who suggested that light might act like a liquid, flowing in waves. Wave theory was supported and extended by Huygens: he proposed and illustrated the wave-fronts that could be produced by points on luminous sources, and he made an analogy between light and sound; diffraction was analyzed in terms of the wave-fronts originating at the aperture. Huygens (1690/1912) wrote:

> "Now there is no doubt at all that light also comes from the luminous body to our eyes by some movement impressed on the matter which is between the two ... If, in addition, light takes time for its passage ... it will follow that this movement, impressed on the intervening matter, is successive; and consequently it spreads, as Sound does, by spherical surfaces and waves: for I call them waves from their resemblance to those which are seen to be formed in water when a stone is thrown into it, and which present a successive spreading as circles.... each little region of a luminous body, such as the Sun, a candle, or a burning coal, generates its own waves of which that region is the centre. Thus in the flame of a candle, having distinguished the points A, B, C, concentric circles described about each of these points represent the waves which come from them. And one must imagine the same about every point of the surface and of the part within the flame." (1912, pp. 4 and 17)

In contrast, Newton (1730) proposed that light consisted of small corpuscles which collided with one another: "Are not the Rays of Light very small Bodies emitted from shining Substances? For such Bodies will pass through uniform Medium in right Lines without bending into the Shadow, which is the Nature of Rays of Light" (p. 345). Despite this statement, Newton did not rule out the operation of light as waves. Thereafter, the theoretical contrast was between Huygens' wave theory and Newton's corpuscular theory of light (see Sabra, 1967; Shapiro, 1980; Ronchi, 1970; Cantor, 1977).

With the appreciation that light could be considered as a physical property, and that its reflections and refractions followed physical principles, its study became the province of physicists, whereas the examination of sight was pursued by physiologists and philosophers. The separation of the physics of light from the philosophy of sight was to reflect the ancient schism between materialists and idealists: light was an external, material phenomenon whereas sight was internal and subjective.

NATURE OF SIGHT

Well over two thousand years ago there were medical practitioners in Babylon, Mesopotamia, and Egypt, some of whom were eye specialists. They must have had a working knowledge of ocular anatomy in order to carry out the operations they are known to have performed. However, the records that have survived (for example in the Ebers papyrus) relate mainly to the fees they charged and the penalties they suffered for faulty operations rather than the conditions they cured. Their skills and understanding would have been passed on to Greek physicians, who both developed and recorded them. Accounts of the history of ophthalmology can be found in Albert and Edwards (1996), Duke-Elder (1961). Hirschberg (1899), and Shastid (1917).

Many Greek texts, through their translations, have been transmitted to us, but any illustrations that they might have included have not survived. This void has been filled by Magnus (1901), who has redrawn diagrams of the eye to reflect the written accounts of ocular anatomy in the Greek period. He produced schematic eyes he believed corresponded to texts by Democritus, Aristotle, Celsus, Rufus of Ephesus, and Galen. Sudhoff's (1907) counsel of caution should be repeated when interpreting these reconstructions: in producing the illustrations Magnus would have found it difficult to exclude his knowledge of both anatomy and perspective, so the reconstructions would have appeared very strange to the authors to whom they are attributed. In this regard, it is instructive to compare Galen's eye with the fragment of a manuscript drawing that is reproduced in May's (1968) translation of Galen. The latter is a much cruder representation that does not bear a great deal of similarity to the reconstruction by Magnus, but both would have been derived from text alone. Moreover, not all those to whom diagrams of the eye are attributed would have based their knowledge on dissections of animal or human eyes. Perhaps only Aristotle and Galen would have recorded their own observations.

Sight will be considered here first in terms of the anatomical structure of the eye and its comparison with a camera, although these aspects are elaborated in Chapter 4. One consequence of equating eye and camera was a concentration on the problem of focusing on objects at different distances (accommodation). Various historians have commented on the struggle to account for accommodation. For example, John Hunter, in a letter to Joseph Banks in 1793, noted:

> "The laws of optics are so well understood, and the knowledge of the eye, when considered as an optical instrument, has been rendered so perfect, that I do not consider myself capable of making any addition to it; but still there is a power in the eye by which it can adapt itself to different distances far too extensive for the simple mechanism of the parts to effect." (Home, 1794, p. 24)

The situation was succinctly summarized by Helmholtz (1873) in one of his *Popular lectures*: "The mechanism by which this [accommodation] is accomplished ... was one of the greatest riddles of the physiology of

the eye since the time of Kepler...No problem in optics has given rise to
so many contradictory theories as this" (p. 205). Corrections for errors of
refraction have a longer history still, and this will be touched upon briefly
before describing some of the early views about the retina and the paths
taken by the optic nerves to the brain.

EYE

The initial Greek speculations about the anatomy of the eye, like those
advanced by Empedocles, were founded in philosophy: the four elements
of earth, air, fire, and water, led to the proposition that there must be four
coats to the eye. The optic nerve was described by Alcmaeon in the sixth
century B.C., and it was thought of as a hollow tube, enabling humors to
pass from the brain to the eye. About a century later Democritus provided
a more detailed description of the eye: it was a simple spherical structure
consisting of two coats enclosing a humor that could pass along the hollow
optic nerve, after the manner proposed by Alcmaeon. Light could pass
through the aperture (pupil) and no lens was represented within the eye.
The optic nerve left the eye in the line of the optic axis.

The dominance of philosophy over observation was partially reversed
for the school of Æsculapius that emerged in the fifth century B.C., of which
Hippocrates (ca. 460–370 B.C.) was a member. Naturalistic observation partially replaced superstition, but the examination of anatomical organs was
prohibited then (see Garrison, 1914; Osler, 1921; Singer, 1925; Choulant,
1945). The moral strictures of the time did not countenance dissection of
dead bodies, although this was soon to change with the Platonic dissoci-
ation of the body from the soul. It is known that Aristotle did dissect the
eyes of animals, and he is believed to have written at least one book (now
lost) on the eye (see Diogenes Laertius, 1925). The dawning of more exact
knowledge of the structure of the eye was marked by drawing on the evidence from dissection rather than dogma. Aristotle's diagram of the eye
shows three coats enclosing the humor, supplied by three ducts:

> "From the eye there go three ducts to the brain: the largest and the medium-
> sized to the cerebellum, the least to the brain itself; and the least is the one
> situated nearest to the nostrils. The two largest ones, then, run side by side and
> do not meet; the medium-sized ones meet—and this is particularly visible in
> fishes,—for they lie nearer than the large ones to the brain; the smallest pair are
> the most widely separate from one another, and do not meet." (Smith and Ross,
> 1910, p. 495a).

The lens was probably not included because its appearance was assumed
to be an artifact of dissecting a dead eye.

In the first century A.D., the Roman writer Celsus (ca. 25 B.C.–29 A.D.) drew together the Greek knowledge of medicine. The drawing of the eye by Magnus (1901) attributed to him represented the lens although it was located in the center of the eye. The anterior chamber was described as an empty space and it was separated from the posterior by a membrane, to which the lens was attached: "This is enclosed by a small membrane, which proceeds from the internal part of the eye. Under these is a drop of humor, resembling the white of an egg, from which proceeds the faculty of vision. By the Greeks it is called chrystalloides" (Shastid, 1917, p. 8581). As was noted above, the notion that the lens was the seat of vision, which was amplified by Galen, was to survive for many centuries.

The lens was more accurately located in Magnus' (1901) drawing based on the writings of Rufus of Ephesus (fl. 100), and the vitreous humor lay between it and the retina. The vitreous was completely enclosed and the optic nerve was not continuous with it, unlike Galen's diagram. In the latter the anterior and posterior curvatures of the lens were distinguished, and two of the extraocular muscles were shown. Rufus wrote of the lens that "at first this had no special name, but later it was named *lentil-like* on account of its form, and *crystalline* on account of the character of its humour" (Singer, 1921, p. 389).

Galen was one of the greatest of the Greek anatomists. He practiced medicine in Alexandria and Rome as well as in Pergamum. He based his anatomy on dissections of animals, particularly monkeys, but most of his ocular anatomy was derived from dissecting the eyes of freshly slaughtered oxen (Siegel, 1970). Galen drew extensively on the anatomical writing of Herophilus (ca. 335–425 B.C.), which are now lost, and on the physiological speculations of Erasistratus (ca. 310–250 B.C.), both of whom based them on dissections of human and animal bodies. The restrictions that were placed on dissections in the early Christian and Islamic worlds resulted in a reliance on Greek (and particularly Galen's) works on anatomy, and they were recounted dogmatically until the time of Vesalius over one thousand years later. The journey from Galen to Vesalius was tortuous, not least for those who required surgery. There was general disinterest in science and medicine after the sacking of Rome in the fifth century, but Greek anatomical wisdom was retained by Islamic scholars, who translated many books into Arabic and eventually transmitted them to late medieval students (O'Leary, 1949).

Galen's medical works were translated into Arabic by Hunain ibn Is-hâq (ca. 807–877). The earliest surviving diagrams of the eye are to be found in Islamic manuscripts (see Meyerhof, 1928; Polyak, 1942, 1957), of which that by Hunain ibn Is-hâq is probably the oldest. It is essentially a functional diagram, since it adopts different viewpoints for different parts of the eye. This could be the reason why the pupil and the lens are shown in circular form, and the lens is situated in the middle of the eye. The extraocular muscles were also illustrated. Hunain ibn Is-hâq's illustration was copied several times in the centuries that followed. Thus, Arabic accounts of the eye drew on Galen for inspiration, but their illustrations reflect a greater concern with geometry than anatomy. This is also the case for the diagrams corresponding to Ibn al-Haytham's text. The Arabic manuscript represents two eyes, and incorporates the meeting of the optic nerves at the optic chiasm (see Polyak, 1942). Ibn al-Haytham (Alhazen) added greatly to the understanding of binocular vision, which was probably the reason for representing two eyes. The illustration of the eye that was printed in Risner's (1572) translation of Alhazen and Witelo is essentially similar to that of Vesalius, and shows a single eye.

As was the case for optics, scholars in the late Middle Ages derived much of their knowledge from manuscript translations of Alhazen into Latin, and the diagrams of the eyes by both Bacon and Pecham showed a similar preoccupation with geometry. Essentially the same principles were operating in later Arabic drawings of the pathways from the eyes to the brain depict the optic nerves extending to the lens itself, and they cross at the chiasm with a geometrical symmetry.

Printed figures of the eye were published from the beginning of the sixteenth century, and some are shown in Wade (1998b). Reisch's (1503) diagram is perhaps the oldest version. However, this is unlikely to have been based on observation of actual eyes, but derived from earlier manuscript drawings; it does bear a close resemblance to a fifteenth century manuscript drawing based on concentric circles (see Sudhoff, 1907; Choulant, 1945). Reisch wrote his *Margarita philosophica* as a guide for the Carthusian monks in his order. The section including the diagram of the eye is but a small part of the work, and does not suggest any active pursuit of ocular anatomy. A similar diagram was printed in a specifically anatomical book by Ryff (1541), with an improvement in the representation of the crystalline: it took on a lenticular rather than a spherical shape. This slight modification does suggest that the benefits of direct observation were beginning to be incorporated into anatomical drawings. Ryff's diagram was frequently copied in the century that followed. Very shortly thereafter, the genius of Vesalius was brought to bear on the topic, and the modern era of anatomy was founded.

In the fourteenth century, sanctions prohibiting dissection of human bodies were relaxed and knowledge concerning anatomy in general slowly began to be based on more secure ground, although the descriptions were not always accurate and observation often remained a slave to Galenic dogma. The dissecting skills of the anatomist were critical, and the major advances came with practitioners like Leonardo da Vinci and Vesalius. Leonardo's detailed drawings of dissections did not make any immediate impact because they remained both in manuscript form and in private hands. Unlike his anatomical drawings of the musculature, those of the eye reflected a conflation of dissection and dogma: his rather crude drawings reflected a reliance on Galen, even though he did prepare the excised eye (by boiling it in the white of an egg) for dissection. His drawings of the eye showed the lens as spherical and central in the eye, and the optic nerves passed to the cerebral ventricles (see McMurrich, 1930; Gross, 1998).

The renaissance of anatomy is associated with Vesalius, who published his book *De humani corporis fabrica* in 1543. It is taken to be a synthesis of science and art because of the high quality of the anatomical illustrations. The blocks from which the woodcuts were printed survived into the twentieth century, and they were reprinted in Saunders and O'Malley (1950). Vesalius presented an account of anatomy that was almost free from the legacy of Galen. While Vesalius could examine the structure of the eye with his own rather than Galen's eyes, he did not pay too much attention to it. His diagram of the eye did not match the detail or accuracy of those for the skeletal musculature and internal organs: a symmetrical lens was still located in the center of the eye and the optic nerve was situated on the optic axis. He listed the various structures, but did not pursue their function in any detail. Felix Platter (1536–1614; 1583) moved the lens towards the pupil and recorded the differences between the curvatures of its front and back surfaces, otherwise the structures were essentially similar to those described by Vesalius, as was the case for Porta's (1593) diagram.

Hieronymous Fabricius ab Aquapendente (1537–1619; 1600) placed the lens appropriately within the eye, and defined the optical centers of several of the refracting surfaces. The optic nerve left the eye centrally in these diagrams, but there is a hint of its lateral shift in the diagram from Aguilonius (1613). A few years later Scheiner (1619) gave the first accurate diagram of the eye; the lens and its curvatures are appropriately represented and the optic nerve leaves the eye nasally. This figure has frequently been reprinted, and it is often claimed that it represents a human eye (e.g. Polyak, 1957; Finger, 1994), even though Scheiner stated that he did not have the opportunity of dissecting one:

"The observation of most animals' eyes tells us all these things; indeed these processes happen in the eyes of cows, sheep, goats, and pigs, on which I have done many experiments in the presence of other people; logical reasoning leads me to suppose a similar process for the human eyes as well, because in every man's eye there is a hole, through which the optical nerve comes out, placed in the same position as in animals; indeed the cavities of each eye are placed in the skull along the sides of the bone which shapes the nasal projection, although in

the case of man we have to rely on reasoning more than on observation, because
I have never had the opportunity to test a human eye." (1619, p. 18)

Scheiner's analysis was rapidly absorbed by both anatomists and philosophers, particularly by Descartes (1637/1902). His illustration of image formation in the eye of the cosmic observer is perhaps one of the most widely reproduced images in visual science. It encapsulates the advances made in the previous four decades: light is refracted from the various curved surfaces in the eye to form an image on the retina, and the eye through which the light passes is accurately depicted.

RETINA

The retina was considered by Galen to be an outgrowth of the brain; it had a net-like structure, and it provided nourishment for the vitreous, which in turn nourished the lens—the "principal instrument of vision". In this way the pneuma, or visual spirit, could communicate between the brain and the lens: the pneuma were considered to travel along the optic nerves and interact with images of external objects carried in the air to the lens. The visual spirit returned along the optic nerves to the cerebral ventricles where they interacted with the animal spirit. The retina was thus relegated to a nutritional role in this theory of vision. The difficulty with reconciling such a theory with the transmission of light through the transparent lens is evident in a statement by Averroes (1126–1198), in which the possibility of the retina being the "perceptive faculty" is entertained:

"The innermost coats of the eye [i.e. the retina] must necessarily receive the
light from the humors of the eye, just as the humors receive the light from the
air. However, inasmuch as the perceptive faculty resides in the region of this
coat of the eye, in the part which is connected with the cranium and not in the
part facing the air, these coats, that is to say, the curtains of the eye, therefore
protect the faculty of the sense by virtue of the fact that they are situated in the
middle between the faculty and the air." (1961, p. 9)

Platter (1583) was explicit in specifying the retina as the receptive organ: "The principal organ of vision, namely the optic nerve, expands through the whole hemisphere of the retina as soon as it enters the eye. This receives and discriminates the form and color of external objects which together with the light enter the eye through the opening of the pupil and are projected on it by the lens" (Koelbing, 1967, p. 72). This view was amplified by Kepler (1604), but how vision occurred was still a mystery, as Kepler acknowledged, and an appreciation of image formation on the retina was not the solution.

Visual Pathways

Ignorance of the anatomy of the eye in antiquity was amplified with respect to the pathways from the eyes to the brain. Indeed, the involvement of the brain itself in perception and cognition was often denied in early Greek science. On the basis of his dissections of animals, Alcmaeon did advance the opinion that these functions were located in the brain, but his view was not widely held (Singer, 1925). Hippocrates also located the pleasures, sensations, and thoughts in the brain, but the most widely held belief made the heart the locus of sentience, and this was supported by the authority of Aristotle. He had observed that stimulation of the exposed brain did not result in any sensation, and that invertebrates did not have a brain. In addition, he believed that the brain was devoid of blood, which was considered to be an essential component of sensation. The heart, on the other hand, was thought to have connections with the sense organs and it was the source of heat in the body. Earlier, Empedocles had advanced the opinion that the heart was the source of the anima or soul, the spirit of which circulated around the body by the blood.

As was noted above, Alcmaeon proposed that the optic nerves were hollow tubes, and this tradition was continued by Aristotle, as is evident from the diagram of the eye attributed to him. Magnus (1901) represented Aristotle's pathways as comprising three ducts which were considered to pass from the eye to the brain; the largest and medium-sized ducts proceeded to the cerebellum, and the smallest to the cerebrum. Contrary to Aristotle, Galen believed that the origin of the visual pathways was located in the anterior ventricle of the brain, where the animal spirit could interact with the visual spirit, borne by the optic nerves. The optic nerves themselves came together at the optic chiasm, but each of the nerves remained on its own side:

> "If one did not prepare this specimen carefully, one might easily believe that the [optic nerves] really cross each other and run one above the other. That, however, is not the true state of affairs. But as soon as they have touched each other inside the skull they unite their central canals; they then separate immediately, as if to show simply and solely that they only came in contact in order to unite their canals." (Siegel, 1970, pp. 60–62)

Hunain ibn Is-hâq restated the Galenic doctrine that the hollow optic nerves unite at the chiasm; it was so depicted by Ibn al-Haytham, and maintained in later Arabic representations.

The anterior ventricle to which Galen referred was likely to have been the thalamus. Three ventricles were innumerated in Galenic anatomy, and Albertus Magnus incoporated them into late medieval philosophy as representing the sites of perception, reasoning, and memory (Dewan, 1980).

The prevalence of this notion is evident in Leonardo's diagram of the visual pathways: in some other drawings the optic nerves lead directly into the first of the three ventricles without even meeting at the optic chiasm (see McMurrich, 1930; Keele, 1955; Gross, 1998). The more detailed dissections by Vesalius (1543), Varoli (1591), and Laurentius (1599) resulted in illustrations of the base of the brain that charted the course of the optic nerves to the chiasm and beyond, but they were restricted to the gross anatomy.

EYE GLASSES

Throughout the turbulent period of debate about the optical properties of the eye, corrections for presbyopia had been available and were widely used. Convex lenses assisted the eyes of the aged in the medieval period, long before the reasons for their efficacy were understood. As is the case with most developmental changes, age-related difficulties in vision were described in antiquity. Aristotle remarked on the recession of the distance of distinct vision in old people, and Seneca (ca. 6–65) related how letters could be magnified when viewed through water-filled glass balls (burning glasses). Until optical corrections were introduced in the thirteenth century, the suggested compensation for old people was to view objects through a small aperture (like the crooked finger) as this was known to sharpen vision.

Roger Bacon wrote about vision and optics during the 1260s, while at Oxford. It is sometimes thought that Bacon introduced optical corrections for presbyopia, but others were engaged in similar practices during the thirteenth century (see Hill, 1915; Rosen, 1956; Schmitz, 1982, 1995). As one author points out: "Bacon is certainly not the 'discoverer' of reading glasses, but he is the one who recognized the significance of visual aids, carried out improvements on them, sought a scientific explanation for their operation, and addressed the problem of optical corrections theoretically" (Schmitz, 1995, p. 27).

Despite the fact that Bacon recognized that sight in the elderly could be improved by convex lenses, an idea with obvious practical ramifications, the basis of accommodation remained mysterious for years to come. What was lacking was as a good theory of optical image formation—a problem stemming from poor ocular anatomy and adherence to ancient theories that failed to recognize the retina as the receptive surface for light penetrating the lens. To cite but one example, Leonardo da Vinci, who suffered from presbyopia and wore glasses in his later years, attributed his problem to loss of binocular convergence in old age (Keele, 1955).

In 1593, Porta recognized that the sharpness of the image is dependent on the diameter of the aperture, and he applied this finding to presbyopia:

"There are two reasons why older people by using convex lenses can see better and more clearly. First because with age the pupil becomes slack and not only the pupil but all the organs and the control of the organs of the body, which becomes incontinent. Because of the slackening of the pupil the rays wander more freely and carry to the crystalline lens the object less well defined. By means of the converging lenses the rays of the simulacrum are once again re-united and the pyramid is more closely composed . . . so that converging lenses by constricting the simulacrum compensate the defect. The second reason is because in old people the vitreous humour becomes altered and less pure . . . and when light enters the eye through a crystal it becomes clearer and brighter." (Ronchi, 1970, p. 72)

Following Platter's (1583) work on the retina, additional dissections led to more accurate representations of the human eye. As indicated above, the principal integration of optics and ocular anatomy took place early in the seventeenth century as a consequence of Kepler's and Scheiner's insights. With the clearer understanding of optics, corrections for presbyopia became routine, although doubts still remained about its cause. Kepler (1611), for example, thought that it was a consequence of experience: those whose work involves observations of distant objects become incapable of seeing near ones as well. However, biconcave lenses were also prescribed for the shortsighted before Kepler conducted his analysis (Smith, 1998). In Florence, which was a major center for optical instrument making in the fifteenth century, both convex and concave lenses of different power were constructed so that they could be matched to the correction required. The power of the convex lenses was specified in terms of the ages of those who required them, in five year intervals, and orders were requested for "those apt and suitable for distant vision, that is for the young" (Ilardi, 2001, p. 167). Maurolico, writing in the sixteenth century, lamented the demise of this practice:

"There is, therefore, a certain assigned limit to vision with either the one or the other type of spectacles. For, as has been already said, and as daily experience shows, we cannot see and cannot read at the same distance with all glasses. I myself, indeed use somewhat different glasses for observing or reading at long, short, and still shorter distances: the more convex spectacles are adapted to seeing at shorter distances because they bring [the rays] together and hasten their union. Even through the same glasses young people can see at shorter distances than the aged because, of course, the juvenile rays are more convergent than the aged, so that, through the same instrument, the rays are brought earlier into the union; and hence they need less distance for seeing distinctly. From this it will be clear that as many different kinds of glasses have been employed for the same vision as there are men of different ages employing the same glasses to secure a different range of vision. Spectacles for any individual should, of course, be suited to his age, so that the far-sighted where the vision is more scattered and where there is more need of convergence may use the more convex glasses. I remember, some time back, that makers of glasses exercised such care

that they indicated by small marks—one for each year—the age for which the
spectacles were suited; but today this is no longer the custom." (Maurolico,
1611, translated by Crew, 1940, p. 118)

The writing of Kepler at the beginning of the seventeenth century has many
features in common with that of Maurolico. Although Maurolico's work
on optics was written in mid-sixteenth century it was not published untill
1611, long after his death. It would not, therefore, have been available to
Kepler.

Although the assistance of convex lenses in presbyopia was readily
appreciated in the thirteenth century, the integration of the lenticular optics with vision, and their relation to accommodation was to wait another
three centuries. Two factors retarded such integration: ignorance of both
the dioptrics and the anatomy of the eye. When these were more clearly
understood, early in the seventeenth century, corrections for both short-
and long-sightedness became routine, notwithstanding the doubts that
remained concerning their causes. Kepler considered that these conditions
were a consequence of experience; those whose work involved detailed
observation of near objects became incapable of seeing distant objects,
and vice versa. Descartes' (1637) analysis was much more mechanistic and
pragmatic. He attributed short- and long-sightedness to the shape of the
eye ball itself, and sought to determine the appropriate optical correction
by, essentially, employing different lenses to define the near and far points
of distinct vision. Thereafter, the corrections for myopia and presbyopia
were amplified and illustrated by many writers. Nonetheless, presbyopia
was the most common error of refraction and it was not distinguished from
hyperopia.

SUMMARY

In an historical sense, veridicality in perception has been taken for granted.
In so far as perception of objects was constant and served as an adequate
guide to behavior, then there was relatively little to study. Errors in perception, as was noted in Chapter 2, were considered to occur when the
assumption of object constancy was contravened, but the perception of
the constant features of objects was rarely investigated. Veridicality has
been analyzed in terms of the stimulus for the senses, and we have focused on light. The initial theories of light conflated its subjective and
objective dimensions—that is, they confused light and sight. The separation of physical optics from physiological and psychological optics has led
to detailed investigations of the former and relative neglect of the latter.

Those who studied visual experience assumed that their perceptions were matched by those of others. Individual differences were rarely examined. Even in the area of color vision and its deficiencies discoveries of differences between individuals were remarkably recent. A multitude of devices for studying the senses was invented in the nineteenth century, and these led to numerous discoveries (Chapter 5). Before that, however, some basic aspects of vision (like accommodation) needed to be resolved, and these were achieved in the two centuries preceding it. Moreover, the emerging science of the senses found itself able to address fundamental features of philosophy, as in the debate about whether the perception of space was innate. It is to these issues that we now turn.

4

Perception in the Seventeenth and Eighteenth Centuries

The seventeenth century heralded the scientific renaissance. The scientific methods that had proved so successful in the physical and chemical sciences were seen as relevant to life processes. The anatomy of the senses and the brain were gradually elucidated, and these anatomical structures were related to function. In addition, the lessons of science were absorbed into philosophy. Descartes did distinguish between the mechanical body and the immaterial mind, but his application of scientific rigor to understanding the senses set psychology on a course from which it has seldom wavered. Interaction with the world through the senses provides the basis for much in philosophy and physiology, the twin precursors of modern psychology.

In the nineteenth century psychology emerged as the interface between philosophy and the natural sciences. It addressed the eternal questions of philosophy by deed rather than by word: it embraced the scientific method to frame the questions empirically. The methods adopted initially were adapted from other sciences, most notably from physics and physiology. From the mid-nineteenth century new methods were developed for studying perception and performance that distinguished psychology from both philosophy and physiology. Nonetheless, the seventeenth and eighteenth centuries did make inroads into the study of the senses, and it is from these that the edifice of nineteenth century psychology was erected. Vision provides the lens through which this history can be observed. Indeed, it is the process of focusing (accommodation) that provided one of the enduring problems throughout the two centuries. Thus, we will commence with an analysis of the impact of optics, particularly the consideration of the eye as a mechanical instrument.

IMPACT OF OPTICS

The overarching analogy that has been applied to the eye is that of the camera. Initially the comparison was between the eye and the *camera obscura*, the simple dark chamber with a small aperture. With a developing knowledge of both physical and physiological optics, devices capable of focusing on objects at variable distances were compared—both eye and camera containing a lens. The problem of focusing then took center stage. Helmholtz repeatedly made the analogy in his popular lectures on vision, stating succinctly: "Regarded as an optical instrument, the eye is a camera obscura. This apparatus is well known in the form used by photographers.... The eye has the same task of bringing at one time near, at another distant, objects to focus at the back of its dark chamber. So that some power of adjustment or "accommodation" is necessary" (1873, pp. 202–203).

Joseph Le Conte (1823–1901) was one of Helmholtz's contemporaries who also compared the eye to a camera. In his book *Sight* which appeared in 1881, he included a chapter with the same title as Helmholtz's popular lecture on optics. Le Conte's chapter opened as follows: "The further explanation of the wonderful mechanism of the eye is best brought out by a comparison with some optical instrument. We select for this purpose the photographic camera. The eye and the camera: the one a masterpiece of Nature's, the other of human art" (p. 30).

The camera analogy had long guided thinking about the eye and its optical functions. Direct comparisons between the eye and the *camera obscura* were made in the sixteenth century, although, as was indicated in Chapter 3, the dioptrical properties of the eye were not really understood until the early-seventeenth century.

Eye as an Optical Instrument

The principles of the *camera obscura* first began to be correctly analyzed in the eleventh century, when they were outlined by Alhazen. His starting point was the division of the visible objects into point sources, each of which emitted perpendicular rays that could be subjected to punctiform analyses. In his *Perspectiva* he described and presented the principles underlying the inverted, reversed, and clear images. For example, some candles on one side of a room would make images on a dark surface situated behind a small aperture: "if there is a fire facing a hole that leads into a dark chamber, the light of that fire will appear in the chamber opposite the hole" (Sabra, 1989, p. 14).

At the turn of the sixteenth century Leonardo da Vinci made an explicit analogy between the *camera obscura* and the eye in his treatise *On the Eye* (Strong, 1967). Like others at the time, Leonardo considered that vision should be analyzed in terms of a pyramid, with its base on the external object and its apex on the surface of (or in) the eye. He drew attention, perhaps for the first time, to the manner in which the pupil widens as light diminishes and becomes smaller as light increases. The lens, long believed to be the receptive surface for sight, also featured in Leonardo's thinking, although he paid more attention to the extremity of the optic nerve as a possible receptive or sensitive area. He did not, however, look upon the retina as a screen onto which the image is projected, an idea that might have emerged from knowledge of how the *camera obscura* worked.

Leonardo was disturbed by the idea that the rays from the visual field must intersect at the pupil to produce an inverted image like that obtained with a pinhole camera. How could the image carried by the optic nerve be anything but upright? One solution was that there was an inversion in front of the lens and a second inversion within the lens, and another was that an inverted image from the back of the eye reflects back upon the lens in a way that makes it erect again. Leonardo's numerous diagrams and notes show that he was never really satisfied with these or any other ideas.

Others, however, continued to make progress, drawing on the camera model. For example, in 1569 Daniello Barbaro (1513–1570) made a closer equation with the eye when he placed a convex lens in the aperture of a *camera obscura*. Twenty years later Porta (1589, 1593) again likened the *camera obscura* to an eye. Although he placed lenses in the camera's aperture and, in his anatomical diagrams, moved the lens more toward the front of the eye, he did not present a new theory of vision—one based on the lens of the eye as a focusing device. Instead, he still retained the ancient theory supported by Alhazen and Witelo, that the receptive process or visual power stems from the lens, which is anatomically connected by the surrounding web or capsule (the *aranea*) to the retina and optic nerve. Porta believed that forming an image on a surface was the solution to vision:

> "Before I part from the operations of this Glass [lens], I will tell you some use
> of it, that is very pleasant and admirable, whence great secrets of Nature may
> appear to us. As, *To see all things in the dark, that are outwardly done in the Sun, with
> the colours of them*. You must shut all the chamber windows, and it will do well
> to shut up all holes besides, lest any light breaking in should spoil all. . . . Now
> will I declare what I ever concealed till now, and thought to conceal continually.
> If you put a small centicular Crystal glass to the hole, you shall presently see all
> things clearer. . . . Hence you may, *If you cannot draw a Picture of a man or any thing
> else, draw it by this means*; If you can but onely make the colours. This is an Art
> worth learning. . . . Hence it may appear to Philosophers, and those that study
> Optics, how vision is made; and the question of intromission is taken away,
> that was anciently so discussed; nor can there be any better way to demonstrate
> both, than this. The image is let in by the pupil, as by the hole in the window;
> and that part of the Sphere, that is set in the middle of the eye, stands instead of
> a Crystal Table." (Porta, 1589, from a translation of 1669, pp. 363–364 and 365,
> original italics)

Kepler (1604) broke new ground early in the seventeenth century when he analyzed how images might be formed in the eye. His primary concern was to construct more accurate optical instruments for astronomical observation. Astronomical problems could only be resolved with a proper understanding of visual theory. This led him to examine the operation of the *camera obscura*, which in turn stimulated the thought that the eye with its aperture must function in a similar but imperfect way. He tried to understand how the crystalline lens focused rays of light by using water-filled glass flasks. Kepler not only constructed what can be thought of as an early artificial eye, but was probably the first Western scientist to analyze pinhole images correctly (Lindberg, 1968, 1976; Park, 1997; Smith, 1998).

Kepler recognized that the functioning eye posed its own special problems which warranted investigation. He concluded that the visual image is not "caught" by the lens but "painted" on the retina, the eye's true sensitive element. He also correctly recognized that the retinal image, which he called a *pictura*, must be inverted and reversed. But it is with the *pictura* on the reddish-white concave surface of the retina that his optics ends. How the reversed and inverted image is corrected was beyond the scope of his mathematical science. Kepler did not determine how the lens may change shape to focus on near and distant objects. He did, however, shift the focus of vision from the lens to the retina. The recognition that the crystalline lens operated like a glass lens directed attention to both the image that was so formed and the surface upon which it was projected. The fact that objects at different distances could be brought to focus on the retina followed from his analysis, but it did not cast light on the manner in which this was achieved.

Kepler, like Alhazen and many others who studied optics, did not actually engage in dissections of eyes. He relied on those trained in anatomy, especially Platter (1583), whose diagrams he reproduced. Platter made a clear and strong statement about how the lens serves only to focus the rays of light converging on it. This was a significant turning point in visual science. Although he did not formulate a theory of the retinal image, understand the geometrical issues, or recognize the inverted nature of the image on the retina, Platter directed new attention on the role of the retina in photosensitivity at a time when most others were still regarding the lens as the sensitive organ.

Platter recognized that the lens is not located in the center of the eye, and in his drawings moved it closer to its proper location. His anatomy, however, was not without fault. Among other things, his diagrams of the eye repeated the error of representing the optic nerve on the visual axis. In this regard, Platter and many of his contemporaries might have been influenced by the descriptions of the eye provided by Vesalius (1543).

Scheiner (1630) was able to demonstrate the image forming properties of the eye by placing an excised animal's eye in the aperture of a *camera obscura* and noting how an image could be seen on the exposed rear surface the retina. His demonstration was considered so valuable that it was repeated and illustrated seven years later by Descartes (1637/1902), who even replaced the retina with an eggshell in some experiments. Later in the seventeenth century, Jacques Rohault (1620–1675; 1671) constructed a much more sophisticated model of the eye:

"I have thought that the same Thing might be done, by making a large artificial Eye, which I accordingly tryed: The opake Coats, or Tunicks, were all made of thick Paper, except the Retina, which was made of a very white thin Piece of Vellum; in the Room of the Tunica Cornea, I put a transparent Glass, and instead of the Chrystalline Humour, was a Piece of Chrystal of the Figure of a Lens, but more flat than this Humour; for since there was nothing in this Machine but Air, in the Places of the aqueous and vitreous Humours, a little less Convexity was sufficient to produce the Refractions required: And because it was very difficult to flatten or lengthen this artificial Eye, in the manner the natural Eye is done by the Muscles, I placed the Vellum in such a manner, that it could be moved backward and forward, at pleasure." (English translation of 1723, pp. 243–244)

Rohault was able to demonstrate the restricted range of focusing with his system. He also showed the need for adjusting the amount of separation of the vellum from the lens for proper focusing of objects at different distances from the eye. By the end of the seventeenth century, the eye was, for all intents and purposes, to be regarded as a sophisticated optical instrument.

IMPACT OF ANATOMY

The gross anatomy of the eye was reasonably well established by the middle of the seventeenth century, but the manner in which it functioned remained mysterious. Old ideas about species were retained by some, like Thomas Willis (1621–1675; 1664), to account for vision, even if the species were carried by the optic nerve to the brain. A truly mechanistic interpretation was given by Newton (ca. 1682) in a work unpublished in his lifetime: light produced vibrations in the retina, and these were conducted to the brain along the optic nerve. It would appear that Newton conducted experiments with cut sections of optic nerve and concluded that vision like hearing is mediated by vibrations, largely because of his lack of success in isolating the animal spirit:

> "tho' I tied a piece of the optic nerve at one end, and warmed it in the middle, to see if any airy substance by that means would disclose itself in bubbles at the other end, I could not spy the least bubble; a little moisture only, and the marrow itself squeezed out.... And that vision is thus made, is very conformable to the sense of hearing, which is made by like vibrations." (Harris, 1775, p. 100)

A somewhat similar mechanical analogy was entertained by Leeuwenhoek (1675), who examined the structure of the retina with his simple microscope. He reported seeing many small "globuls", which could have been rods, cones, or optic nerve fibers. He likened a glass of water to the optic nerve which contained the globules or filaments; when the surface of the water is touched, the pressure is transmitted to the base, as the filaments might transmit to the brain. It was over a century and a half later before the microanatomy of the retina was revealed in greater detail (see Polyak, 1957). Zinn (1755) did provide an illustration of the microscopic appearance of the net-like patterning over the retina, but the early microscopes could not resolve the detail of its cellular structure. This was to await the application of compound achromatic microscopes available in the early nineteenth century.

Porterfield (1759) appreciated that the retina was a necessary but not sufficient component of visual perception. In this regard, he was able to draw upon the experience of his own phantom limb, since he was often aware of feelings in the amputated part of his leg (see Chapter 2). These he attributed to the continued activities of the severed nerves in his stump, which would have transmitted signals to the brain.

Visual Pathways

While little could be said about the microscopic structure of the retina, the visual pathways were more amenable to study. The separate and ipsilateral projection of the optic nerves was to be repeated by Vesalius, and it was integrated into Descartes' analysis of vision. The diagrams in *Dioptrique* (1637) and in his *Traité de l'homme* (1664) retain the ipsilateral projection of the optic nerves to the brain, but those from each eye are combined in the pineal body in the latter. The illustration from the *Traité* has been reproduced many times, particularly in the context of historical analyses of binocular vision (Polyak, 1957; van Hoorn, 1972; Held, 1976; Wade, 1987; Crone, 1992; Howard and Rogers, 1995). However, it is instructive to compare it with the monocular representation made for *De homine* (1662): both engravings were derived from essentially the same text, which does not mention stimulation of two eyes. A number of similar illustrations from *De homine* all depict one eye only, whereas their corresponding figures from the *Traité* display two. It would seem that the illustration has played a greater role in historical interpretations than the text from which it was derived, and the credit should be placed with the artist as well as Descartes. It is particularly significant in this case because neither of the series of diagrams was produced by the author of the text (Hall, 1972). *Dioptrique* was published during Descartes' life, but the *Traité* first appeared over a decade after his death, and two separate versions of it were printed. The first, in 1662, was translated into Latin (*De homine*) and illustrated by Schuyl, who is said to have worked from a defective manuscript copy of the French. The French version (*Traité de l'homme*) appeared in 1664: the text was given to two illustrators (van Gutschoven and La Forge), who each made a complete set of drawings independently of the other; van Gutschoven's were the ones most generally printed, though some of La Forge's were included, too. The whole set of La Forge's illustrations can be found in the Latin edition of 1677.

Descartes did stress the correspondence between points on the object, those on the retina, and their projection to the brain, but it is unlikely that he was addressing the issue of corresponding points in the two retinas. His analysis of binocular vision was by the ancient analogy with a blind man holding two sticks, and it was not physiological. The union that was depicted in the pineal body reflected an attempt to match singleness of vision with a single anatomical structure. Thus Descartes' speculative physiology defined his visual anatomy. His achievement was in presenting an account of the visual pathways in terms of their topographical organization. In the same year that the *Traité* was published Willis (1664) established that the optic nerves projected to the optic thalami, although the distinction between the thalami and the striate cortex had not been made at that time (see Neuberger, 1981; Finger, 1994).

Descartes' analysis of vision was based on his conception of light: when light strikes the eye it applies force to points on the retina which are transmitted along the optic nerve to the brain. Rohault (1671), on the other hand, was specifically concerned with binocular projections, delineating sympathetic (or corresponding) points on each eye. Although he retained the independence of the two optic nerves, the fibers from corresponding points were united in an undefined part of the brain. Rohault used evidence from brain injury and disease to localize sensation in the brain rather than the nerves:

> "And because we have no Sensation likewise, when any Object makes an Impression upon a Nerve, if its Communication with the Brain be hindred, or if the Brain it self be affected with any particular Distemper; therefore it is reasonable to think, that the Nerves are not the immediate *Organs* of the Soul, but they are so formed by Nature, as to transmit the Impression which they receive, to the Place in the Brain where the Origin of them is, and where probably the immediate Organ of the Soul's Sensation is." (From a translation of 1723, p. 245, original italics)

The concept of the hollow optic nerves, which had survived since Alcmaeon in the fifth century B.C., was gradually being replaced. Rohault described transmission along the nerves and Briggs (1682) represented the optic nerves as composed of fibers. Not only did he produce a delightful illustration of the visual pathways, retaining the independence of the optic nerves, but he also had them terminating in the thalami. Moreover, he stimulated Newton's interest in the visual pathways, and in the ways in which messages from the two eyes could be combined. Briggs proposed a mechanistic principle involving tension applied to the individual nerve fibers "like *unisons* in a *Lute*" (p. 172); only when the tension was equal in the two sets of fibers did single vision occur. He sent his paper to Newton and their correspondence indicates the latter's reserve concerning it (see Brewster, 1855; Turnbull, 1960). In order to rise above the level of opinion, Newton conducted the experiment on cutting nerves (referred to above), made the first representation of partial decussation at the optic chiasm, and proposed a theory of binocular single vision based upon it in around 1682.

The subtlety of Newton's analysis was not, however, widely disseminated. He did make passing reference to it in Query XV of his *Opticks* (1704), but it was not accompanied by a diagram:

> "Are not the Species of Objects seen with both Eyes united where the optick Nerves meet before they come into the Brain, the Fibres on the right side of both Nerves uniting there, and after union going thence into the Brain in the Nerve which is on the right side of the Head, and the Fibres on the left side of both Nerves uniting in the same place, and after union going into the Brain in the Nerve which is on the left side of the Head, and these two Nerves meeting in the Brain in such a manner that their Fibres make but one entire Species or Picture, half of which on the right side of the Sensorium comes from the right side of both Eyes through the right side of both optick Nerves to the place where the Nerves meet, and from thence on the right side of the Head into the Brain,

and the other half on the left side of the Sensorium comes in like manner from the left side of both Eyes. For the optick Nerves of such Animals as look the same way with both Eyes (as of Men, Dogs, Sheep, Oxen, &c.) meet before they come into the Brain, but the optick Nerves of such Animals as do not look the same way with both Eyes (as of Fishes and of the Chameleon) do not meet, if I am rightly informed." (Newton, 1704, pp. 136–137)

In presenting this as a query, rather than the report of an experiment (as in the unpublished manuscript), its speculative nature would have been reinforced. The manuscript passed into the possession of William Jones in the eighteenth century, and was later purchased by the Earl of Macclesfield (see Westfall, 1980). Prior to its purchase Joseph Harris (1702–1764) saw the manuscript, and published a copy of it in his posthumously published *Treatise of optics* (1775). Harris's *Treatise* started life as a book on microscopes in 1742, but his work as assay master to the Mint probably prevented its completion. He died in 1764, and his friends collected the manuscript and arranged for its publication 11 years later. An illustration based on Newton's description was included in Harris' book. A copy of Newton's drawing can be found in Grüsser and Landis (1991) and Crone (1992).

Despite the authority of Newton's analysis, it was not immediately accepted. Perhaps this was in part due to the brief nature of the published version in the *Opticks*, in contrast to the longer, unpublished manuscript account. Porterfield (1737) was well aware of Newton's description of partial decussation, and reprinted Query XV in full. While concluding that "This is indeed the most beautiful and ingenious Explication of the Manner how an Object appears single from the Coalition of the Optick Nerves that ever appeared" (p. 197), he rejected it largely on the authority of anatomists like Vesalius. His diagram, which was essentially like Rohault's, showed ipsilateral projection to the brain, and it was reprinted unchanged in his *Treatise* (Porterfield, 1759).

Newton was almost correct in his analysis: partial decussation was appropriate, but he represented the nerves themselves as uniting at the chiasm. That is, optic nerve fibers from corresponding points on each eye formed single fibers in the optic tract. This detail was rectified by John Taylor (1708–1772; 1738) in an accurate representation of the partial crossing over and independence of the nerve fibers: fibers in the optic nerve diverged after the optic chiasm, with those from the left halves of each retina projecting to the left part of the brain, and vice versa. Taylor (1750) reprinted this figure in a translation of the earlier French book on ophthalmology into German; it is this later diagram that has often been cited as the first correct representation of the optic pathways (e.g., Polyak, 1957; Finger, 1994).

Taylor had represented the partial decussation at the optic chiasm, but this was based more on speculation than dissection. Despite the existence of Taylor's diagram, the precise paths pursued by the two optic nerves to the brain were the subject of much debate, which was not finally resolved until the late nineteenth century.

IMPACT OF PHYSIOLOGY

The analogy between eye and camera, together with an appreciation that the retina was the receptive organ, introduced a new set of problems in the study of vision. If the camera can only focus on objects at a particular distance, how is the eye able to focus upon objects over a wide range of distances? This is the problem of accommodation, the term that Porterfield (1738) coined: "our Eyes change their Conformation, and accommodate themselves to the various Distances of Objects" (p. 126). Boring (1942) claimed that the term "accommodation" was not introduced until a century later. From the time of Kepler to the middle of the nineteenth century accommodation was one of the most intensively studied and controversial topics in vision, as is indicated by the earlier quotations from Hunter and Helmholtz. Not surprisingly, since the equation of the eye with a camera had proved so popular, the solutions were often derived from characteristics of cameras. A camera with a small aperture has a much greater depth of focus than one with a larger aperture; moving the camera lens towards or away from the screen onto which images are projected will vary the distance at which objects are sharply focused; conversely, moving the screen itself will have the same effect. Each of these physical speculations was advanced, together with others that were physiological.

ACCOMMODATION

Kepler (1611) favoured the view that the lens moved forward and backward in the eye. Scheiner (1619) supported this proposal largely on the basis of observations with a camera, but he did also mention that the lens could vary in shape. However, Scheiner's greatest contribution to this area was his experiment with closely spaced pinholes: when their separation was less than the diameter of the pupil, objects seen through them were multiplied at all but one distance of the object from the eye:

> "Make a number of perforations with a small needle in a piece of pasteboard, not more distant from one another than the diameter of the pupil of the eye ... if it is held close to one eye, while the other is shut, as many images of a distant

object will be seen as there are holes in the pasteboard . . . at a certain distance, objects do not appear multiplied when they are viewed in this manner." (p. 38)

Scheiner described and illustrated the consequences of viewing points of light and also the spire on a tower through closely spaced apertures, although later in his book he did present a diagram of what has become called "Scheiner's experiment".

Porterfield (1738) provided a similar, though more detailed, diagram of the experiment and gave the correct interpretation of it. He improved on Scheiner's experiment by using as a stimulus "a small luminous Point in a dark Place", and on this basis made the first optometer. Porterfield extended his experiments to refute La Hire's (1685) contention that the eye did not need to accommodate to objects at different distances, because of the contraction of the pupil when observing near objects and because it could function well by ignoring blurred images. Despite the analogies of accommodation with focusing in a camera, Descartes' (1664) earlier physiological speculations were to prove particularly astute. The lens itself was considered to change its curvature, becoming more convex for focusing on near objects, and less convex for more distant ones. He even suggested that accommodation provides a source of distance information for objects that are close to the eye.

To these speculative mechanisms could be added another: the cornea increased its curvature in order to focus on near objects. This was advanced by Jean Théophile Desaguliers (1683–1744; 1719) who proposed that the lens was fixed in curvature, and pressure on the humors of the eye forced it forwards, thus increasing the corneal curvature. Another possibility that was entertained concerned the elongation of the eye as a consequence of the action of the extraocular muscles. Associated to such elongation would have been an increase in corneal curvature. The most systematic experiments on accommodation, prior to those of Young (1793, 1801), were conducted by Porterfield (1738). He devised an optometer for determining the near and far points of vision, and he was able to discount both of the speculations above by recourse to sight following removal of the crystalline lenses. He examined such an aphakic individual who was unable to accommodate at all without the aid of a convex lens, and the power of the lens required to be modified for objects at different distances. Porterfield concluded that since elongation of the eye was still possible for such a person, the crystalline lens must be involved in accommodation, although he remained unsure of the manner in which it functioned. The involvement of the ciliary process was acknowledged, but its location and attachment to the lens led him to the conclusion that its action moved the lens forward and backward in the eye itself. As Priestley (1772) remarked: "That the eye does, by some conformation, adapt itself to the view of objects at different distances, seems to have been indisputably proved by Dr. Porterfield; but among those who suppose a conformation of the eye for this purpose, independent of a variation in the aperture, it is by no means agreed in what it consists" (p. 646).

Thus, writers on the eye and vision selected one or more of these hypotheses as their candidates for accommodation until the late eighteenth century, when Young reported his experimental enquiries. His logical and physiological conclusions were initially presented in a paper to the Royal Society of London in 1793, upon which was founded his election as a Fellow. There followed a remarkable series of experiments that were published in 1801, supporting changes in lens curvature. Such support was not derived from direct evidence, but rather from the rejection of all alternative hypotheses. Changes in corneal curvature were excluded in two ways: the sizes of images of candle flames reflected from the cornea did not change with variations in accommodation, and immersion of the eye in water did not abolish accommodation. Elongation of the eye was rendered untenable because accommodation was still possible when considerable external pressure was applied to the eye.

The association of accommodation of the eye to convergence of the eyes was made by many writers, and it was discussed principally in the context of depth or distance perception. In the seventeenth century, both Aguilonius and Descartes discussed them as cues to distance, and they formed a cornerstone of George Berkeley's (1685–1753; 1709) theory of muscular involvement in distance perception (see Baird, 1903; Boring, 1942). However, their close physiological connection was emphasized by both Porterfield and William Charles Wells (1757–1817; 1792).

OPTICAL INSTRUMENTS

In order to determine the range of accommodation with greater precision, Porterfield (1738) invented the optometer and gave it its name. It was based on the observation made by Scheiner (1619), who had described the consequences of viewing an object through two apertures. In the words of Helmholtz:

> "Two pinholes are made in a card at a distance apart less than the diameter of the pupil of the eye. With one eye closed, the observer looks through both holes at a small object sharply delineated against a contrasting background, for example, at a needle held in front of a bright window. The needle should be adjusted at right angles to the line joining the two holes. If the eye is focused on the needle itself, it appears single; but if it is focused on something else, nearer or farther away, the needle appears double." (1924/2000, pp. 124–125)

Porterfield's optometer consisted of a metal plate with two narrow and close vertical slits, so that when it was held close to the eye the slits were separated by less than the diameter of the pupil. The distance of a line of light from the vertical slits could be changed so that the near and far points of vision could be measured; that is, the nearest and farthest positions at which the line could be seen as single. Near the end of the eighteenth century, Young (1793) wrote his first paper on accommodation. He argued that it is not due to changes in the cornea, the humors of the eye, or the length of the eye. Instead, Young argued from experiments that the eye's ability to accommodate is due to a change in the curvature of the lens. In his words, it is mediated "by the ciliary processes to the muscles of the crystalline, which, by the contraction of its fibres, becomes more convex, and collects the diverging rays to a focus on the retina" (1793, p. 174).

In 1801, Young returned to the topic of accommodation, having been stimulated by Porterfield's analysis of it. He praised his predecessor for developing the optometer, but expressed concern about its precision: "Dr. Porterfield has employed an experiment, first made by Scheiner, to the determination of the focal distance of the eye; and has described, under the name of an optometer, a very excellent instrument, founded on the principle of the phenomenon. But the apparatus is capable of considerable improvement" (Young, 1801, pp. 33–34).

Young's first objective was to modify the device to make it more sensitive. The process involved incorporating a lens and a graduated scale. His new optometer provided measurements across the range over which accommodation could operate, and he even provided tables to assist in the prescription of lenses for myopic and presbyopic eyes. What Young's device did not do was to shed new light on the process itself. Despite the force of all the arguments for the involvement of the lens in accommodation, not to mention what Young himself had written in 1793, its mechanism of action remained unclear. For example, one year following Young's (1793) suggestion that the curvature of the lens itself changes, Wells remarked that he had attempted to observe such variations "by applying to the crystallines of oxen, which had been felled from thirty seconds to a minute before, chemical and mechanical stimuli, and those of Galvanism and electricity; but in no instance was any alteration of figure, or other indication of muscular power, observed" (Wells, 1811, p. 390).

A major problem was that it was still assumed that a change in the shape of the lens could only be effected by muscular activity within the lens itself. Since the anatomists were still unable to provide evidence of muscular fibers in the lens, earlier theories remained intact, namely, those that held the lens does not change shape yet can move forward or backward in the eye. Young (1801), who also presented the first good description of astigmatism and its possible correction, agreed that the lens could only change its shape by internal muscular action. But unlike just about everyone else, he proposed that this is precisely what does in fact happen during accommodation. Young's new theory, however, was neither widely circulated nor well received, even though it represented a significant advance in physiological optics. Later, Helmholtz, who had great respect for Young and proceeded to resurrect his trichromatic theory of color vision, had this to say about Young's second paper on the optometer and accommodation: "This is a work of astonishing perspicacity and originality, which was qualified to settle the question as to accommodation even at that time, but, on account of its conciseness, it is often hard to follow, and, moreover, it presupposes the most thorough knowledge of mathematical optics" (1924a/2000, p. 167).

ACCOMMODATION AND AGE

Descartes (1637/1902) benefited greatly from the earlier analyses of eye and camera and made some shrewd speculations about the nature of long-sightedness and short-sightedness, as well as about accommodation. He surmised that "as we grow old, they [the crystalline lenses] become flatter and wider" (p. 116). Following Descartes, corrections for presbyopia were addressed and illustrated by many writers, some of whom tried to reconcile the corrections with possible causes. Newton linked his physical with physiological optics and sought an explanation of presbyopia. In his *Opticks* of 1704 he proposed that the cornea shrinks and the lens grows flatter with old age.

Thus, convex lenses can correct the age-related defects, resulting in better vision for nearer objects. Moreover, Newton pointed out that myopic individuals, who require concave lenses at the prime of life, may slowly acquire the ability to see distant objects more distinctly as they age. However, the lifespan changes in the range of accommodation continued to be accounted for by the progressive use of more powerful spectacles. The situation changed during the final decade of the eighteenth century, as a consequence of studies by Wells (1792). In his book on binocular vision (published in1792 and reprinted in Wade, 2003a), he wrote:

"For the change, in the conformation of the eyes, which renders them useful, seems to be one of those which nature has destined to take place at a particular age, and to which there is no gradual approach through the preceding course of life. A person, for instance, at forty, sees an object distinctly, at the same distance that he did at twenty. When he draws near fifty, the change I have spoken of commonly comes on, and obliges him in a short time to wear spectacles. As it proceeds, he is under the necessity of using others with a higher power. But, instead of supposing that his sight is thus gradually becoming worse, from a natural process, he attributes the increase of the defect in it to his too early and frequent use of glasses." (1792, pp. 126–127)

Nineteen years later, Wells (1811) examined the effects of belladonna on accommodation; when one eye was so treated the power of accommodation was lost, whereas the untreated eye was unaffected. Purkinje described similar studies on himself in 1825. He also reported that the power of accommodation was lost following the application of belladonna (see Wade and Brožek, 2001).

It was not until Helmholtz's day that his Dutch contemporary, Frans Cornelis Donders (1818–1889), made the difference between hyperopia and presbyopia explicit. In his *Treatise on physiological optics*, Helmholtz described the most common errors of refraction: "A near-sighted or myopic eye is one for which the far point is a short distance away, sometimes only a few inches from the eye; the near point being, of course, even closer. A far-sighted or presbyopic eye, on the other hand, is one for which the near point is quite a little distance away, perhaps several feet from the eye" (1924a/2000, p. 128). Helmholtz further noted that far-sightedness is more common in old age, but he did not distinguish between hyperopia and presbyopia (Helmholtz, 1855).

The developmental course of presbyopia was more intensively studied by Donders (1864). Prior to his analysis, presbyopia had been confounded with hyperopia and both were contrasted with myopia. Donders distinguished between errors of refraction, which are anomalous conditions of the eye, and presbyopia which is "a normal condition of the normally constructed, emmetropic eye, at a more advanced period of life" (1864, p. 84). Accordingly, he proposed: "The term presbyopia is, therefore, to be restricted to the condition, in which, as a result of the increase of years, the range of accommodation is diminished and the vision of near objects is interfered with" (1864, p. 210).

When the physiological basis for accommodation became better understood its psychological significance waned.

SEPARATION OF THE SENSES

Vision was not the only sense subjected to scrutiny before the nineteenth century. While the five senses, specified by Aristotle, were rarely questioned, the foundations of the edifice were beginning to crumble. It was a consequence of a closer examination of perceptual experience and the early stirrings of experimental science. This was evident in the fractionation of feeling into more discrete modes. Aristotle's struggles with the sense of touch or feeling were evident from the material surveyed in Chapter 1. Despite the many perceptual consequences of stimulating the skin senses, the belief that it was a single contact sense was retained. The attacks on this position that emerged in the seventeenth and eighteenth centuries were not restricted to the skin surface, but delved beneath it also. Movement was the source of much of the disquiet—either through the action of the muscles themselves or through the consequences of movement as in vertigo.

MUSCLE AND TEMPERATURE SENSES

Boring (1942) credited Bell with establishing the concept of the muscle sense, although Bell's claim had been rejected by William Hamilton (1788–1856) in his brief but scholarly history of the muscular sense (Hamilton, 1846). The behavioral basis for an addition to Aristotle's five senses was clearly founded in experiments conducted in the eighteenth century. For example, the term "Muskelsinn" had been used by German writers in the eighteenth century, and it was suggested that the idea was described even earlier: Julius Cæsar Scaliger (1484–1558) distinguished between active and passive dimensions of touch:

> "And indeed this seems to be the case, for heaviness and lightness are perceived by touching, and everybody thinks that they recognise heaviness and lightness by handling. However, I am not convinced. I accept that motion is perceived by touch, but I deny that heaviness is. The most powerful argument is as follows. Heaviness is the object of motive power, which certainly consists in *action*. But touch only occurs by being *acted upon*. Therefore heaviness is perceived by a motive power, not by touch. For since there are two organs (I mean the nerves and the spirits), for sensing and for being moved, which are distinct from each other, it will be a mistake if we confuse the object of a motive force, with the object of a moved force. For touch is moved, and does not act. But a motive force moves a heavy body, but is not moved by it. This is obvious in the case of paralysis: heat is sensed, but the heaviness of the motive force is not sensed, because the organs have suffered.—But is heaviness *sensed*? It is indeed sensed by the motive force, and judged by it; just as when something difficult is expressed through the power of the intellect itself, this power is active, not passive, when it expresses it. For it is common to all things in our world, which depend on matter, that they cannot act without also being acted upon. An objection could be raised about compression.... There are two further reasons: because we sometimes sense heaviness even without touch, and because we do not sense by touch. The former is the case when someone's hand is placed on a heavy body, but they do not sense its heaviness. But the motive power senses without touching. A lead weight attached to a string is sensed as heavy, even though the hand does not touch the lead. Then in the latter case, when one's arm drops under its own weight, it is sensed as heavy. But it touches nothing." (Scaliger, 1557, in Hamilton, 1846, p. 867, original italics)

Classical divisions of touch into independent qualities were often repeated up to the nineteenth century, when they were given some experimental support. For example, Thomas Reid (1710–1796; 1764) noted that: "by touch we perceive not one quality only, but many, and those of different kinds. The chief of them are heat and cold, hardness and softness, roughness and smoothness, figure, solidity, motion, and extension" (p. 99). The complexities of touch were drawn out thereafter, and the arguments could be made explicitly for temperature. Some experimental support for the distinction between the touch and temperature senses was provided by Erasmus Darwin (1794) on the basis of an observation made by his son, Robert:

> "The following is an extract from a letter of Dr. R. W. Darwin, of Shrewsbury, when he was a student at Edinburgh. 'I made an experiment yesterday in our hospital, which much favours your opinion, that the sensation of heat and touch depend on different sets of nerves. A man who had lately recovered from a fever, and was still weak, was seized with violent cramps in his legs and feet; which were removed by opiates, except that one of his feet remained insensible. Mr. Ewart pricked him with a pin in five or six places, and the patient declared he did not feel it in the least, nor was he sensible of a very smart pinch. I then held a red-hot poker at some distance, and brought it gradually nearer till it came within three inches, when he asserted that he felt it quite distinctly. I suppose some violent irritation of the nerves of touch had caused the cramps, and had left them paralytic; while the nerves of heat, having suffered no increased stimulus, retained their irritability.'. . . . The organ of touch is properly the sense of pressure, but the muscular fibres themselves constitute the organ of sense, that feels extension. Hence the whole muscular system may be considered as one organ of sense, and the various attitudes of the body, as ideas belonging to this organ, of many of which we are hourly conscious, while many others, like the irritative ideas of the other senses, are performed without our attention." (E. Darwin, 1794, pp. 122–123)

Thus the stirrings of experimental evidence to question the unity of Aristotle's feeling sense were emerging, and were to be extended in the nineteenth century.

Movement Sense

Similar arguments could be summoned to support a movement sense. What became known as the movement sense is mediated by the vestibular and muscle systems. The behavioral consequences of vestibular stimulation have long been appreciated, but they were not integrated with the anatomy and physiology of the semicircular canals until the late-nineteenth century. Thus, the earlier claims for a movement sense were based almost entirely on behavioral evidence relating to apparent visual or body movement. That is, the vestibular system had been examined indirectly through studies of vertigo.

The early modern era of research on this sense was heralded by Platter (1583) and Willis (1672), who suggested mechanistic interpretations for vertigo in terms of motion of the animal spirit in the brain. Platter observed that: "An intense, uniform, and extended movement of the head transfers itself in a similar way to the spiritus. Despite holding the head still afterwards, it appears to continue moving for a while, before it eventually feels still. This is the basis for dizziness, if one rotates the head and body in a circle for a long time" (Koelbing, 1967, p. 89).

Willis defined vertigo as "an affection in which visible objects appear to rotate" (1672, p. 353), and devoted a chapter of his book to describing its pathology and the conditions that can induce it, including body rotation in healthy individuals. Platter and Willis interpreted vertigo in terms of Galen's animal spirit: motion of the spirit in the head produced apparent body and visual motion during rotation, rather like smoke in a flask lagging behind that of the rotating vessel. Moreover, Willis described the visual motion that continues after body rotation ceases, and this was attributed to the continued motions of the animal spirit relative to the stationary head. Willis gave a graphic description of it in his Oxford lectures:

> "Vertigo arises from the circular motion of the spirits, and, as it were, their rotations in the brain and its medullary part. It takes place just as smoke and vapour contained in a glass or phial are sent into similar motion if you spin the vessel round. This motion lasts longer in the smoke or vapour than in the vessel. Thus we find people whose spirits are very thin, and therefore flexible and weak, pass into vertigo as soon as the body or head is rotated and this sensation persists after the body has ceased its turning motion." (Dewhurst, 1980, pp. 113–114)

So little was then known about the functions of the brain that this interpretation was long held. Even when the attraction of the animal spirit was waning, the logic of the explanation was retained. In his medical text on vertigo, Marcus Herz (1786) modified the interpretation slightly by referring to movement of nervous humors in the brain rather than animal spirits, but how these humors moved remained mysterious.

In the eighteenth century, François Boissier de Sauvages (1706–1767) discussed vertigo in his classification of diseases, and described it as: "an hallucination which takes place when stationary objects appear to move and rotate around us...The cause of vertigo is nothing other than an impression on the retina which is equivalent to that excited by objects that paint their images successively on different parts of that membrane" (1772, p. 50). He drew parallels between vertigo and visual persistence with rapidly moving lights, and suggested that the sensitivity of the retina was changed by the retrograde movements of blood in the vessels supplying it. He did discuss the effects of body rotation, and the possibility of unconscious eye movements was entertained.

An alternative to speculating on processes in the retina or brain was to study the phenomenon of vertigo itself. Eighteenth century interest in vertigo was principally medical, and most observations on it were made in that context. For example, Robert Whytt (1714–1766) included giddiness amongst the symptoms for nervous diseases:

> "Many people of a delicate, nervous, and vascular system, after stooping and suddenly raising their head, are apt to be seized with a *vertigo*, which is sometimes accompanied by faintness. In this case, the vessels of the brain being too weak, seem to yield more than usual to the weight of the blood, when the head is inclined; and afterwards, when it is suddenly raised, and the blood at once descends towards the heart, those vessels do not contract fast enough, so as to accommodate themselves to the quantity of blood remaining in them: At the same time the brain, on account of its too great sensibility, is more affected than usual, by any sudden change in the motion of the fluids through its vessels." (1765, p. 309, original italics)

Diseases of the inner ear were discussed by Bell (1803/2000), but their association with vertigo was not explicitly entertained. While he mentioned that "Of the diseases of the labyrinth, there is little on record" (p. 451), he did observe that inflammation around the auditory nerve was accompanied by an increased sensitivity to slight head movements and to vertigo. The paradox of these investigations is that the gross anatomy of the labyrinthine organs was reasonably well known at that time. Albrecht von Haller (1708–1777) gave the following description of its structure:

> "Two other passages lead from the tympanum to the *labyrinth*, or innermost chamber of the ear. . . . There is a nervous pulp in the vestibulum distinguished from the parietal bone by the vapour surrounding it. Into this open the five mouths of the semicircular canals, the foramen ovale, and the passages of the nerves and the arteries. . . . The larger posterior and lower of these circles is perpendicular; also the middle and upper one is placed towards the perpendicular; but the outermost and least is horizontal." (1786, pp. 283–284, original italics)

No functions were assigned to the labyrinth, but its inclusion in the chapter on hearing conformed to the received view that the semicircular canals are implicated in auditory localization. The structures of the inner ear were represented with accuracy and clarity by Antonio Scarpa (1752–1832) towards the end of the eighteenth century (Scarpa, 1789), and his "beautiful plates" were copied by Bell (1803).

VERTIGO

Experiences associated with vestibular stimulation are unlike those of seeing or hearing because they are referred to other bodily organs. Thus, motion illusions based on body rotation relate to the feelings of body rotation, as well as of visual motion. It is these aspects that were investigated before galvanic studies were undertaken, and it is in this regard that the essential aspects of vestibular function had been outlined experimentally. The investigations were conducted initially by Wells (1792), although they were not related to the vestibular system itself, nor were they recognized by historians. The received opinion was clearly stated by Boring:

> "The history of what has been called vestibular equilibration, the static sense, ampullar sensation, giddiness, vertigo, the sense of rotation, and the sensibility of the semicircular canals is voluminous and simple. It is voluminous because there has been so much written about it: in 1922 Griffith cited 1685 titles from 1820 on. It is simple because it can all be organized about Purkinje's description of dizziness (1820–1825), Flourens' discovery that lesions of the semicircular canals produce muscular incoordination in the plane of the affected canals (1824–1830), the Mach-Breuer-Brown experiments and their theory of the function of the canals (1873–1875), and the discovery of vertiginous habituation by the psychologists of the U.S. Army (1918), Griffith (1920) and Dodge (1923)." (1942, p. 535)

The history is certainly voluminous, but it is not simple. Robert Bárány (1876–1936), who was awarded the Nobel Prize in 1914 for his vestibular researches, surveyed its history. He remarked that he had come across (but did not cite) over one hundred dissertations on vertigo from the sixteenth to the eighteenth centuries. These were, however, dismissed as adding little to what had been known to the ancients:

> "The reality is that they all say much the same thing. In the Middle Ages one had become fully accustomed to the complete description. Whoever wrote a book studied the texts of his predecessors and wrote more or less the same thing with small variations. For example, regarding the interesting question of vertigo from rotation, many authors have speculated whether it is accompanied by unconscious eye movements. It did not occur to any of them to rotate themselves a few times and to feel if their eyes were moving, or to ask his good friend to rotate and observe his eyes. The often insightful considerations would only be carried out at the writing table. The first to make the observations that will be discussed here was *Purkinje* in 1825." (Bárány, 1913, pp. 396–397)

Both Bárány and Boring were correct in citing the physiological experiments of Pierre Flourens (1794–1867), and the hydrodynamic theory of Ernst Mach (1838–1925), Josef Breuer (1842–1925), and Alexander Crum Brown (1838–1922). However, Boring placed undue reliance on the historical accuracy of Griffith's (1922) monograph, as have others

(Kornhuber, 1974, Wendt, 1951). Perhaps all of them were in thrall of Mach's historical authority, which was amplified in his book on movement perception (Mach, 1875; Young, Henn, and Scherberger, 2001). Mach commenced: "The work before you attempts, for the first time, to present a complete chapter of physiology, to which the incontestable Purkinje (Purkyně), Flourens and Goltz have laid the foundations.... The elder Darwin and Purkyně have studied the remarkable subjective sensations of rotation that take place if one rotates rapidly several times and then stops suddenly" (Mach, 1875, pp. iii and 1). Brown (1878a) similarly surveyed the past in Purkinje's favor. With regard to the aftereffects of body rotation he wrote:

> "Purkinje studied the conditions under which this apparent rotation occurs, and arrived at the following conclusions, which have been confirmed by all succeeding observers: – 1. That the direction of apparent motion of surrounding objects depends upon the direction of the preceding real motion of our body, and is always opposite to it. 2. That the axis about which the apparent motion takes place is always that line in the head which was the axis of the preceding real rotation." (Brown, 1878a, p. 634)

In a second article by Brown (1878b) mention is made of Erasmus Darwin's investigations of body rotation; post-rotational nystagmus is both described and illustrated, but again its initial observation is credited to Purkinje.

Eye Movements and Vertigo

Erasmus Darwin was also mentioned by Griffith (1922) and Boring (1942), but they did not recount the reasons why he chose to carry out his studies. It was Porterfield (1759b) whose speculations regarding the link between eye movements and post-rotational visual motion stimulated renewed interest in the visual dimension of vertigo in the late-eighteenth century. Motion was the last of the phenomena of vision described in the second volume of Porterfield's *Treatise on the eye, the manner and phænomena of vision*, and his analysis of it was subtle. Vertigo was the final phenomenon discussed in the final section:

> "But, before I dismiss this Subject, I shall endeavour to explain another *Phænomenon* of Motion, which, tho' very common, and well known, yet, so far as I know, has not as yet had any Solution given to it. If a Person turns swiftly round, without changing his Place, all Objects about will seem to move in a Circle to the contrary Way, and the Deception continues, not only when the Person himself moves round, but, which is more surprising, it also continues for some time after he stops moving, when the Eye, as well as the Objects, are at absolute Rest." (1759b, pp. 424–425)

The evidence that the eyes do not move following rotation was sub-jective. Porterfield was not conscious of any movements of his eyes and so he was convinced that they remained stationary following rotation. The situation was clarified by Wells (1792); he distrusted the recourse to sub-jective experience in deciding upon a matter of science, and he found that experiments with afterimages were preferable because of their increased objectivity. It was Wells' monograph that galvanized Erasmus Darwin to deliberate further on vertigo, and it was Wells who engaged in a public dispute with Darwin concerning the involvement of eye movements in visual vertigo following body rotation.

It is clear that all these commentators have ignored Wells' (1792) sem-inal studies on vertigo. He conducted sophisticated experiments on post-rotational vertigo and nystagmus long before Purkinje's studies. Wells' analysis of vertigo should be considered as heralding the first clear behav-ioral evidence for the vestibular sense. His experiments satisfied Müller's requirement "that external causes should excite in it a new and pecu-liar kind of sensation different from all the sensations of our five senses" (1843/2003, p. 1087); the external causes are linear and angular accelera-tions, and the sensation is one of rotation both of the body and the visual scene.

A common feature of many of Wells' experiments on vision was the use of afterimages to assess the manner in which the eyes moved. He used the term 'spectra' to describe afterimages; they were so called by Robert Darwin (1786). Wells enlisted afterimages to determine how the eyes move during post-rotational vertigo, although his initial observation was accidental:

"During a slight fit of giddiness I was accidentally seized with, a colored spot [afterimage], occasioned by looking steadily at a luminous body, and upon which I happened at that moment to be making an experiment, was moved in a manner altogether independent of the positions I conceived my eyes to possess." (Wells, 1792, p. 95)

Wells capitalized on this happy accident and provided experimental evidence to link the pattern of eye movements to the direction of visual vertigo. Wells proceeded to examine the effects systematically. He gave the first clear description of the fast and slow phases of post-rotational nystag-mus, and its decreasing amplitude with time. Furthermore, he described how the direction of post-rotational afterimage motion was dependent on head position during rotation. Wells was not aware of feeling his eyes moving after rotation and so he asked another person to rotate and then stop "and I could plainly see, that, although he thought his eyes were fixed, they were in reality moving in their sockets, first toward one side, and then toward the other" (p. 97). In the space of a few pages, Wells encapsulated the essential features of vestibular function as they are expressed through eye movements and post-rotational vertigo.

Robert Darwin's (1786) article was reprinted in full as the final chapter in the first volume of his father's book *Zoonomia*, which was published two years after Wells' *Essay upon single vision*. Darwin's *Zoonomia* was the culmination of many years of thought and writing, and so the chapter entitled "Vertigo" reflected ideas that had been nurtured prior to the appearance of Wells' *Essay*. He commenced by noting that "the disease called vertigo or dizziness has been little understood" (1794, p. 231). Darwin listed the conditions which can induce vertigo and the symptoms accompanying it. The inducing conditions are visual, as in looking down from a tall tower or viewing a whirling wheel, or postural, as in seasickness or rotating the body. These were related to the importance of vision in maintaining postural equilibrium.

Darwin also described the vertigo and double vision that accompanies drunkenness. The example of post-rotational vertigo is described thus:

> "When a child moves round quick upon one foot, the circumjacent objects become quite indistinct, as their distance increases their apparent motions; and this great velocity confounds both their forms, and their colors, as is seen in whirling round a many colored wheel; he then loses his usual method of balancing himself by vision, and begins to stagger, and attempts to recover himself by his muscular feelings. This staggering adds to the instability of the visible objects by giving a vibratory motion besides their rotatory one. The child then drops to the ground, and the neighbouring objects seem to continue for some seconds of time to circulate around him, and the earth under him appears to librate like a balance. In some seconds of time these sensations of a continuation of the motion of objects vanish; but if he continues turning somewhat longer, before he falls, sickness and vomiting are very liable to succeed." (Darwin 1794, p. 235)

The first volume of *Zoonomia*, containing Darwin's deliberation on vertigo, appeared in May or June of 1794, two years after Wells' monograph. Wells must have read it with mounting indignation, as he wrote two rejoinders as letters to the September and October issues of *The Gentleman's Magazine* for the same year (Wells, 1794a, 1794b). In the first, Wells demonstrated that visual vertigo occurs with rotation in darkness, contrary to the Darwins' speculation. It was concerned principally with the logic of Darwin's theory, although it did mention some experimental observations, too. In the second, Wells described experiments indicating that the eyes move following body rotation and provided more details about how they move.

One significant factor that emerged from Erasmus Darwin's deliberations on vertigo was the invention of the human centrifuge (see Wade,

2004e). This was described and illustrated in the third edition of *Zoonomia* (Darwin 1801); however, it was not initially enlisted to study vertigo, but employed as a device for treating the insane! The links between vertigo and the vestibular system remained mysterious when Wells and Darwin were engaging in their heated dispute. It was not established until the closing decades of the nineteenth century (see Chapter 7).

EMERGENT PHILOSOPHIES

Certain visual problems were under examination throughout the seventeenth and eighteenth centuries, whereas others were addressed seriously for the first time during that period. Color vision, visual direction, eye movements, accommodation and binocular vision belong to the first category and visual vertigo to the second. In the eighteenth century, vision was examined in the context of either optics or medicine, and both were influenced by philosophy. Newton published his *Opticks* in the first decade of the century and Young made his initial observations on vision in the last decade. Newton and Young adopted contrasting theories of light; Newton's theory was based on its corpuscular properties whereas Young provided further evidence (mainly from studies of interference) for its action as a wave. Despite differences in physical optics that separated Newton and Young, the methods that Newton proposed remained dominant throughout the eighteenth century. They were appositely summarized by one of his most ardent advocates: "All the Knowledge we have of Nature depends upon Facts; for without Observations and Experiments, our natural Philosophy would only be a Science of Terms and an unintelligible Jargon" (Desaguliers, 1745, p. v).

Newton made many astute comments about vision and his optics were extended further in the visual domain by Desaguliers (1716a), Robert Smith (1689–1768; 1738), and Harris (1775). The medical dimension was represented by William Cheselden (1688–1752), John Hunter, Erasmus and Robert Darwin. Porterfield, Wells, and Young combined optics and medicine with a flavoring of philosophy. Students of optics and medicine shared an interest in unraveling the enigma of accommodation.

The philosophical climate of the eighteenth century was immersed in the continuing debate between rationalists and empiricists, between those who based their philosophy on thought as opposed to the senses. The extreme positions of the seventeenth century had been leavened, but the philosophical divisions were still plain for all to see. Belief in the innate organization of perception extends well into antiquity, but it was given its modern guise by Descartes (1664/1909). He searched for new methods of enquiry rather than adopting those of past philosophers. His method was to reject all ideas about which there could be any doubt. That is, Descartes' skeptical enquiries led him to the view that only thought and reason were beyond doubt; they were the foundations upon which philosophy should be built and they were the province of humans alone. The body, on the other hand, worked by mechanical principles the understanding of which Descartes did much to advance, particularly in the context of vision.

Thus, Descartes gave to the mind properties that were not shared by the body, which was treated as a machine. His mechanistic approach to the senses clarified many issues in perception, but he had to grasp the thorny problem of accounting for the interaction of the rational mind with the mechanistic body. Kant (1781, 1786) tried to address the same question: he developed a transcendental theory of mind which drew upon both rationalism and empiricism without being allied to either. Rather than accounting for ideas in terms of experience, he adopted the opposite strategy of accounting for experience in terms of concepts. That is, our conscious, phenomenal world is a cognitive construction. He accepted that all knowledge arises from the senses, but it is not treated in a passive way: "Though all our knowledge begins with experience, it by no means follows that all arises out of experience. For, on the contrary, it is quite possible that our empirical knowledge is a compound of that which we receive through impressions, and that which the faculty of cognition supplies from itself" (translation in Watson, 1979, pp. 80–81). Certain concepts, like intuitions of space and time, were considered to be independent of experience and are used to order perception. "Space does not represent any property of objects as things in themselves, nor does it represent them in their relations to each other" (Watson, 1979, p. 85). The case for nativism was advocated by Kant in a more specific way than Descartes had proposed. Perception was taken to be an active process of organization rather than a passive accretion of sensations. Kant made a distinction between the world of things and that of appearances, and was pessimistic about whether the latter (and hence psychology) was open to scientific enquiry. That is, he did not consider that the inner world was open to precise measurement, and therefore could not be classified as a science. Essentially, Kant was arguing that the experimental study of perception was beyond the scope of science.

Kant did not deny that all knowledge begins with experience, but he did not believe that it all arises out of experience either. He considered that certain aspects of knowledge are innate, most particularly the ideas of space and time. That is, Kant suggested that the individual is born with the ability to organize experience in both space and time. Perception is then an active organizing process for Kant, rather than a passive receptive process. The distinction between innate and learned processes in perception became enshrined in nativist and empiricist philosophies, respectively. The nativists believed that we are born with the ability to perceive space, whereas the empiricists argued that we have no such knowledge of the world at birth, but we need to learn to see the spatial attributes like size, shape and distance. Kant was responding to empiricist philosophers who had reacted strongly to Descartes' nativism. Modern empiricist philosophy was expounded by John Locke (1632–1704) at the end of the seventeenth century. In his *Essay concerning human understanding*, published in 1690, he wrote:

> "Let us suppose the Mind to be, as we say, white Paper, void of all Characters, without any *Ideas*; How comes it to be furnished? Whence comes it by that vast store, which the busie and boundless Fancy of Man has painted on it with an almost endless variety? Whence has it all the materials of Reason and Knowledge? To this I answer in one word, from *Experience*: In that all our Knowledge is founded, and from that it ultimately derives it self." (Locke, 1690, p. 41, original italics)

For Locke the mental element is the idea, which is based upon sensory experience. Ideas could be simple (like whiteness) or compound (like snow), and compound ideas are made up from associations between simple ones, by a process like 'mental chemistry'. Similar associative links can account for our ability to generalize across stimuli: for instance, to form a general idea of a triangle from many different specific instances. Thus, Locke was an empiricist and an associationist: knowledge derives from the senses and we learn to perceive the objects in the world by association. Locke charted the course for empiricism, but many of the details were provided by later philosophers. Berkeley argued, in *An essay toward a new theory of vision*, that we learn to perceive the dimensions of space by associating muscular sensations with those of vision. He commenced by stating:

> "My Design is to shew the manner, wherein we perceive by Sight the Distance, Magnitude, and Situation of Objects. Also to consider the Difference there is betwixt the Ideas of Sight and Touch, and whether there be any Idea common to both Senses. It is, I think, agreed by all that Distance of itself, and immediately cannot be seen. For Distance being a Line directed end-wise to the Eye, it projects only one Point in the Fund of the Eye, Which Point remains invariably the same, whether the Distance be longer or shorter." (Berkeley, 1709, pp. 1–2)

Berkeley proposed that we learn to see distance by associating sight with touch. Moreover, the degree of muscular contraction involved in converging the eyes are also correlated with distance, and provide a source of association with sight for perceiving distance. Thus, in order to perceive distance visually we learn the relationship between the visual stimulation and the states of the muscles controlling the eyes. The muscular and touch systems were considered to provide direct and undistorted spatial information that could be used to teach vision the dimensions of space.

The empiricist philosophy of Locke was refined by Berkeley who argued that appearances are all: existence is perception. That is, the matter from which materialism is constructed is itself open to question. If all we have are our perceptions, how can we prove the existence of an external world? A problem with this position is that if perceptions are transitory so is existence. Does an object cease to exist when the eyes are closed? Berkeley sought to salvage this slide into solipsism by arguing that God alone perceived an external reality. Despite this idealist stance, Berkeley made important steps towards understanding how we perceive space, and how the different spatial senses are integrated. Most specifically, he implicated eye movements in the perception of space.

Reid (1764) reacted to Berkeley's idealism by arguing that the evidence of external reality is provided by the common activities of the senses and is supported by common sense intuition. Thus, Reid is considered to be a founder of the Scottish common-sense school of philosophy, whose ideas were to be influential in the development of psychology in America in the nineteenth century. The school was opposed to associationism, particularly when it was couched in physiological language. Reid also proposed a faculty psychology; faculties were innate properties of the mind which exerted control over habits, or behavior. His descriptive psychology could be studied by reflection on mental activity, by an analysis of the use of language, and by observations of behavior. He provided a bridge between the extreme rationalists and empiricists. His belief in the power of reason was tempered by a desire to accumulate evidence empirically. Reid placed perception at the heart of his philosophy: "All that we know of nature, or of existence, may be compared to a tree, which hath its root, trunk, and branches. In this tree of knowledge, perception is the root, common understanding is the trunk, and the sciences are the branches" (1764, p. 424).

Porterfield was in the nativist tradition, as he argued that perception of *"the Situation and Distance of visual Objects, depends not on Custom and Experience, but on an original connate and immutable Law"* (1737, p. 215, original italics). That is, he placed his philosophy at the service of his vision, and visual direction was the particular topic he examined: the perceived direction and distance of objects is available without recourse to learning. Porterfield was, therefore, opposing Berkeley's theory of perception. However, a test of the theory was to appear in an unexpected guise.

Empiricism and Cheselden's Case

A topic that fused medical and philosophical issues was Cheselden's (1728) report of vision in a young man recovering from removal of a cataract. Cheselden was seen as presenting a case that could answer a question that had been posed by empiricist philosophers; it was an attempt to address an empiricist issue by empirical procedures. Could someone who had been blind from birth name objects that were familiar to them by touch when sight was restored? Philosophers rarely questioned whether the person with sight restored would be able to see post-operatively, but only whether they could name objects by sight alone. Physicians, on the other hand, were faced with the practicalities of vision in those with sight restored. In the early nineteenth century the uniqueness of Cheselden's case became apparent because of the difficulties involved in making similar general statements from other cases.

Cataract operations have been performed for thousands of years (see Magnus, 1901), but Cheselden's case assumed particular significance because of the philosophical context in which it was placed. Despite this long history, the problem of restoring vision following operations to remove congenital cataracts became of central importance to theories of space perception in the eighteenth century. Empiricist philosophers, like Locke and Berkeley, argued that we learn to perceive visual space by associating it with touch and muscular movement.

Locke addressed the issue of restoring sight from a philosophical rather than an experimental vantage point. The question was not related to whether the patients with restored sight could see following removal of a cataract, but whether they could name objects that they had previously distinguished by touch. That is, it was a matter of philosophical debate between empiricists and nativists. The catalyst for raising this as an empirical issue that can be addressed by empiricist philosophy was William Molyneux (1656–1698). The question had been posed rhetorically by Molyneux in a letter to Locke; it was occasioned by reading Locke's (1690) *Essay concerning humane understanding* and it was printed in the second edition:

> "*Suppose a Man born blind, and now adult, and taught by his touch to distinguish between a Cube and a Sphere of the same metal, and nighly the same bigness, so as to tell, when he felt one and other, which is the Cube, which the Sphere. Suppose then the Cube and Sphere placed on a Table, and the Blind Man to be made to see. Quære, Whether by his sight, before he touch'd them, he could now distinguish, and tell, which is the Globe, which the Cube. To which the acute and judicious Proposer answers: Not. For though he has obtain'd the experience of, how a Globe, how a Cube, affects his touch; yet he has not yet attained the Experience, that what affects his touch so or so, must affect his sight so or so; Or that a protuberant angle in the Cube, that pressed his*

hand unequally, shall appear to his eye as it does in the Cube." (Locke, 1694. p. 67, original italics)

This was music to Locke's ears, and he added his endorsement: "I agree with this thinking Gent... and am of opinion, that the Blind Man, at first sight, would not be able with certainty to say, which was the Globe, which the Cube, whilst he only saw them: though he could unerringly name them by his touch, and certainly distinguish them by the difference of the Figures felt" (pp. 67–68).

This has become known as Molyneux's Question, and it has stimulated considerable interest and speculation ever since (see von Senden, 1960; Morgan, 1977; Zemplen, 2004). The question remained one of debate until Cheselden's case was examined by philosophers, who considered that the post-operative vision in the patient represented an attempt to address it empirically. In Cheselden's words:

"Tho' we say of the Gentleman that he was blind, as we do of all People who have Ripe Cataracts, yet they are never so blind from that Cause, but that they can discern Day from Night; and for the most Part in a strong Light, distinguish Black, White, and Scarlet; but they cannot perceive the Shape of any thing. . . . When he first saw, he was so far from making any Judgment about Distances, that he thought all Objects whatever touch'd his Eyes (as he express'd it) . . . He knew not the Shape of any thing, nor any one thing from another, however different in shape, or Magnitude; but upon being told what Things were, whose Form he before knew from feeling, he would carefully observe, that he might know them again. . . . We thought he soon knew what Pictures represented, which were shew'd to him, but we found afterwards we were mistaken; for about two Months after he was couch'd, he discovered at once, they represented solid Bodies, where to that Time he consider'd them only as Party-colour'd Planes, or Surfaces diversified with Variety of Paint; but even then he was no less surpriz'd, expecting the Pictures would feel like the Things they represented, and was amaz'd when he found those Parts, which by the Light and Shadow appear'd now round and uneven, felt only flat like the rest; and ask'd which was the lying Sense, Feeling, or Seeing? Being shewn his Father's Picture in a locket at his Mother's Watch, and told what it was, he acknowledged a Likeness, but was vastly surpriz'd; asking, how it could be, that a large Face could be express'd in so little Room, saying, It should have seem'd as impossible to him, as to put a Bushel of any thing into a Pint" (Cheselden, 1728, pp. 447–449)

Cheselden was held in high regard both as a surgeon and as a scholar. Voltaire said he was "one of those famous surgeons, who unite a great extent of knowledge with dexterity in operations" (Morgan, 1977, p. 23). Cheselden carried out a number of informal tests on the vision of the operated boy in order to determine what could be discriminated—he could not differentiate the distances, sizes, and shapes of objects.

The outcome of Cheselden's case was commented on extensively by James Jurin (1684–1750) in his essay appended to Smith's (1738) *Opticks* and by Porterfield (1759b), both of whom disagreed with Locke's conclusion. However, it was Voltaire's (1738) description of the operation and its theoretical import, in his *Elements of Newton's Philosophy*, that awakened the interests of French philosophers (see Pastore, 1971). Following that, Diderot (1749, 1750) published *An essay on blindness* in which he considered the theoretical implications of the Cheselden case in some detail. Both Diderot and Condillac (1754, 1982) suggested ways in which post-operative testing could be improved to address the theoretical issues raised. Condillac's discussion was in the context of his speculations concerning how a statue could be constructed so that it derived knowledge of the world through its senses.

EMERGENT EMPIRICAL METHODS

Descartes and Newton set in train the mechanistic investigation of natural phenomena, but their trains ran in different directions. For Newton, observation and experiment were all important, whereas for Descartes, rational analysis reigned supreme. Those who investigated natural phenomena tended to contrast these two approaches. Nowhere was this more evident than in the writings of Desaguliers, an ardent advocate of Newtonian philosophy. He studied natural philosophy at Christ Church, Oxford and attended lectures on optics and mechanics. In 1710 Desaguliers was requested to deliver lectures on experimental philosophy (physics) at Christ Church, and he subsequently published his lecture notes in 1719. His demonstrations of phenomena to students were a great innovation, about which there was much debate at the time, and his two textbooks based on his lectures (Desaguliers, 1719, 1744 and 1745) were very popular.

Desaguliers used Newtonian philosophy to disparage that of Descartes:

> "It is to Sir Isaac Newton's *Application of Geometry to Philosophy, that we owe the routing of this Army of* Goths *and* Vandals *in the philosophical World...Our* incomparable Philosopher *has discovered and demonstrated to us the true Nature of Light and Colours, of which the most sagacious and inquisitive Naturalists were entirely ignorant.*" (Desaguliers, 1745, p. vi, original italics)

At Newton's behest Desaguliers (1716a, 1716b, 1728) repeated some basic experiments in optics that Newton's detractors had failed to replicate; their confirmation by Desaguliers was such that "no person, who chose to give his name to the public, or whose name is worth recording, made any more opposition to it" (Priestley, 1772, p. 351). These experiments were included in his first series of lectures and demonstrations on experimental philosophy (published in 1719), but not in the second series: "*As the Treatise of Opticks, I design'd to publish, was only intended to be easy and popular; I refer the Readers who are desirous of seeing the Subject treated of in that manner, to the Book of Opticks published by the Reverend and Learned Dr.* Smith" (1744, p. vii, original italics). The lectures themselves were not only very popular and but some were attended by royalty. Newton in turn was a supporter of Desaguliers's popularization of his theories. During the period of Newton's presidency of the Royal Society (1703–1727), Desaguliers was elected a Fellow in 1714, and became the Society's demonstrator and curator. He was awarded the Society's Copley Medal three times. His experiments in binocular vision and size perception will be described below.

BINOCULAR COLOR COMBINATION

Throughout the eighteenth century binocular vision was studied in terms of singleness rather than depth. In the context of experiments on binocular single vision Desaguliers (1716b) devised a method of combining different stimuli in the two eyes that was to become widely employed in other studies of binocular vision, namely, placing an aperture in such a position that two adjacent objects were in the optical axes of each eye. Desaguliers used the method to examine both binocular single vision and binocular color combination, and to provide experimental evidence to support Newton's theory of binocular combination. The latter involved the concept of corresponding points and physiological union in the visual system (see Chapter 3).

The existence of retinal disparities was clearly enunciated by several students of optics in the eighteenth century, but the purpose to which they could be put—stereoscopic vision—was not appreciated. For example, Sébastien Le Clerc (1637–1714; 1712), an authority on perspective, represented the disparate projections of objects to the two eyes, but used these as evidence against Descartes' theory of binocular union in the pineal body. Both Smith (1738) and Harris (1775) provided clear diagrams of crossed and uncrossed disparities, but these were used to specify the locations of double images.

The combination of different colors presented to corresponding regions of each retina became an issue of theoretical importance following Newton's experiments on color mixing and his theory of binocular combination. Indeed, Desaguliers (1716b) was amongst the first to draw attention to the phenomenon. In particular, he showed that dichoptically presented colored lights rival rather than combine as in Newton's experiments on color mixing. Using the same experimental apparatus as he employed for his studies of binocular single vision, he replaced two candles with patches of different colored silks and observed that color mixing did not occur. Moreover, if the colored patches were made more intense, the rivalry was more compelling. That is, no color combination took place dichoptically, and the color rivalry is more evident with intense stimuli. Newton had stated that it was impossible for two objects to appear in the same place—because he believed that fibers from corresponding locations in each eye united at the chiasm. A similar argument would apply to color, and Desaguliers' observation was certainly in line with Newton's prediction. Nonetheless, the report set in train a series of studies that attempted to examine the phenomenon.

Desaguliers' method of binocular combination was applied by Taylor (1738), who added the refinement of placing colored glasses in front of candle flames; he found that colors combined rather than engaged in rivalry. Etienne-François Du Tour (1711–1784; 1760) provided a clear description of binocular color rivalry. He achieved dichoptic combination by another means: he placed a board between his eyes and attached blue and yellow fabric in equivalent positions on each side, or the fabric was placed in front of the fixation point. When he converged his eyes to look at them they did not mix but alternated in color. Du Tour also applied the method of observing the colors through an aperture, as has been adopted by Desaguliers, and obtained similar results. Yet another technique was to view different colored objects through two long tubes, one in each optic axis. This was used by Reid (1764), and he saw the colors combined although his description was not without its ambiguity: the colors were not only said to be combined, but also one "spread over the other, without hiding it" (p. 326). In these early reports of binocular color combination we have the origins of a dispute that was to extend beyond the eighteenth century, and was the source of much acrimony between two towering theoretical opponents in the second half of the nineteenth century—Helmholtz and Ewald Hering (1834–1918): do colors fuse when presented to corresponding regions of each eye, or do the undergo rivalry?

SIZE PERCEPTION

Desaguliers also conducted experiments on size perception. The knowledge that some objects were too small to be seen is an ancient one, but it was usually associated with their distance from the observer rather than their projected size. Desaguliers was able to demonstrate that although visual resolution was dependent on visual angle, visual size was not. Statements about apparent size were rarely given empirical weight prior to his experiments, apart from the reports of the difference in the apparent size of the moon at the zenith and near the horizon—the moon illusion (see Chapter 2). Desaguliers (1736a) compared judgments of the size of stimuli (candles) at different distance but matched for apparent size. When two candles of equal physical size were so perceived (even when one was twice the distance of the other), he substituted a smaller one of equal visual subtense for the far one, with no change in perceived size. He concluded that apparent distance, rather than physical distance, determines apparent size. It is noteworthy, too, that Desaguliers did not base his conclusions on his own observation but on those of "any unprejudic'd Person". Using naive subjects in perceptual studies was indeed a novelty, and one which was not adopted by many others until the late nineteenth century.

Desaguliers' experiments on apparent size were stimulated by his speculations on the link between size and distance perception in the moon illusion. He pointed out, as had many others previously, that the horizon moon is perceived as more distant than at its zenith. The suggestion that the vault of the heavens was flat was made by Alhazen in the eleventh century, and Desaguliers (1736a) expressed this concept diagrammatically. His figure was modified by both Smith (1738) and Young (1807), and is usually associated with one of the latter. Desaguliers also considered aerial perspective (reduced contrast with increased distance) as a cue to distance. The issue of size-distance invariance was not new at that time, but Desaguliers (1736b) attempted to place it on an empirical footing with a simple experiment using two spherical balls. He noted that when the two spheres subtended equal angles the one of lower contrast was seen as more distant and larger.

Thus, Desaguliers adopted Newton's natural philosophy and he applied experimental methods to the psychological domain of binocular vision and size perception. Not only did he apply control to the stimulus and viewing conditions but he also tested naive observers. The involvement of larger samples of observers probably derived from his lectures and demonstrations which were both novel and very popular. He clearly delighted in his demonstrations, and in the year of his death he wrote: "*About the Year* 1713, *I came to settle at* London, *where I have with great Pleasure seen the* Newtonian Philosophy *so generally received among Persons of all Ranks and Professions, and even the* Ladies, *by the Help of Experiments;.... the present* Course, *which I am now engag'd in, being the* 121st *since I began at* Hart-Hall *in* Oxford, *in the Year* 1710" (1745, p. x, original italics).

COLOR

Descartes and Newton both examined the color spectrum using prisms. Although the occurrence of colors due to light passing through or reflected from glass or crystals had been known about since antiquity, experimental examination of them had not been undertaken. A preliminary study of the prismatic spectrum was conducted by Harriot at the beginning of the seventeenth century, and the spectrum was subjected to more detailed analysis later in the century. Descartes' method of producing the prismatic spectrum was different to that adopted later by Newton. For Descartes, sunlight fell normally on one face of the prism, and was refracted at the second face, upon which the aperture was placed; he noted that the distinctness of the spectrum was dependent on the size of the aperture. Newton, on the other hand, only allowed a narrow pencil of sunlight to fall on the first face of the prism.

The optical instruments used to study color vision were relatively simple. With Newton's formulation of the color circle primary colors also became those from which compounds could be derived. Color wheels, discs with sectors painted in different colors, had been in use since the time of Ptolemy, but they were applied with greater precision in the eighteenth and nineteenth centuries. Young (1802a) stated that color vision could be mediated by retinal mechanisms that responded selectively to each of the three primaries, red, yellow, and blue. He later modified his selection to red, green, and violet (Young, 1802b, 1807). The debate about primary colors was frequently based upon the practice of painting, and the three primaries that they eventually established were red, yellow, and blue.

Newton distinguished between mixing pigments and mixing parts of the spectrum, noting that pigments reflected the incident light selectively. This could have proved useful to artists and scientists alike, but it was not pursued, perhaps because artists did not adopt the seven Newtonian primaries. The stimulus to differentiating light from pigment mixtures was Young's specification of a different set of primaries for light (red, green, and violet) to those adopted by artists (red, yellow, and blue). When Young's trichromatic theory was adopted, first by James Clerk Maxwell (1831–1879; 1855) and then by Helmholtz (1867), support for it was provided by experiments using color wheels. The resolution of the difference between mixing pigments and mixing lights was to await Helmholtz's clarification of the rules governing additive and subtractive color mixing. The primary lights when mixed yield white whereas primary pigments produce black (Helmholtz, 1852).

SUMMARY

The advances achieved in the seventeenth and eighteenth centuries were considerable, both with regard to the physics of stimulation and the psychology of the response. Less was achieved with regard to the physiology of the senses. In the context of vision, the major transformation was the separation of light from sight. Light was in the domain of physics and its properties could be isolated and examined. The formation of images in artificial eyes directed attention to similarities between eyes and cameras containing lenses. This in turn stimulated interest in the problem of accommodation—how can objects at different distances be focused in an optical system. The analogy between eye and camera was less than helpful in this regard, and the more open speculations of Descartes were found to offer more fruitful solutions for eyes.

The separation of white light into the spectral colors enabled the enigma of color to be investigated experimentally. Rules for color combinations were determined and the appearance of color could be related to the refrangibility of light, later to be specified in terms of wavelength. Waves and corpuscles vied for prominence in the analysis of light. Sight was not omitted from this scheme. Newton acknowledged that the rays were not colored and so the experience of color retained a subjective dimension. Those who studied light and color were philosophers, although their hues differed. There were experimental philosophers, like Newton, who wished to remain in contact with the phenomena they examined. For them observation and experiment provided the bedrock of science. Newton did not wish to entertain hypotheses—principles that could not be supported by experiment. Rationalist philosophers, like Descartes, were not so constrained, although he did add to the mechanistic approach in a multitude of ways.

The anatomy of the senses received benefits from both shades of philosopher, and this was clearly displayed in binocular vision. Both Descartes and Newton brought their brilliance to bear on binocular combination. However, they took the nerves in different directions. Descartes combined them in the pineal body, sacrificing anatomy to philosophy. Newton observed and experimented on the pathways from eyes to the brain, or sensorium, where the signals coalesced. Neither could be confident in their conclusions because so little was known about nerves and their central connections.

The psychology of the senses remained more firmly grounded. Experiments on color and size perception were conducted, and characteristics of binocular vision were examined, too. At the end of the eighteenth century, Wells was in the vanguard of vision—not only in the binocular domain but also concerning the movement sense. Unease with Aristotle's restriction of the senses to five had long been voiced, but Wells gave it substance. In true Newtonian style, he observed and experimented on visual vertigo. By examining the ways in which the eyes moved following body rotation, he established the principal features of semicircular canal function. Alas, neither he nor any of his contemporaries knew that the semicircular canals were involved in the maintenance of balance. Wells provided the behavioral evidence to link the vestibular receptors to vertigo, but he was not able to specify the mechanism by which it came about. This was to change in the following century. All the dimensions of the senses would explored in greater detail, and this would be assisted by a new array of instruments that could be enlisted to study them.

5

The Instrumental Revolution in the Nineteenth Century

The nineteenth century witnessed an explosion of experimental ingenuity in all areas of science. The senses were at the center of many of the dramatic departures, and the experimental advances in turn influenced theories of perception. As an example, the stereoscope was invented in the 1830s; it transformed not only the vision of pictures but also the picture of vision. The hallmark of the century was the invention of instruments which enabled the experimental investigation of phenomena. At its outset, Alessandro Volta (1745–1827; 1800) invented a battery which enabled electricity to be harnessed in a manner that could be applied with ease to living matter. He not only realized that the senses could be stimulated by electricity, he applied it to his own senses. Thus, a novel means of stimulating the senses became available, not to mention the myriad instruments that could be powered by this source.

Vision, as opposed to optics and ophthalmology, became an experimental discipline rather late. Of course, experiments were conducted in the previous centuries, but an accepted armory of methods and machines was not available until the 1830s. In that decade: Ernst Heinrich Weber (1795–1878; 1834) demonstrated that the nuances of visual discrimination could be measured, by applying what became called psychophysical methods; Joseph Plateau (1801–1883; 1833) devised a contrivance for synthesizing visual motion from a series of static pictures; Charles Wheatstone (1802–1875; 1838) demonstrated, by means of his invention, the stereoscope, that depth perception was influenced by retinal disparity; Gottfried Reinhold Treviranus (1776–1837; 1837) employed the new achromatic microscope to describe the cellular structure of the retina, heralding a new era for visual science, in which function could be related to microscopic structure. These instruments, and many others that were invented in the latter half of the nineteenth century, greatly expanded the range of visual phenomena, and the ways in which they could be investigated.

The essence of experiment is control, both of the stimulus and the response it generates. Measurement of these aspects was carried out to a higher degree in the nineteenth century. The initial impulse derived from instruments for stimulus control. They could be applied to visual motion and visual space, and it is these aspects that are considered initially. At about the same time, advances in microscopy exposed a greater degree of structure in sensory systems than had previously been imagined. Receptors were identified, and concerted efforts were made to relate structure to function.

STIMULUS CONTROL—THE IMPACT OF PHYSICS

Since the scientific revolution in the seventeenth century, instruments had been applied to investigate natural phenomena. An obvious example in the context of vision was the prism, which facilitated the analysis of light and experiments on the perception of color. However, in the early nineteenth century, the instruments of sensory discovery, particularly in vision, were found to have a popular as well as a scientific attraction. They were called philosophical toys (see Wade, 2004b). Turner (1998) has made a distinction between philosophical instruments and philosophical toys. The term philosophical instrument was applied to a contrivance which could demonstrate scientific phenomena. Their use represented an appreciation that nature can be examined by experiment as well as by observation, and they reflected the foundations upon which science is built. Philosophical toys were also designed for the experimental study of natural phenomena, but they could provide amusement, too. In the context of vision, there are many philosophical instruments and toys, and discussion will be confined to those that have been applied to the examination of spatial vision. First, however, their use in the development of understanding light and the eye will be mentioned, as this involved simple philosophical instruments.

Philosophical instruments reflected the emergence of science as an experimental discipline. In the context of vision, this scientific revolution is associated with the mechanistic speculations of Descartes and the experiments of Newton. Philosophical toys were more concerned with the manipulation of motion and space than color.

The advance of visual science as an experimental discipline has essentially been determined by the invention of instruments, like the stereoscope and stroboscope, to examine visual phenomena. They were philosophical toys as they were adapted for amusement and adopted by the public at large. The stereoscope sold in millions, as it could be combined with paired photographs to provide a more compelling impression of scenes otherwise unseen. The stroboscopic disc proved to be the engine for the perception of apparent motion, to be experienced later in the century as movies. It could be said that development of visual science was as dependent on these devices as biology had been upon the microscope.

Philosophical toys were usually based on simple optical or visual principles that were expressed in novel ways. For example, David Brewster's (1782–1868) kaleidoscope was based on mirror reflections. It took the popular imagination by storm in the second decade of the nineteenth century, but it remained an instrument of amusement rather than science. The stereoscope, on the other hand, was of vital importance to visual science, in addition to providing immense popular entertainment. The kaleidoscope was enlisted by artists to form symmetrical patterns, and Brewster (1819) included a chapter 'On the application of the kaleidoscope to the fine and useful arts' in his treatise on the kaleidoscope.

In the eighteenth century, physics had made advances by isolating variables and then manipulating them, and much the same applied to visual science in the nineteenth century. Indeed, the principal inventors of the instruments to be discussed, like Wheatstone and Plateau, were themselves physicists. Physics remained concerned with the control and measurement of naturally occurring events, like gravity, magnetism, and electricity, and with the development of theories to account for them. Other physicists who extended their enquiries into the operation of the senses were also preoccupied by stimulus control and manipulation. The measurement of responses was generally ignored. What is now called physics was referred to as natural or experimental philosophy, and these instruments were employed by physicists as well as being adapted for popular use. For example, the mirror stereoscope was a simple device, based on reflecting two slightly different perspective drawings of a three-dimensional object, but its scientific impact was dramatic, as was its popular appeal. Its invention by Wheatstone in the early 1830s made possible the experimental study of binocular space perception. Wheatstone (1827) had previously invented the phonic kaleidoscope for studying visual persistence, and later devised a chronoscope for measuring short intervals of time (Wheatstone, 1845). The former reflected a mounting interest in the integration of space and time. Together with considerations of the personal equation, the chronoscope opened the way to more precise measurements of reaction time. The instruments to be discussed below were based on long known visual phenomena, and were used experimentally to establish new facts concerning vision. The first of these to be discussed, visual persistence, is one of the earliest recorded phenomena.

MOTION

Aristotle, in the fourth century B.C., described persisting visual effects like afterimages, and in the first century Seneca described the trailing tails of shooting stars, comets, and lightning, and appreciated that this was due to the inability of vision to resolve very brief intervals of time. These common examples of visual persistence were frequently referred to as 'the duration of visual impressions' because the effects of a brief stimulus were visible for a short but sensible period beyond its extinction. Thus, the study of visual persistence also has a long history, which has proved of particular interest because the phenomenon lies at the heart of apparent motion, and therefore the simulated motion that we observe in films (see Eder, 1932).

Visual persistence was one of the first spatio-temporal phenomena to be subjected to quantification. The basic procedure was initially described by Ptolemy, and in more detail by Alhazen in the eleventh century. A rapidly moving flame will be seen in positions it no longer occupies; if it is rotated rapidly then a circle will be seen. Leonardo da Vinci repeated this observation and demonstrated that a similar effect occurs when the eye moves with respect to a stationary flame (MacCurdy, 1938). In the second edition of his *Opticks*, Newton (1717) used this phenomenon to estimate the duration of visual persistence; he suggested it was less than a second. More precise measurements were made by Chevalier Patrice D'Arcy (1725–1779; 1765): he built a machine with rotating arms onto which a glowing coal could be attached. By measuring the velocity required to complete a visible circle of light (in an otherwise dark room), he calculated the duration of visual persistence to be 8/60 s, or about 130 ms.

At the beginning of the nineteenth century, visual persistence was enlisted to produce a bewildering variety of philosophical toys. The phenomenon was manipulated in three ways. First, by rendering visible rapidly moving lights during continuous viewing. Secondly, by successive stimulation of the eyes by slightly different figures. Thirdly, by briefly presenting parts of a single figure in rapid succession.

The kaleidoscope did lead to an important offshoot bearing a similar name—the phonic kaleidoscope or kaleidophone—which rendered visible the paths of rapidly vibrating rods. The kaleidophone was an extension of a method described by Young (1800), in which silvered wire was attached to a piano string so that its vibration could be observed with the aid of a magnifying glass. Wheatstone (1827), whose background was in musical instrument manufacture, constructed the kaleidophone to amplify the vibrations so that they could be seen by the naked eye. Silvered glass beads were attached to the ends of rods having different cross-sections and shapes; when the rods were bowed or struck Chladni figures could be seen in the light paths traced by reflections from the beads. Wheatstone described the kaleidophone in the following way:

> "The first rod is cylindrical, about 1–10th of an inch in diameter, and is surmounted by a spherical bead which concentrates and reflects the light which falls upon it. The second is a similar rod, upon the upper extremity of which is placed a plate moving on a joint, so that its plane may be rendered either horizontal, oblique, or perpendicular; this plate is adapted to the reception of the objects, which consist of beads differently coloured and arranged on pieces of black card in symmetrical forms. The third is a four-sided prismatic rod, and a similar plate is attached to its extremity for the reception of the same objects. Another rod is fixed at the centre of the board; this is bent to a right-angle, and is furnished with a bead similar to the first-mentioned rod.... A hammer, softened by a leather covering, is employed to strike the rods; and a violin-bow is necessary to produce some varieties of effect." (Wheatstone, 1827; reprinted in Wade, 1983, pp. 206–207)

The kaleidophone was but one instrument of several that appeared in London during the 1820s. In 1827, John Ayrton Paris (1785–1856) described the thaumatrope, or wonder turner, which was even simpler in design. A circular piece of card had different drawings on each side, and its ends were connected by string. When it was whirled both designs were seen superimposed: birds could be seen caged during rotation but free when the disc was stationary; fragments of words written on each side of the disc could be rendered complete due to visibility of their persisting parts.

The impetus for these devices derived from observations made of the motions of spoked wheels behind or in front of railings. The initial description appeared in a brief note over the initials J.M.: "When a spoked wheel, such as that of a carriage, or the fly of an engine, is viewed in motion, through a series of vertical bars, spokes assume the peculiar curvatures which are represented" (1821, pp. 282–283). Peter Mark Roget (1779–1869), better known for his *Thesaurus* than for his experiments on vision, was fascinated by this phenomenon. In 1825 he provided illustrations and a mathematical analysis of the phenomenon, relating it to persisting visual images. In the conclusion to his article he observed that it "might therefore, if accurately estimated, furnish new modes of measuring the duration of the impressions of light on the retina" (Roget, 1825, p. 140).

London scientific society was intrigued by the phenomena as well as by the instruments, and the fashion ensnared many whose names are not normally associated with toys or even vision. For example, Michael Faraday (1791–1867; 1831) cast his scientific eye over the effects and wrote a very influential article on optical deceptions. He was disparaging about Paris' thaumatrope, referring to it as a schoolboy trick, but he was attracted by Roget's analysis of rotating spokes, and by his own observation of counter-rotating cogwheels. When viewed so that one wheel was aligned with the other "there was immediately the distinct, though shadowy resemblance of cogs moving slowly in one direction" (1831, p. 205). He constructed a simple arrangement of cut-out sectored-discs to examine the effects further.

Faraday wrote: "The eye has the power, as is well known, of retaining visual impressions for a sensible period of time; and in this way, recurring actions, made sufficiently near to each other, are perceptibly connected, and made to appear as a continuous impression" (1831, p. 210). This statement excited the interests of others to construct instruments that could synthesize motion from a sequence of discrete images. In 1833, both Plateau, with his phenakistoscope or fantascope, and Simon Stampfer (1792–1864), with his stroboscopic disc, developed similar instruments for presenting a series of still pictures in rapid succession. Plateau (1833) described the instrument as: "a cardboard disc pierced along its circumference with a certain number of small openings and carrying painted figures on one of its sides. When the disc is rotated about its center facing a mirror, and looking with one eye opposite the openings... the figures are animated and execute movements" (p. 305).

Stampfer's stroboscopic disc was very similar to Plateau's phenakistoscope, and both acknowledge the stimulus provided by Faraday's article. Stampfer (1833) described it in similar terms to Plateau:

> "The principle on which this device is based is that any act of vision which creates a conception of the image seen is divided into a suitable number of single moments; these present themselves to the eye in rapid succession, so that the ray of light falling on the change of the images is interrupted, and the eye receives only a momentary visual impression of each separate image when it is in the proper position." (Translated in Eder, 1945, pp. 499–500)

The issue of priority of invention inevitably ensued, and it is generally accorded to Plateau (Boring, 1942). However, Roget (1834) suggested in his *Bridgewater Treatise* that he had made such a device even earlier. His interests in visual persistence had been rekindled by Faraday's article:

"About the year 1831, Mr. Faraday prosecuted the subject with the usual success which attends all his philosophical researches, and devised a great number of interesting experiments on the appearances resulting from combinations of rotating wheels ... This again directed my attention to the subject, and led me to the invention of the instrument which has since been introduced into notice under the name of the *Phantasmascope* or *Phenakistiscope*. I constructed several of these at that period (in the spring of 1831), which I showed to my friends; but in consequence of occupations and cares of a more serious kind, I did not publish any account of this invention, which was reproduced on the continent in the year 1833." (Roget, 1834, p. 416, original italics)

Plateau (1833) appreciated that there were limits to the visibility of such apparent motion: if the rotation was too slow then each individual figure was seen; if it was too fast then they were all seen together in a confusion. These instruments could be used by just one person at a time, whereas William Horner (1789–1837; 1834) developed a variant for group viewing: it consisted of a cylinder mounted on a vertical axis, with slits at regular intervals, and a sequence of drawings on the opposite inside surface of the cylinder. He called it the *dædaleum*, but it became widely used in the latter half of the nineteenth century under the name of *zoetrope*.

Stroboscopic discs presented stimuli discretely, briefly, and in succession; that is, a sequence of drawings differing slightly from one another were viewed successively through slits in a rotating disc. To the astonishment of observers a single figure appeared in motion: perceived movement was synthesized from a sequence of still pictures. Stroboscopic discs were used to study visual persistence and apparent motion, and Purkinje made a variant of one in 1840; he called it the phorolyt or kinesiscope, and it was sold commercially as a magic disc (Matousek, 1961). Purkinje used his phorolyt to produce dynamic images of a range of natural movements generated from a sequence of static drawings. These varied from the pumping action of the heart to the walking movements of newts; he also used it to display his own rotating posture (see Wade and Brožek, 2001).

Successive exposure of a moving window in front of a fixed scene has received sporadic description since the time of Leonardo da Vinci. He made passing reference to: "the movement of certain instruments worked by women, made for convenience of gathering their threads together ... For these in their revolving movement are so swift that through being perforated they do nor obstruct to the eye anything behind them" (MacCurdy, 1938, p. 272). A more detailed description was given by Robert Darwin (1786). He made a simple paper sail which he could rotate:

"This is beautifully illustrated by the following experiment: fix a paper sail, three or four inches in diameter, and made like that of a smoke jack, in a tube of pasteboard; on looking through the tube at a distant prospect, some disjoined parts of it will be seen through the narrow intervals between the sails; but as

the fly begins to revolve, these intervals appear larger; and when it revolves
quicker, the whole prospect is seen quite as distinct as if nothing intervened,
though less luminous." (R. Darwin, 1786, p. 324)

Wheatstone's (1827) examination of visual persistence with the kaleidophone had alerted him to the possibilities of such a device, and he constructed one to demonstrate this effect more precisely: a sector in a metal
disc exposed part of a design painted on glass in transparent colors; when
the sector was rotated rapidly enough, the whole design was visible.

In the philosophical toys described above, an aperture moved in front
of a scene or picture. In 1829, Plateau investigated the effects of moving
a pattern behind both moving and fixed apertures (Plateau, 1829, 1836,
1878); the instrument was similar to the phenakistoscope, involving rotating discs, and he gave it the name anorthoscope. Regular geometrical
patterns moving behind a fixed aperture appeared deformed, or deformed
figures appeared regular, like anamorphoses. The device was elaborated
by Zöllner (1862), who demonstrated the importance of pursuit eye movements to the perceptual distortions. The aperture was typically a vertical
slit, and the shapes were moved horizontally behind it. Simple shapes, like
circles, appeared like ellipses with the long axis vertical for fast movements
and horizontal for slow.

Depth

The philosophical toys described above manipulated both space and time,
so that an object presented successively could be seen simultaneously.
Wheatstone, who was involved in developing two of the three manipulations of visual persistence, was also a close acquaintance of Faraday, who
stimulated interest in the third form (the stroboscopic disc). However, it
was in the context of space perception that Wheatstone was to have the
greatest impact on the development of visual science and on visual art. The
stereoscope, perhaps more than any other instrument, ushered in the era of
experimentation to vision. The stereoscope is a simple optical device that
presents slightly different figures to each eye; if these figures have appropriate horizontal disparities then depth is seen. Whereas the stroboscope
simulated motion, the stereoscope simulated depth. Paired photographic
images of distant scenes could be seen in depth, and this intrigued a public
eager for enhancement of the senses.

Paradoxically, knowledge of retinal disparity has a history stretching
back to Ptolemy and Galen, but the use to which it was put was only
appreciated with the invention of the stereoscope. That is, the existence
of retinal disparity was considered to introduce a problem in interpreting

binocular single vision. Prior to the invention of the stereoscope, theories of binocular vision were based on either the combination of corresponding points to yield singleness, or the suppression of signals from one eye (see Wade, 1983).

Wheatstone was able to free-fuse stereopairs with ease; he also used the then long-known method of viewing figures down two viewing tubes. However, many of his acquaintances found difficulties with these techniques, and so Wheatstone made the stereoscope. In the early 1830s he constructed both mirror and prism stereoscopes, but only the mirror model was described in his first publication on binocular vision (Wheatstone, 1838). With the aid of the stereoscope and suitably drawn stereopairs, Wheatstone was able to demonstrate that apparent depth could be synthesized. The sign of the depth, whether nearer or farther than the fixation point, was dependent upon the direction of disparity; reversing the disparity reversed the direction of depth seen. There were limits to the extent of disparity that yielded depth perception, and radically different figures, like letters of the alphabet, when placed appropriately in the stereoscope engaged in binocular rivalry. Wheatstone was acutely aware of the theoretical significance of stereoscopic depth perception with regard both to the binocular circles of Vieth (1818) and Müller (1826a) and to Müller's concept of identical retinal points.

Wheatstone analysed the factors that normally accompany an approaching object: increases in retinal image size, retinal disparity, convergence, and accommodation. In his second contribution, Wheatstone (1852) examined each of these factors in isolation, after the manner of experiments in physics. He modified the mirror stereoscope to have adjustable arms, so that changes in convergence could be studied without changes in retinal disparity; he had a variety of stereophotographs taken of the same object with variations in disparity; he viewed the images through artificial pupils to bypass accommodation; retinal magnitude was increased without change in retinal disparity. The factors of greatest importance were retinal disparity and convergence.

The most popular model of stereoscope was Brewster's (1849) lenticular version, although he illustrated a wide variety of methods for combining stereopairs (Brewster, 1851), as did Heinrich Dove (1803–1879; 1851). The optical manipulation of disparities was also achieved with Wheatstone's (1852) pseudoscope, which reversed them, and with Helmholtz's (1857) telestereoscope, which exaggerated them. The anaglyph method, enabling overprinted red and green images to be combined through similarly colored filters was introduced at about the same time (d'Almeida, 1858).

In the year after Wheatstone's first article on the stereoscope appeared, his friend, William Henry Fox Talbot, made public his negative-positive photographic process. In fact the term 'photographic' was used first by Wheatstone (Arnold, 1977). He immediately grasped the significance of photographing scenes from two positions, so that they would be seen in depth when mounted in the stereoscope. In 1840, he enlisted Talbot's assistance to take stereo photographs for him; when they were sent to him the angular separation of the camera positions used to capture the two views was too large (47.5 deg) and Wheatstone suggested that 25 deg would be more appropriate. Klooswijk (1991) has reprinted a section of Wheatstone's letter to Talbot, and has himself taken stereophotographs of the bust Talbot probably employed from camera angles of 47.5, 25.0, and 1.75 deg. Wheatstone also asked Henry Collen (1800–1875) to take stereoscopic photographs of Charles Babbage (1792–1871); a single camera was used to take photographs from different positions because it was difficult to find two cameras that were optically equivalent. Collen (1854) described it thus:

> "In 1841, when I was one of the very few who undertook to make use of Mr. Talbot's process, Mr. Wheatstone not only had the idea of making photographic portraits for the stereoscope, but at his request, and under his direction, in August of that year, I made a pair of stereoscopic portraits of Mr. Babbage, in whose possession they still remain; and if I remember rightly, Mr. Wheatstone has previously obtained some daguerreotype portraits from Mr. Beard for the stereoscope." (p. 200)

The *camera obscura* had been applied to equating image formation in the eye with that in an artificial device. Wheatstone showed how the photographic camera, in combination with the stereoscope, could be employed to reintroduce the dimension of depth to the perception of pictures. In Wheatstone's obituary notice in *Nature* the following comments were added by Signor Volpicelli of the Academia dei Lincei:

> "Our countryman, Leonardo da Vinci, in 1500, or thereabouts, conceived and was the first to affirm, that from a picture it was not possible to obtain the effect of relief. But Wheatstone, reflecting profoundly in 1838, on the physiology of vision, invented the catoptric stereoscope, with which he philosophically solved the problem of the optical and virtual production of relief." (Volpicelli, 1876, p. 502)

TIME

In the eighteenth and early nineteenth centuries the accurate estimation of short intervals was of importance to astronomy and physics, and they often had to rely on the eye as an instrument of measurement. An appreciation of the personal equation and reaction time arose precisely from individual differences in such estimations (see Boring, 1929; Mollon and Perkins, 1996). The chronoscope also had its origins in the measurement of physical phenomena, although it was to become a vital instrument in the experimental psychologists' armory. Descriptions of earlier chronographs can be found in Dove (1835).

Time, however, was much too serious an issue to be the source of popular amusement. Time, or our perception of it, was implicitly manipulated in the stroboscopic discs, which when wedded to the camera could produce apparently moving images. The instruments that were concerned directly with time, other than measuring its passage with accuracy, fractionated it into smaller units. These were philosophical instruments rather than philosophical toys, and there use was generally confined to the laboratory. The instruments, like chronoscopes and tachistoscopes, were often applied to the experimental study of vision (see Wade and Heller, 1997). Their developments were, however, closely associated with phenomena that did have an enormous popular impact and appeal, such as the electric telegraph.

In his lectures on natural philosophy and the mechanical arts, delivered in 1802, Thomas Young not only appreciated the importance of measuring short durations, but he also made an instrument "by means of which an interval of a thousandth part of a second may possibly be rendered sensible" (1807/2002, p. 190). A descending weight rotated a drum on which marks could be made by a pointer:

> "By means of this instrument we may measure, without difficulty, the frequency of the vibrations of sounding bodies, by connecting them with a point, which will describe an undulating path on the roller. These vibrations may also serve in a very simple manner for the measurement of the minutest intervals of time; for if a body, of which the vibrations are of a certain degree of frequency, be caused to vibrate during the revolution of an axis, and to mark its vibrations on a roller, the traces will serve as a correct index of the time occupied by any part of a revolution, and the motion of any other body may be very accurately compared with the number of alternations marked, in the same time, by the vibrating body." (Young, 1807/2002, p. 191)

In this short statement, and with his chronometer, Young set down the principles upon which most measurements of brief intervals were to be made in biology for much of the nineteenth century. Moreover, the mechanism of its operation inspired Wheatstone to wed it with electricity in order to measure the velocities of projectiles. In producing the electromagnetic chronoscope he "borrowed the idea of the chronoscopic part of this apparatus from an instrument intended for measuring small intervals of time, invented by the late Dr. Young" (Wheatstone, 1845, p. 92). In 1840, as an offshoot from his research in developing the electric telegraph, Wheatstone refined the measurement of short intervals by incorporating an electromagnet, and produced the chronoscope. It consisted of a clock that was started and stopped by the action of an electromagnet. In the following year he demonstrated this instrument to scientific societies in Brussels and Paris; its principal function was "for the purpose of measuring rapid motions, and especially the velocity of projectiles" (Wheatstone, 1845, p. 86). When slight modifications were introduced and reported by others, Wheatstone (1845) sought to establish his priority in its invention. Matthias Hipp (1813–1893) also adapted the chronoscope for use in astronomy, and it was his instrument that became widely used in measurements of the personal equation after about 1860 (see Edgell and Symes, 1906).

The tachistoscope was a device which presented visual stimuli for very short intervals, so that the eyes could not move during exposure. It was employed to examine whether stereoscopic depth was still seen without eye movements. The first attempts to address this problem were by Dove (1841), who used an electric discharge to observe stereopairs. The problems associated with electric sparks resulted in the search for alternative methods of brief presentation for controlled durations. Volkmann (1859) gave the name tachistoscope to an instrument of his invention, and it was developed initially for observing stereoscopic images. He confirmed Dove's observation of stereoscopic depth without eye movements. In addition, he did appreciate the instrument's wider applicability in experimental psychology.

Philosophical instruments were applied to study natural phenomena experimentally. In the context of vision, they removed space and time from their object base. Newton had established that color could be examined independently of objects and Wheatstone's stereoscope, similarly removed binocular depth perception from its object base. In many instances the instruments were also adopted for popular amusement, and were called philosophical toys. The manipulations of space and time together, in toys like the stroboscopic disc, resulted in the synthesis of motion from discrete presentations of static images. Many versions of stereoscopes and stroboscopes were made, and when combined with realistic photographic images, either paired or in sequence, their popular appeal was enormous.

ANATOMY

Anatomy changed dimensions in the nineteenth century. A microscopic world unfolded beneath the achromatic lenses of the new microscopes. The microscopic world had remained rather blurred throughout the eighteenth century, due to the simple optical magnifiers employed. It was transformed by the introduction of powerful achromatic instruments in the 1820s, and rapid advances were made thereafter. Cell doctrine was most clearly articulated at the end of that decade by Schwann: "there is one common principle of development for the most diverse elementary parts of the organism, and that this principle is the formation of cells" (1839, p. 196). The staining procedures introduced later in the nineteenth century verified speculations about the continuity between nerve cells and their fibers but they did not clarify the anatomical relationship between the nerves themselves. There were two opposing the camps: on the one hand, the reticularists argued that all nerves were linked continuously in a vast network; the anti-reticularists, on the other hand, believed that neurons were structurally independent units of nervous activity. It was not until the end of the nineteenth century that the neuron doctrine began to be widely accepted (see Robinson, 2001; Shepherd, 1991; Spillane, 1981).

In 1832 Purkinje obtained an achromatic microscope made by Plössl. He directed it at the large cells in the cerebellum, thereby identifying the cells that bear his name. Purkinje is more widely known in visual science for the range of subjective phenomena he described, some of which also bear his name (see Wade and Brožek, 2001; Wade et al, 2002). He carried out relatively little further research on vision after he appreciated the power of the new microscope. Together with his students, most notably Gabriel Valentin (1813–1883), a wide range of structures was examined. In a letter to one of his students Purkinje wrote that: "There should be nothing in the whole organic body that cannot be investigated and identified with regard to its detail and its local and general function" (Thomsen, 1919, p. 1). The cerebellum was one of the structures examined. Purkinje reported the microscopic characteristics of the large cells in the 'yellow' (white) matter on 23 September 1837 to a meeting of natural scientists held in Prague:

> "Similar corpuscles are present everywhere in the folia of the cerebellum, arranged in great numbers in rows delimiting the yellow matter. Each of these corpuscles is turned with its rounded end inward, towards the yellow matter, and in its head, apart from the inner space, there is also distinctly shown a central nucleus. Its tail is turned outward and, mostly ending in two projections, buries itself in the grey matter almost as far as the outer periphery, where the surface is surrounded by the vascular membrane." (Translated in Kruta, 1971, p. 127)

These observations were made before any adequate staining methods had been developed. Purkinje used alcohol to fix his preparations, and he made thin sections so that they could be examined microscopically. Kruta (1971) noted that "Purkyně was one of the first—at least after Leewenhoek—to observe tissues in thin sections and he thus contributed considerably to the improvement of microscopic technique" (p. 127). The independence of nerves, and the neuron doctrine, were firmly established when Charles Sherrington (1857–1952; 1906) described the synapse and proposed a mode of chemical transmission across synaptic junctions.

Among the other cells that were isolated and described were specialized cells, called receptors; they could be related to the stimuli that excited them. Those located in well-defined sense organs were named on the basis of their morphology (rods, cones, hair cells, etc), whereas the receptors in or beneath the skin were generally named after those who first described them (e.g., Golgi tendon organs, Krause end bulbs, Meissner corpuscles, Merkel discs, Pacinian corpuscles, and Ruffini cylinders). The isolation of receptors that were specialized to respond to specific forms of environmental energy was adopted as a criterion for defining the senses. Particular attention was directed to the receptors in the retina, and the complexity of retinal structure became apparent as a result of the many microscopic investigations undertaken.

STRUCTURE OF THE RETINA

When achromatic microscopes were directed towards retinal fibers in the 1830s a greater degree of structure was discerned, but the nature of the receptors was not immediately apparent. Moreover, the previous hypotheses linking visual acuity to the dimensions of retinal elements influenced the initial representations of their structure. Treviranus, like Purkinje, had the benefit of a Plössl microscope for his studies, and from 1833 he measured the dimensions of many nerves in sensory systems and in the brains of a variety of animals. He considered that the brain was comprised of cylindrical cells arranged in parallel. For example, the diameters of fibers in the optic nerves of rabbit were given as 0.0033 mm. Prior to these microscopic investigations, he had measured his own visual acuity: the value he derived for distinguishing between two points was 30″ (Treviranus, 1828).

With his measurements of visual acuity and his microscopic studies of the retina, Treviranus was in a position to fuse the indirect estimates of retinal cell size with the direct measurement of them. He did not cite the earlier indirect estimates, but he did relate his value with those derived from his microscopic studies of other species. Treviranus (1835) inferred that the radius of the papillae (the name he gave to the extremities of the retinal elements) in humans was 0.0006 of a Paris line (equivalent to a diameter 0.003 mm). It was in close correspondence with those of swans and rabbits, measured microscopically.

In his posthumously published volume on the inner structure of the retina, Treviranus (1837) presented drawings based on vertical and horizontal microscopic sections of cells in the visual systems of many species. His diagram of the crow's retina indicated a wider variation in retinal structure than had previously been represented, and the layers within it were clearly shown. He did, however, make the error of directing the papillae towards the incoming light rather than away from it. In this regard, Treviranus was reflecting the earlier ideas (from Descartes onwards) that the terminations of the optic nerves were the receptive elements in the retina, and that they were directed towards the lens. The years following 1840 saw rapid advances in fixing, sectioning, and staining microscopic preparations (see Finger, 1994; 2000). Nonetheless, Treviranus described and illustrated cylindrical cells in the retinas of a variety of animals, and opened the way for others to examine the microscopic structure of the retina in more detail. As Polyak (1957) remarked: "The work of Treviranus, though erroneous in almost every point, was beneficial because it stimulated an immediate series of investigations" (p. 48).

Müller (1843/2003) described seeing "rod-shaped" bodies in the retina, but their relationship to the optic nerve fibers remained uncertain:

"Although the three layers of the retina certainly exist, and although rod-shaped bodies composing its internal lamina are very distinct, having been seen by Volkmann, E. H. Weber, Gottsche, Ehrenberg, and myself, yet the essential nature and mode of connexion of these bodies with the fibres of the fibrous layer are still involved in obscurity. It is a question, namely, whether the rod-shaped bodies correspond exactly in number to the nervous fibres, and whether each fibre actually corresponds to one of those bodies; or whether the latter are superposed in series upon the fibres of the fibrous layer." (Müller, 1843/2003, p. 1123)

The possibility of more complex connections within the layers of the retina were alluded to by Müller, but the receptive elements were considered to be 'rod-shaped'. Within a few years, cones as well as rods had been isolated and structure was related to function, largely due to the microscopical studies of Bowman, Kölliker, and Schultze.

The correct anatomical orientation of the retinal elements was described shortly after Treviranus by Bidder (1839); the terminations of the optic nerve structures were directed towards the choroid rather than the lens. Bidder then rejected the possibility that they could be receptive elements because of their orientation. A decade later, William Bowman (1816–1892; 1849) provided a diagram of the retina, which distinguished between what he called rods and bulbs. He described the constituents of the retina in the following way:

"Now, the retina contains in itself all the structural elements which are found in other parts of the system, *except nerve-tubules*, which are not present in the human retina, nor in the retina of the higher animals, but only in the optic nerve; and it moreover contains, besides these, other structural elements not elsewhere met with, but peculiar to this part, and which we are therefore led to suspect may be in some way or other subservient to the proper action of the retina as a recipient of the vibratory impressions of light. . . . The *elements peculiar to the retina* are . . . of two kinds—*Columnar particles, or rods*, arranged vertically in a single series; and *Bulbous particles*, interspersed at regular intervals among the former." (Bowman, 1949, pp. 79–80, original italics)

Bowman drew attention to the disagreements about the interpretations of the terminal structures of the retina, and to the difficulties of obtaining good specimens for microscopical study. He also described the characteristic structure of the retina in the yellow spot: "The two elements . . . are found over the yellow spot as on the surrounding parts of the retina; the rods are of the same length, but thicker, and the bulb-like bodies are nearer together" (1849, p. 92). The texture of the retina was quite different around the yellow spot: "the grey fibres do not pass over it in a direct course from the optic nerve to the side of the retina beyond the spot, but take a circuitous course, so as to avoid the spot, and only that small number which properly belong to it, and terminate in it" (p. 91). Bowman did describe differences in the numbers of rods and bulbs in different species, but no generalization was drawn from this. He described the bulbs as "globular or egg-shaped, and sometimes to have a small blunt spur upon them, turned towards the choroid" (p. 87), but Hannover's (1844) 'cônes' was the name for them that was generally adopted. In German they were called Zapfen, and this is the term used by Helmholtz (1867).

Helmholtz drew upon the burgeoning microscopical research that was emerging from German laboratories. The authorities on retinal structure were Alfred Kölliker (1817–1905) and his collaborator Heinrich Müller (1820–1864). The figure Helmholtz used to illustrate retinal structure in the first volume of his *Handbuch* was from Kölliker, but he changed it in the second edition of 1896 to that by Schultze, together with Schultze's diagram of the single rod and cone. The numerical ordering of the layers in the retina was reversed, too. For Kölliker's diagram the sequence started with the rod and cone layer; for Schultze's the number of layers was extended to ten, and the sequence terminated with the choroid. The English translation of Helmholtz (1924a/2000) confounds the two accounts; the text is taken from the first edition, but Schultze's diagram from the second edition replaces that of Kölliker. The third German edition (and therefore the English translation) is based on Helmholtz's first edition, and so contains this conflation.

Schultze succeeded Helmholtz in the chair of anatomy at Bonn in 1859, when Helmholtz moved to Heidelberg. In the first volume of his *Treatise on physiological optics* Helmholtz (1924a/2000) was able to state that: "The retina is composed partly of the microscopical components of the nervous system (nerve fibres, ganglion cells and nuclei), and partly of certain characteristic elements, the so-called rods (*bacilli*) and cones (*coni*)" (p. 24).

In the Supplement to the first edition Helmholtz (1867) gave the dimensions of rods and cones (approximately 0.002 and 0.005 mm, respectively) as determined by Schultze. Only cones were present in the fovea, and outer segments were small (0.002 mm). Schultze (1866) also examined the complement of rods and cones in a variety of animals, and was able to suggest that rods and cones have different functions.

By the end of the nineteenth century the cell doctrine was universally accepted, and the neuron doctrine was receiving added support. Receptors for the various senses were observed, and the characteristics of perception were related to receptor structure. The dimensions of nerve fibers were found to vary widely, depending upon the state of myelination, although they were within the range of the estimates derived indirectly in the eighteenth century.

PATHWAYS TO THE BRAIN

At the beginning of the nineteenth century, Bell (1811) tried to stimulate his medical colleagues to abandon the notion "that the whole brain is a common sensorium" and to encourage exploration of nerve pathways:

> "It is not more presumptuous to follow the tracts of nervous matter in the brain, and to attempt to discover the course of sensation, than it is to trace the rays of light through the humours of the eye, and to say, that the retina is the seat of vision. Why are we to close the investigation with the discovery of the external organ?.... That the external organs of the senses have the matter of the nerves adapted to receive certain impressions, while the corresponding organs of the brain are put to activity by the external excitement: That the idea or perception is according to the part of the brain to which the nerve is attached, and that each organ has a certain limited number of changes to be wrought upon it by the external impression: That the nerves of sense, the nerves of motion, and the vital nerves, are distinct through their whole course, though they seem sometimes united in one bundle; and that they depend for their attributes on the organs of the brain to which they are attached." (Bell, 1811/2000, pp. 3 and 5–6)

The pathways from the receptors to more central sites, and to areas of the brain, took rather longer to trace. Even in the case of vision, where the optic nerve, chiasm, and tract had been described by Galen, the precise paths pursued remained hotly debated until the late nineteenth century. In the second edition of his *Opticks*, Newton (1717) had hinted at partial decussation of fibers at the chiasm, and he had provided evidence of it in an earlier unpublished manuscript (see Chapter 3). The situation was complicated by the differences that were observed between species. When Bell (1803/2000) was writing, the consensus was that there was no decussation at the optic chiasm. This was challenged in the decades following, in part because William Wollaston (1766–1828; 1824) was able to marshal evidence from his own hemianopia as well as from anatomy to support partial decussation. He combined two sources of evidence regarding the pathways from the eyes to the brain—clinical observation and anatomy. Both were to play critical roles in the clarification of visual pathways later in the century, but few speculated on the more central pathways of vision. This was to become a topic of considerable interest, largely as a consequence of David Ferrier's (1843–1928; 1876) studies of electrical stimulation and ablation of the occipital cortex. The detailed anatomy of the crossings was described by Bernhard von Gudden (1824–1886; 1870) and by Hermann Munk (1839–1912; 1879), but there remained powerful detractors. It was not until the end of the nineteenth century that the partial decussation of the optic pathways in humans was considered as established.

SPATIAL ILLUSIONS

The second half of the nineteenth century was the era of illusions. Despite the fact that illusions have fascinated students of the senses for over 2,000 years, many of the geometrical optical illusions graced by the names of their discovers derive from this period. Helmholtz, writing in 1867, did describe a few illusions, but not many. The avalanche descended in the later decades. Magicians were the masters of illusion in the first half of the century. Probably each individual's first contact with illusions is through magic, and it certainly reaches a larger section of the population than the illusions studied in science. We now accept that magic involves tricks that comply with natural laws, but this was not always so. Magicians of the past appreciated the laws of light and could manipulate attention with far greater subtlety than was the case for students of the senses. They were able to beguile and bamboozle those who did not share their knowledge, which they kept as secret as possible. As Brewster wrote in 1832 in his book on *Natural Magic*:

> "The secret use which was thus made of scientific discoveries and of remarkable inventions, has no doubt prevented many of them from reaching the present times; but though we are ill informed respecting the progress of the ancients in various departments of the physical sciences, yet we have sufficient evidence that almost every branch of knowledge had contributed its wonders to the magician's budget, and we may even obtain some insight into the scientific acquirements of former ages, by a diligent study of their fables and their miracles." (p. 3)

Magicians are applied scientists, using knowledge of illusions (and selective attention) with consummate skill without wishing to delve too deeply into their underlying basis. The optical illusions devised in the nineteenth century are not so magical, but they are robust and they have had an enormous impact on the development of psychology.

ILLUSIONS AND THE ORIGINS OF EXPERIMENTAL PSYCHOLOGY

Geometrical optical illusions are quintessentially phenomena of the late-nineteenth century, when the likes of Ponzo, Poggendorff, Mach and Müller-Lyer described their eponymous phenomena. These illusions have an important place in the history of psychology, because they were amongst the factors that led Wundt to establish his Psychological Institute at Leipzig in 1879—he could not envisage how illusions could be accounted for in physiological terms, and so they, along with consciousness, required a separate discipline. Wundt took as his yardstick the proximal stimulus (the retinal image)—and he could not accept that, say, two linear extents that produced equivalent retinal extents could yield perceptual inequality due to physiological processes. Thus, geometrical optical illusions are important in the context of establishing psychology as an independent discipline: there was considered to be no physiological correlate of perception. Psychologists like Wundt sought to determine correlates, and the one most favored at that time was in terms of eye movements, although other higher-level alternatives were also entertained.

It is, however, instructive to examine why there should have been this burst of illusory activity in the late nineteenth century. Put another way, why did outline drawings assume such a central role in the study of perception? It could have been due to the combination of two powerful strands of thinking about vision. The first stems from the seventeenth century, when Kepler and later Descartes elucidated the dioptrical properties of the eye. They thereby set in train the idea that the problem of perception has as its starting point the static, two-dimensional retinal image. The retinal image was considered as static, and the problem was seen as restoring the missing dimension of distance from the ambiguous projection. However, this is both a physical and a physiological fiction. The static retinal image is a convenient physical fiction because it allows us to draw ray diagrams that describe the dioptrical properties of the eye. It is a physiological fiction because the eye is never still and the receptors collect energy at differential rates. Nonetheless, these fictions continue to drive our models of vision.

The second strand relates to the experimental approaches to the study of perception introduced in the mid-nineteenth century. Wheatstone and Helmholtz argued that experimental rigor of the physical sciences should be brought to bear on the study of perception. Thus stimulus variables should be isolated and manipulated in quite unnatural ways in order to determine how perception is modified. It is difficult to manipulate solid objects, but it is exceedingly easy to create novel pictures. Moreover, Wheatstone himself had shown that the perception of three-dimensional space can be synthesized from the use of two appropriate flat drawings. So pictures became the accepted stimuli for the study of vision. Once accepted, the psychologists then rediscovered tricks that had been a part of the artist's armory for centuries and they devised some novel ones, too.

Are pictures so central to understanding perception? What is the relationship between the perception of pictures and of the objects they portray? Will understanding pictures facilitate our interpretations of vision, or vice versa? And how do those peculiar pictures, geometrical optical illusions, relate to other forms of pictorial representation? It could well be argued, as Gibson (1966, 1979) has, that the study of perception will not be furthered by the examination of such oddities. When Purkinje remarked that "visual illusions reveal visual truths", he was not referring to geometrical optical illusions.

To question the appropriateness of pictures as the stimuli for vision is more subversive than it might at first appear, because it is attacking both theoretical strands mentioned above. Are not our ideas of the retinal image also pictorial? We have certainly progressed in our physiological knowledge since Wundt; indeed, there are now physiological interpretations of illusions. But have our ideas about the nature of the retinal image advanced also? Thus, the study of illusions was used to argue for the independence of psychology from physiology. The static proximal stimulus had been described, and so the two lines of the Ponzo illusion would project equal length lines on the retina and visual neuroscience stopped at the retina—so physiologists could not account for the illusion.

Illusions were studied in the late nineteenth century because they were not amenable to the extant physiology—hence their place in psychology. They also fostered the use of two-dimensional stimuli in perceptual experiments, giving vision the aura of scientific respectability.

MOTION AFTEREFFECTS

One illusion that excited attention in the early nineteenth century was not so called until much later in that century. It is now referred to as the motion aftereffect (MAE). Aristotle had described the apparent motion seen in stationary stones at the riverside after he had observed pebbles beneath the flowing water. A more detailed description was provided by Lucretius, also in the context of flowing water (see Wade, 1994; Wade and Verstraten, 1998 for historical reviews of MAEs). Unlike most other phenomena described in antiquity, this motion illusion disappeared from view for many centuries: there do not seem to be any other descriptions of it until early in the nineteenth century when it was rediscovered frequently. The two most notable accounts were made by Purkinje (1820, 1825) and by Addams (1834). Purkinje first briefly described the MAE in an article concerned with vertigo:

> "Another form of eye dizziness can be demonstrated if one observes a passing sequence of spatially distinct objects for a long time, e.g. a long parade of cavalry, overlapping waves, the spokes of a wheel that is not rotating too fast. When the actual movement of the objects stops there is a similar apparent motion in the opposite direction." (Purkinje, 1820, pp. 96–97)

Purkinje (1825) amplified one aspect of the MAE in his second book on subjective visual phenomena. This report is more frequently cited: "One time I observed a cavalry parade for more than an hour, and then when the parade had passed, the houses directly opposite appeared to me to move in the reversed direction to the parade" (1825, p. 60). Purkinje specified the direction of apparent motion, and he interpreted it in terms of involuntary eye movements over the houses. A few years later Robert Addams (ca. 1800–1875) observed what later became called the waterfall illusion at the Falls of Foyers in northern Scotland (see Wade and Hughes, 2002). This was a noted, though remote, cascade visited in the eighteenth century by Dr. Johnson on his Highland tour and celebrated in verse by both Robert Burns and William Topaz McGonagall. Addams described the waterfall illusion thus:

> "Having steadfastly looked for a few seconds at a particular part of the cascade, admiring the confluence and descussation of the currents forming the liquid drapery of waters, and then suddenly directed my eyes to the left, to observe the vertical face of the sombre age-worn rocks immediately contiguous to the water-fall, I saw the rocky face as if in motion upwards, and with an apparent velocity equal to that of the descending water." (Addams, 1834, p. 373)

The full text of Addams' brief but insightful article can be found in Dember (1964) and in Swanston and Wade (1994).

Despite the fact that Purkinje's book was well known in Germany, and that Addams' article was translated into German (Addams, 1835), both were often overlooked by German sensory physiologists, and the MAE was rediscovered independently several more times. Some of the rediscoveries were in the context of flowing water (Müller, 1838; Oppel, 1856; Aitken, 1878). Travelling on the railways also provided a platform for observing MAEs (Brewster, 1845; Helmholtz, 1867/1925; Thompson, 1877), and Thompson extended the MAE to depth as well as direction:

> "Thus, if from a rapid railway train objects from which the train is receding be watched, they seem to shrink as they are left behind, their images contracting and moving from the edges of the retina towards its centre. If after watching this

motion for some time the gaze be transferred to an object at a constant distance
from the eye, it seems to be actually expanding and approaching." (Thompson,
1877, p. 32)

MAEs in the third dimension were examined more systematically by
Sigmund Exner (1846–1926; 1888) and Adolf von Szily (1847–1920; 1905).
Thompson (1880) did make reference to Addams' report and was probably
the first to refer to the phenomenon as the "waterfall illusion" (p. 294).

Addams appreciated that the waterfall illusion could be investigated
experimentally, and he suggested that the motion of falling water could
be simulated in the laboratory by moving stripes, but this was not put
into practice until Oppel (1856) reached the same conclusion independently. Oppel had experienced the MAE initially at the dramatic Rheinfall
at Schaffhausen, and this stimulated his interest in it. A few years earlier,
Plateau (1849, 1850) stumbled across the MAE in the course of conducting experiments using the phenakistoscope (or stroboscopic disc). He had
been studying the effects of rotating patterns on perception and noticed the
motion visible in stationary objects following prolonged exposure. He introduced the stimulus employed most widely throughout the second half
of the nineteenth century—a black disc with a white Archimedes spiral on
it—which became called the Plateau spiral. Plateau described the MAE in
the following way:

"If the disc rotates in the direction indicated by the arrow, and one looks at it
with the eyes fixed on the centre for a time sufficiently long, but not long enough
to tire the eyes, then one immediately directs the eyes to another object, such as
the face of a person, for example, one experiences a singular effect: the head of
the person appears to shrink for some time. If the disc is turned in the opposite
direction, the resulting effect is opposite: it is as if the head of the person appears
to expand." (Plateau, 1849, p. 257)

The description is all the more remarkable because Plateau was blind
at the time of writing it (see Verriest, 1990). Many of the nineteenth century
studies of MAEs used the Plateau spiral, or some variant of it, like concentric counter-rotating spirals (Dvorak, 1870). Other stimuli were introduced,
however, some of which have a remarkably contemporary ring to them.
Oppel (1856) constructed an instrument for producing continuous linear
motion of parallel stripes. Bowditch and Hall (1881) added a further modification to the moving stripes, surrounding them with stationary ones. It
was with such a stimulus that Wohlgemuth (1911) carried out many of his
experiments.

Linear motion in two directions simultaneously was examined by
Exner (1887) and by Borschke and Hescheles (1902). Horizontal and vertical gratings were moved vertically and horizontally, respectively, behind

a circular aperture. Exner reported that the motion seen during adaptation was in a diagonal direction, with an MAE in the opposite diagonal. Borschke and Hescheles developed the stimulus further with sets of vertical and horizontal rods: they systematically changed the relative velocity of the two components, thereby modifying the direction of the resultant vector and also of the MAE.

The sectored disc was described independently by Wundt (1874) and by Aitken (1878), although it was by no means as widely used as Plateau's spiral. Rotating sectored discs continue to be used in experiments, and they are particularly good for demonstrating the paradoxical aspect of the MAE: following inspection the stationary sectors appear to rotate but not to change position.

The earliest interpretations of the waterfall illusion were in terms of eye movements (Purkinje, 1820; Addams, 1834; Helmholtz, 1867/1925) despite the logical difficulty of accounting for the phenomenon in this way: any after-movement of the eyes would affect all contours in the visual field, rather than being restricted to regions exposed to prior motion. Mach (1875) pointed to the problems associated with eye movement interpretations and the difficulty they would have in accounting for radial motion seen in the spiral MAE. Kleiner (1878) rotated a central sectored disc in the opposite direction to two adjacent ones, and reported oppositely directed MAEs that were visible simultaneously.

Thus, considerable experimental ingenuity was invested in studies of the waterfall illusion, and perceptual studies of it continue apace (see Chapter 8).

SUMMARY

The instrumental revolution in the nineteenth century reflected the desire to investigate the senses in the laboratory rather via observation of nature. Stimuli in the laboratory could be isolated and controlled so that the effects of varying a single feature could be examined. The method had proved successful in the physical sciences in the preceding two centuries, and Newton had shown how it could be applied to study color. The perception of space could be similarly investigated. Allied with a host of novel instruments for delivering the stimulus, the study of perception could be considered as a science. In the 1830s instruments for manipulating stimuli for space and motion were devised. That is, both space and motion were removed from their object base in order to synthesize apparent depth from paired pictures and apparent motion from sequences of still images. The reverberations from the stereoscope and stroboscopic disc spread far beyond science and engaged the popular imagination—they became philosophical toys. In addition to advancing science they provided amusement and entertainment.

The success of the instruments in terms of stimulus control was immense. Experimental stimuli were much easier to construct, and many features of phenomena became amenable to study for the first time. They not only fuelled the study of the senses, they played a part in liberating them from medicine and philosophy. Initially this was through sensory physiology, but later in the century it provided planks for the platform from which psychology could spring. The negative aspect of this development was that perception and its phenomena became more rarefied, having less contact with the object base from which the phenomena arose. Space perception was reduced to viewing paired pictures with defined disparities, and motion perception was largely confined to the sequences of static stimuli. Simulated depth and simulated motion were the topics of study, and the apparent dominated the real.

Instruments were applied in other areas, too. The achromatic microscopes developed from the 1820s had a liberating influence on the senses. The exposed cells in all their intricate specializations, particularly receptors and the nerve tracts from them to the brain. Aristotle's constraint of the senses could not be maintained with such a bounty of biology. The number of senses slowly expanded, and anatomical support was found for behavioral distinctions that were well-established.

By the end of the century, the cell and neuron doctrines were widely accepted, but relatively little was known about the brain. That was to await yet new techniques in the twentieth century. The success of the instruments for stimulus control tended to divert attention from the diversity of perception itself. That is, the variations that could occur both within an individual as well as between them were not accorded the same concern. Unlike the stimulus, the response was initially neglected. Some did examine the variabilities in perception, and sought ways of measuring them. It is to the response that we now turn.

6

The Response Revolution in the Nineteenth Century

The strides made up to the middle of the nineteenth century at stimulus control, via novel instruments, were not matched by attempts to measure the characteristics of the ensuing percepts. The response was not accorded the attention that was lavished on the stimulus. This was about to change, and the measurement of responses became a prominent component in establishing psychology as a discipline independent of philosophy or physiology. In fact, the changes had been quietly afoot for some time. Weber reported his experiments on sensory discriminations of touch and temperature in 1834 and 1846. This was followed by the synthesizing studies of Gustav Theodor Fechner (1801–1887), who integrated Weber's fraction to provide the basis for the new discipline of psychophysics—the investigation of the links between psychological dimensions of perception and their physical correlates. From the mid-nineteenth century new methods were developed for studying perception and performance that distinguished psychology from both philosophy and physiology, and the arbitrary birth of the independent discipline is often taken as the founding by Wundt of the Institute of Experimental Psychology at Leipzig in 1879. The founding fathers of psychology—Weber, Fechner, and Helmholtz—who

133

influenced Wundt were all students of perception, and their more general contributions were based firmly on their perceptual research. Responses were measured in a variety of ways at Wundt's Institute. Foremost was the application of the new psychophysics, but this was followed by measurement of reaction times. Wundt, like Helmholtz, was an empiricist and an associationist, and the motor components of perception and learning were of central importance. Concern with eye movements had been of considerable theoretical significance but their measurement lagged behind. Eye position following an eye movement was taken to be of greater significance than the manner in which the eyes moved.

Obtaining useful measurements of perceptual experience can be very difficult. The attempt to communicate subjective experience to other people has fascinated and frustrated writers, painters and other artists for centuries. It is only through communication that we can convey what we see, hear, taste, small, and feel. Our language is replete with words relating to the senses, but this abundance can provide problems for understanding perception, and alternative procedures have been developed that rely less on language and more on other responses.

PHENOMENOLOGY

One of the standard procedures developed for scientific enquiry into complex natural phenomena is to reduce them to simplified situations in which relevant features can be isolated and controlled. In the case of color vision, a stimulus would be required to produce light of a known wavelength and intensity. The size of the stimulus and perhaps its shape could be controlled, too. Other sources of light would need to be eliminated, unless the effect of these was to be specifically studied. Such control over stimulation would generally require laboratory conditions, and usually special apparatus as well. Experiments carried out in this way can provide unambiguous and detailed measurements of visual performance. This approach has been very influential in studies of perception, which often involve visual environments so restricted as to be far removed from natural visual experience. Measurements of perception are obviously easier to obtain when the perceptual experience is itself very simple; for example, sitting in a dark room and pressing a button if and when a single faint light source is seen. The measurements obtained in an experiment are used to infer the nature of perceptual processes, since we can never measure perception directly.

Thus, a response of some kind is required in order for such inferences to be made. The simplest approach is to ask someone to describe their experience, and to draw conclusions from their reports. Descriptions of the same scene or event can be compared across observers, and it may be possible to classify the verbal reports to give some degree of quantification. In principle, free description of experience offers potentially the richest source of information, since language is the most flexible means of communication we have. For many centuries, philosophers and others interested in perception, relied upon verbal description as the only means of obtaining data for analysis. Although perceptual experience is subjective, we are able to communicate quite effectively with other people regarding the nature of the world around us; disagreements about experience are much less likely than agreement. While language is a powerful means of communication, it is nevertheless restrictive; in the limit, only those experiences for which we have words can be described, and only those who can use language can be studied. Reliance on verbal descriptions has not always clarified our understanding of perception.

Some perceptual experiences vary in intensity so that the question "How much?" can be applied to them. For example, length is such a dimension: variations in length can be measured physically (say in cm) and perceived intensity can be given a value—a number (often in similar units) can be attributed to the length of an object. There are many such dimensions of sensations, like loudness, brightness, duration, and temperature. These experiences of sensory intensity can be called prothetic (see Stevens, 1975). They are distinguished from other (metathetic) experiences for which the dimension of intensity is inappropriate, even though there is a systematic change in the underlying stimulus dimension. For example, variations in the wavelength of light do not result in variations in intensity, but in color. The appropriate question here is "What kind?" rather than "How much?"

Perceptual experience has always been described in words, when possible, but this has not been the only way of assessing it. Language reflects the nuances that can be applied to the richness of perception, and it has been considered by some, like Goethe, to be the most appropriate vehicle for conveying experience. Goethe, in line with many Romantic philosophers, rejected the experimental approach to the study of nature because it was too constrained. In its place he proposed the astute and intuitive observation of natural phenomena, setting in train the method of phenomenology. This is best seen in his *Zur Farbenlehre* (1810/1840), which contrasted his observational approach to color with what he considered to be the physicalism of Newton. The purity of white light was taken to be fundamental and indivisible, rather than white being a mixture of different colored lights. Goethe chose to observe and describe instead of experiment on color vision. He distinguished between what he called physiological colors (the experience of color) and physical colors produced by optical refraction. He did borrow a prism to repeat Newton's experiment of separating the spectral components of white light, but failed to conduct it appropriately; when asked to return the prism he simply directed it to a light and concluded that it still looked white! Despite the fact that Goethe's theory of color did not influence the scientific community, his observations were most astute. He described many phenomena like positive and negative color afterimages, irradiation, color shadows, and color blindness, in addition to contrast effects—both in the chromatic and achromatic domains. For example, the color or brightness of a piece of paper can be changed by surrounding it by differently colored or bright papers, as can its apparent size.

The methods of phenomenology were given a more methodological twist by Purkinje, whose interests in vision were stimulated by reading Goethe's analysis of color. He was encouraged in his researches by Goethe because of his use of the phenomenological method (Wade, Brožek, and Hoskovec, 2002). When Purkinje gained access to one of the new large achromatic microscopes in the early 1830s he put his observational skills to good use. He has left his mark throughout the body. There are Purkinje cells in the brain, Purkinje fibers around the heart, Purkinje images are reflected from the optical surfaces of the eye, a Purkinje tree (the shadows of the retinal blood vessels) can be rendered visible, and at dawn and dusk we can experience the Purkinje shift (the difference in the visibility of colored objects when seen in daylight and twilight—blue objects appear lighter and red ones darker in twilight). As a medical student he investigated subjective visual phenomena in part because he did not have access to any physiological apparatus, but also because he believed that visual illusions revealed visual truths. Most of his experimental research in both physiology and histology was conducted in Germany, but at the age of sixty three he was called to the chair of physiology in Prague, where he became one of the most ardent advocates of Czech nationalism. He was followed in that chair by Hering, who also embraced phenomenology (see Baumann, 2002).

PSYCHOPHYSICS

The general characteristics of perception can be determined by verbal description, which provides a qualitative index of what we perceive. In order to study perception in more detail, quantitative measures are required; that is, measures to which numbers can be assigned. With quantitative measures experimental manipulations become possible and hypotheses about the nature of phenomena can be tested. For example, the phenomenology of color has been very successful in highlighting the aspects of color vision that require explanation, like color naming, primary colors, and contrasts between colors. However, in order to study any of these phenomena in more detail it is necessary to relate aspects of the stimulus (like its wavelength) to features of the response. Stimulus definition is in the domain of physics and the response to stimulation is the province of psychology—relating one to the other was called psychophysics by Fechner in his book with this title published in 1860. For color many possible response measures could be taken: detecting the presence of one color amongst other similar ones; matching the color of one stimulus to that of another; judging whether pairs of colored stimuli are the same or different. The physical aspect of psychophysics is the measurement and control of the stimulus, and the psychological feature is the measurement and control of the response. It is generally the case that very simple responses are required rather than detailed descriptions of experience.

Weber (1834, 1846) introduced new methods of measuring sensitivity, establishing perception as an experimental rather than an observational discipline. Working initially with the discrimination of lifted weights, Weber demonstrated that the smallest appreciable difference was a constant fraction of their actual weights. He wrote: "It appears from my experiments that the smallest difference between two weights which we can distinguish by way of feeling changes in muscle-tension is that difference shown by two weights roughly bearing the relation 39 to 40, i.e. when one is 1/40 heavier than the other" (Ross and Murray, 1978, p. 220). This was so irrespective of the absolute weights compared. Weber further showed that different fractions resulted from passively held weights, visual judgments of the lengths of lines, and auditory discriminations of pitch. That is, a general law of discrimination was proposed that applied to all modalities but with fractions specific to the judgments involved. Weber did not provide a generalized mathematical description of what we now call Weber's law; this was left to Fechner. Weber did note that there were clear individual differences in sensitivity, but judgments of a particular individual tended to be constant.

Weber did much more than compare lifted weights. He introduced the use of calipers to measure two-point thresholds on the skin surface and found that sensitivity varied enormously, with greatest sensitivity around the lips and least on the trunk. The magnitude of the thresholds depended on the area of the skin stimulated, which led Weber to introduce the concept of sensory circles—areas on the skin surface that can result in the stimulation of a single peripheral nerve. He developed a method of delayed comparison, varying the interval between presentations of the first and second stimuli: "In this way one can measure and quantitatively express the clarity of the memory for sensations as it decreases from second to second.

As we rarely have the opportunity of measuring such mental processes, I commend these experiments to the attention of psychologists" (Ross and Murray, 1978, p. 206). Temperature and kinesthetic sensitivity were also examined by Weber. His work represents a distinct shift in the psychology of perception from philosophy towards physiology, from speculation to experimentation, and from qualitative to quantitative approaches.

The psychophysical procedures set in train by Weber have been employed to determine the limits or thresholds of perception in all its modalities. These were called absolute thresholds, as they were thought to represent the absolute limits of detection. Now they are referred to as detection thresholds. They are concerned with detecting the presence of a stimulus of low intensity—e.g., is a light on or off? Difference thresholds are of much greater use: they concern discrimination (the detection of a difference) between two stimuli—e.g., is one light brighter or dimmer than another? Typically, a standard stimulus is presented against which a comparison is judged. The observer indicates whether the comparison is greater or less than the standard on some dimension (e.g. brightness). When they are of similar intensity the judgments can be very difficult, and the observer can make different decisions when the same stimuli are presented on separate trials. Because there is some uncertainty in the observer's decision, and therefore variability in the response, it is essential to measure the same conditions many times. Accordingly, the threshold is a statistical concept; it does not signify an abrupt change between not detecting then detecting a difference between two stimuli. Rather it is an arbitrarily defined point in the gradual transition between these states.

There are various psychophysical methods that can be applied to measure perception. Most are based on the methods developed in the nineteenth century by Weber and Fechner in Leipzig. The classical methods are now called: the method of limits, the method of constant stimulus presentation, and the method of adjustment. The method of constant stimulus presentation provides data that can be represented graphically; the graphs can be either in terms of the obtained values or of some smoothed function derived from statistical curve-fitting procedures. The curve-fitting procedure produces an S-shaped relationship which is called the psychometric function. Most information can be derived from judgments that are difficult, i.e., those in the area of uncertainty.

PSYCHOPHYSICAL SCALING

The classical psychophysical methods were described by Fechner not only to provide systematic techniques for measuring thresholds but also to establish a quantitative index of sensory magnitude. That is, he wanted to use the results to scale the intensity of sensations with the precision that scientists apply to scaling physical dimensions, like light intensity, weight, or length. In short, he wanted to devise units in which sensory intensity could be measured. The unit he selected was the difference threshold or just noticeable difference (jnd). Therefore any sensation could, in principle, be measured as so many jnds. Fechner chose the absolute (or what we would now call the detection) threshold as the zero point on the scale. Weber had earlier found that the value of the jnd increases with the intensity of the stimulus with which it is being compared. This is now called Weber's law and it can be described very simply: $dI/I = k$, where dI is the jnd, I is the stimulus intensity against which a variable is compared, and k is a constant called the Weber fraction.

Fechner also made a critical assumption—that equal differences in jnd give rise to equal sensation differences. Applying these assumptions to any stimulus continuum results in a curve that rises rapidly and then levels off. It can be represented as a straight line if the magnitude of sensation (S) is plotted against the logarithm of stimulus intensity (I). More generally, the relationship can be expressed as: $S \propto \log I$, which we now call Fechner's law. In words, the magnitude of sensation is proportional to the logarithm of the stimulus intensity.

Fechner tested the validity of this relationship indirectly. It would have been very tedious to measure an ascending range of jnds, and Fechner did not believe that sensation could be scaled directly. That is, he did not consider that observers could report the magnitude of sensation. Instead, he used an indirect technique called category scaling. This involved presenting observers with a wide range of stimuli, and asking them to order some of them into, say, seven categories, so that the differences between categories were subjectively equal. Results using this method generally supported Fechner's law. However, with more research, doubts were cast both on the method of category scaling and on the assumptions Fechner made. Firstly, the validity of Weber's law has been questioned by results from experiments on signal detection. Detection and difference thresholds can be modified by the motivation of observers and by the likelihood of stimuli occurring. Secondly, all jnds do not appear subjectively equal: jnds at the extreme ends of a stimulus dimension do not seem the same as those in the middle region (see Stevens, 1951).

Fechner's insight was that the mental and material worlds could be united mathematically in the domains of sensory and stimulus intensities. The new discipline was defined in his *Elemente der Psychophysik* (1860): "Psychophysics should be understood here as an exact theory of the functionally dependent relations of body and soul or, more generally, of the material and the mental, of the physical and the psychological worlds"

(Fechner, 1966, p. 7). Fechner distinguished between an outer and an inner psychophysics; the former was concerned with the sensation and stimulus intensities, and the latter with the relation between brain process and sensations. He realised that experiments in his day would be confined to outer psychophysics, but these were seen as necessary steps towards understanding inner psychophysics.

Fechner refined the methods Weber employed to measure difference thresholds, but this was by no means his only contribution to psychology. He received a medical training at Leipzig University, where Weber lectured, though he never practiced medicine. After graduation Fechner was more attracted to physics than physiology, later lecturing and conducting research on electricity. He also undertook a series of experiments on subjective colors and on the visibility of long lasting afterimages (Fechner, 1838, 1840). These latter probably resulted in a temporary blindness, accompanied by a protracted depression, which led to his resignation from the chair of physics at Leipzig in 1840. After several years of isolation he returned to his earlier philosophical speculations, and eventually found a unity between his physical and philosophical views. Fechner began writing satirical and speculative pamphlets under the pseudonym of Dr. Mises when he was a medical student, and continued in this vein throughout his life; they reflected a continuing mental conflict between his scientific materialism and his philosophical pantheism (Kuntze, 1892). In his eighth decade, Fechner applied his quantitative approach to the study of beauty and founded the subject of experimental aesthetics. Nonetheless, it is Fechner's psychophysics that did most to chart the course of psychology in the latter half of the nineteenth century.

REACTION TIME

Leipzig was the intellectual center of the new psychology. Weber and Fechner worked there, and it was at its university that Wundt established his Institute of Experimental Psychology. Wundt received a medical education at Heidelberg, and returned there to become an assistant in physiology to Helmholtz. In 1862, Wundt published his first book *Beiträge zur Theorie der Sinneswahrnehmung* (Contributions to a theory of sense perception) which provided an outline of the course he considered the new psychology should follow. In 1875 he moved to Leipzig, where both Weber and Fechner were still active. On his arrival, Wundt had some difficulty in persuading the authorities that he required space for his apparatus and for conducting experiments, but his arguments prevailed. The institute had limited facilities for formal laboratory experiments on psychophysics and reaction time, but it did attract enthusiastic students, and in 1881 a new journal, *Philosophische Studien*, was founded in which the results could be published.

Wundt called his experimental approach to the study of conscious experience physiological psychology, and his text bearing that title, first published in 1874, was widely adopted as expressing the new psychology. He sought to unite physiology and psychology: "The present work shows by its very title that it is an attempt to bring two sciences which have for a long time followed very different paths although they are concerned with almost one and the same subject matter, that is, human life" (Diamond, 1974, p. 750). Wundt clearly derived a great deal of experimental knowledge from the period with Helmholtz. Most particularly, he was able to discern the insights that can be inferred from measuring the time taken to respond to stimuli. Helmholtz had applied the method to determine the speed of nerve transmission, and Donders saw its significance for measuring decision time.

Helmholtz demonstrated the advantages of reaction time as a consequence of his measurements of the velocity of nerve impulses (see Finger and Wade, 2002a; 2002b). His research on sensory nerves began in 1850, while he was still analyzing frog motor nerve speeds. Human subjects were asked to make movements with a hand or with their teeth as quickly as possible when a weak shock was applied to some part of the body. The movement again broke a current, which was used to measure the elapsed time. He estimated the rate of sensory nerve conduction from his measurements of time and distance, noting that "a message from the big toe arrives about one thirteenth of a second later than from the ear or face" (see de Jaager, 1865/1970, p. 42). Helmholtz initially thought that the sensory nerves conduct at about 60 meters (approximately 200 feet) per sec, or about twice as fast as frog motor nerve conduction. Additional studies, including some from other laboratories (Hirsch, 1862; de Jaager, 1865/1970), soon convinced him that his initial estimates were too high, and that human sensory nerves only conduct at about 30 meters per second. "Happily," Helmholtz later declared, "the distances our sense-perceptions have to traverse before they reach the brain are short, otherwise our consciousness would always lag far behind the present" (Koenigsberger, 1906, p. 71).

The last question he asked was whether the speed of human motor nerve conduction is comparable to that of the frog. How to conduct good experiments in this domain bothered him for years. He ultimately solved the problem with the help of Russian scientist Nikolai Baxt (1843–1904), who also studied recognition time for optical stimuli in Helmholtz's laboratory (Helmholtz, 1870, 1871; Boring, 1950). The two men immobilized an arm by putting it in a special cast; they then stimulated the nerves to the ball of the thumb, either at the wrist or farther away at the elbow. When the automatic twitching of the thumb was measured with Helmholtz's myograph, human motor nerve conduction was also found to be about 33 meters per second.

Helmholtz provided scientists with a way to measure mental processing. The new idea to emerge from Helmholtz's work was to subtract simple reaction times (time taken to respond to the presentation of a stimulus) from complex reaction times, in which subjects were asked to respond in different ways to different stimuli. By determining how much longer it took to respond in the complex reaction time experiment than in the simple one, measurements began to be made of the 'mind-time' needed to make choices. Choice reaction time, decision time, mental chronometry, or what was also called physiological time (Hirsch, 1862), was the subject of many new experiments in Utrecht, home to Donders. In Holland, Donders and de Jaager, a student who wrote his dissertation on reaction time under Donders' direction, conducted many important reaction time studies between 1865 and 1869 (see Brožek and Sibinga, 1970, for a review of these early reaction time studies).

Donders (1865, 1869) and de Jaager (1865/1970) acknowledged the role played by Helmholtz as they quantified mental operations by measuring latencies to tactile, visual, or acoustic stimuli under various discrimination conditions often demanding different responses. In the first reaction time study in de Jaager's thesis the subject was required to respond as quickly as possible to a mild electrical stimulus to one foot or the other using the hand on the stimulated side of the body. On some trials the site of stimulation was revealed beforehand, whereas on other trials (those associated with more mental processing as evidenced by longer latencies) it was not.

Donders introduced reaction time as a measure of mental processing. In 1865 he presented a paper to the Royal Netherlands Academy of Sciences outlining his initial experiments on timing mental processes. A more elaborate report was published in 1868, and again in 1869. Donders introduced his paper of 1869 by lamenting the difficulty of applying the rigor of physiology to the study of mental processes:

> "But will all quantitative treatment of mental processes be out of the question? By no means! An important factor seemed to be susceptible to measurement: I refer to the time required for simple mental processes. For answering the question whether we are entitled to apply the generally proved relation to special cases—in other words, whether we may assume that there is an absolute correspondence between diverse functions in the brain and the diversity in each particular sensation, each private mental picture, each expression of the will—it seems that the determination of that duration of time is not without importance." (Donders, 1969, pp. 413–414)

Donders was able to build on Helmholtz's measurements of the velocity of nerve conduction, and the durations of simple response times: "The idea occurred to me to interpose into the process of physiological time some new components of mental action. If I investigated how much time this would lengthen the physiological time, this would, I judged, reveal the time required for the interposed term" (1969, p. 418). The expression 'reaction time' was introduced in 1873 by Exner, and Donders distinguished between various types: a-type was to single stimuli, b-type was to several stimuli, and c-type was to one but not to an alternative stimulus. Donders' c reaction times are longer than a or b. Much of the early research in Wundt's laboratory was concerned with confirming Donders' extensive work on reaction times.

Donders was trained in medicine at Utrecht and his abiding interests were in physiology. He became engaged in ophthalmology almost by accident, when he translated a book from German to Dutch, repeating many of the experiments reported in it. He became professor of ophthalmology at the University of Utrecht in 1852, and wrote extensively on anomalies of refraction and accommodation (Donders, 1864). Although his main research was concerned with vision, his impact on psychology has been a consequence of his use of reaction time as an index of cognitive functioning. This sort of mental chronometry is still of great interest to cognitive neuroscientists. In part because of his role in initiating reaction time studies, Helmholtz and Donders are now looked upon as having played a pivotal role in the "cognitive revolution" that is currently in vogue in the brain and behavioral sciences.

SENSORY-MOTOR INTERACTIONS

Helmholtz's studies of the velocity of nerve transmission drew attention to similarities between sensory and motor processes, and to physiological interpretations of psychological phenomena. This in turn led theorists to make closer associations between sensation and the ensuing behavior. One such was Alexander Bain (1818–1903); he placed physiology at the heart of psychology in his textbook *The senses and the intellect* (1855). He integrated sensory-motor physiology with traditional associationist philosophy to espouse an independent discipline of psychology "conceiving that the time has now come when many of the striking discoveries of Physiologists relative to the nervous system should find a recognized place in the Science of Mind" (Bain, 1855, p. v). He extended the union to an associationist treatment of higher mental processes and voluntary action, emphasizing the importance of sensory feedback in the control of movement:

"In treating of the Senses, besides recognising the so-called muscular sense as distinct from the five senses, I have thought proper to assign to Movement and the feelings of Movement a position preceding the Sensations of the senses; and have endeavoured to prove that the exercise of active energy originating in purely internal impulses, independent of the stimulus produced by outward impressions, is a primary fact of our constitution." (Bain, 1855, pp. v–vi)

By stressing the motor component of perception he was the harbinger of behaviorism: "action is a more intimate and inseparable property of our constitution than any of our sensations, and in fact enters as a component part into every one of the senses" (1855, p. 67). Bain also appreciated those actions connected with the alleviation of pain or the increase of pleasure would occur with greater frequency.

In his book, *Mind and body*, Bain (1873) set out an account which related the processes of associative memory to the distribution of activity in neural groupings—or neural networks as they are now termed. In the course of this account, Bain anticipated certain aspects of connectionist ideas that are normally attributed to 20th century authors—most notably Hebb (see Wilkes and Wade, 1997). As Bain stated in his autobiography:

"The whole subject had been simmering for a number of years. More particularly was the attempt made to deal with the connexion of mind and brain by numerical estimates; namely by taking, on the one hand, the number of psychical situations, and, on the other hand, the nervous groupings rendered possible by the approximately assignable number of nerve cells and fibres...The chief novelty consisted in the treatment of the intellect upon the method of innumeration just referred to." (1904, pp. 312–313)

Bain presented an early version of the principles enshrined in Hebb's neurophysiological postulate. His words were:

"I can suppose that, at first, each one of the circuits would affect all others indiscriminately; but that, in consequence of two of them being independently made active at the same moment (which is the fact in acquisition), a strengthened connexion or diminished obstruction would arise between these two, by a change wrought in the intervening cell-substance; and that, afterwards, the induction from one of these circuits would not be indiscriminate, but select; being comparatively strong towards one, and weaker towards the rest." (1873, p. 119)

Bain eventually rejected his own hypothesis because he did not believe that there were enough nerves in the brain to sustain all the associations considered possible in human cognition. Nonetheless, he did signal the direction to which neuroscience would turn over a century later. He also drew attention to the close links between sensory and motor processes, and these were to be the subject of detailed experiments within his own lifetime. The particular motor processes that came to prominence in the late nineteenth century were those associated with movements of the eyes.

EYE MOVEMENTS

It might appear obvious that a response as evident as movement of the eyes would be investigated with regard to the ensuing perception. This was not the case, however. Even though we can feel the movement of our eyes in their sockets, and we can observe the ways the eyes of others move, their measurement arrived rather late in the history of perception. Investigations of the ways in which the eyes move came to prominence in the nineteenth century, but techniques for measuring them more precisely emerged in the twentieth century.

Porterfield (1737, 1738) wrote two essays on the motions of the eye. The first was concerned with their external motions and the second with their internal ones. Internal eye movements, as involved in accommodation, were discussed in Chapter 4. The first essay, concerned with the actions of the extraocular muscles, specified both the problem of restricted spatial resolution in vision and suggested a solution to it:

> "Now, though it is certain that only a very small Part of any Object can at once be clearly and distinctly seen, namely, that whose Image on the *Retina* is in the *Axis* of the Eye; and that the other Parts of the Object, which have their Images painted at some Distance from this same *Axis*, are but faintly and obscurely perceived, and yet we are seldom sensible of this Defect; and, in viewing any large Body, we are ready to imagine that we see at the same Time all its Parts equally distinct and clear: But this is a vulgar Error, and we are led into it from the quick and almost continual Motion of the Eye, whereby it is successively directed towards all the Parts of the Object in an Instant of Time." (pp. 185–186)

The quick movements of the eye were not given a name, but they are now called saccades, nor were they open to measurement other than by observation of another's eyes or the awareness of one's own eye movements. Porterfield was by no means the first to consider the problem of variations in visual acuity across the visual field. Heller (1988) has drawn attention to the medieval prehistory of eye movement research, and particularly the impact that the translation of the *Optics* by Alhazen had on Western thought. Alhazen provided an empirical demonstration of distinct vision using a viewing board. He fixed two equivalently written words in central and peripheral locations; the central word was more easily read than the lateral one and the indistinctness of the lateral word increased with movement into the periphery. The poverty of peripheral vision is such that in order to sample the environment effectively, the fovea must be moved around the scene. The first step toward understanding the eye movement strategy of sampling the visual surroundings is recognizing the pattern and nature of eye movements themselves.

Nystagmus

In the nineteenth century, Mach, Crum Brown, and Breuer, examined the consequences of body rotation on eye movements (see Tatler and Wade, 2003). All noted that the eye rotations decline with constant body rotation, but recommence when the body is stopped. Mach had devised a rotating chair in which the visual and motor consequences of body rotation could be examined (see Young et al, 2001). Mach (1875) was explicit in relating the eye movements to angular accelerations of the head, rather than angular velocities. He also discovered independently Wells' (1792) technique of generating an afterimage before rotation and noting its apparent motions after rotation ceases.

Brown (1874, 1875) used a rotating stool to determine thresholds for detecting body rotation. Because the thresholds were lowest when one of the semicircular canals was in the plane of rotation, he related the sense of rotation to these organs, and suggested their mode of operation. He became increasingly interested in the eye movements that accompany and follow body rotation, and gave lucid accounts and illustrations of their discontinuity:

> "When a real rotation of the body takes place the eyes do not at first perfectly follow the movement of the head. While the head moves uniformly the eyes move by jerks. Thus, in the diagram, Fig. 3, where the abscissæ indicate time and the ordinate the angle described, the straight line *a b* represents the continuous rotatory motion of the head and the dotted line the continuous motion of the eye. Here it will be seen that the eye looks in a fixed direction for a short time, represented by one of the horizontal portions of the dotted line *a b*, and then very quickly follows the motion of the head, remains fixed for a short time, and so on. After the rotation has continued for some time the motion of the eye gradually changes to that represented by the dotted line *c d* in Fig. 4. The eye now never remains fixed, but moves for a short time more slowly than the head, then quickly makes up to it, then falls behind, and so on. At last the discontinuity of the motion of the eye disappears, and the eye and the head move together. If now the rotation of the head be stopped (of course the body stops also) the discontinuous movements of the eyeballs recommence. They may now be represented by the dotted line in Fig. 5. The intermittent motion of the eyes gradually becomes less, passing through a condition such as that shown by the dotted line in Fig. 6, and at last ceases." (Brown 1878, p. 658)

Breuer's work on vestibular function led him to the study of eye movements during and after body rotation, and indeed it was Breuer (1874) who gave an indication of a saccade-and-fixation process in the vestibulo-ocular reflex. He argued that during rotation the eyes lag behind the head in order to maintain a steady retinal image; then they make rapid jerky motions in the direction of head rotation. The eye movements reduce in amplitude and can stop with rotation at constant angular velocity. When the body rotation ceases the eyes rotate in the same direction as prior head rotation, and the visual world appears to move in the opposite direction interspersed with rapid returns. He also stated that there is no visual awareness during these rapid returns. This is a clear reference to saccadic suppression, although he did not use the term saccade.

Hering (1879a) examined eye movements in the contexts of the fixation reflex and following rapidly moving objects, rather than following body rotation. He noted how moving peripheral images engage our attention and initiate eye movements to fixate them, and that some movements are too rapid to be perceived. However, when the eyes are moved in the same direction some object motion can be seen:

> "It is impossible to see a movement at too high a speed, because of the after-duration of the stimulus. Thus the falling rain drops appear as threads when we hold the eyes still. But if we move the eyes rapidly in the same direction with the moving object, it is possible to see the object and the movement. Even the falling rain drop may be captured in its flight." (Hering, 1942, p. 183)

Even before Mach, Breuer, and Brown had conducted their experiments, galvanic stimulation had been applied to the ears by Purkinje (1820) and by Eduard Hitzig (1838–1907). Hitzig (1871) applied electrical currents between the mastoid bones and noted not only the direction of apparent visual motion but of actual body and eye movements, too. He described the nystagmus induced, and he called it by that name. The eye movements were likened to a fisherman's float drifting slowly in the water and then being snatched back. The fast phase of nystagmus was always in the direction of the anode.

While there exist numerous earlier nineteenth century studies of eye movements outside the context of nystagmus, an appreciation of the distinction of saccades as a specialized family of movements, or of their importance in vision is absent from most of these works. Helmholtz devoted a section of his *Handbuch* to the analysis of eye movements (Helmholtz, 1867, 2000); it offered an exquisitely detailed exploration of eye rotations, but he was more concerned with the position of the eye following a rotation, rather than the kinetics of the eye movements themselves. When eye movements were investigated it usually involved attempts to measure their velocity. For example, Volkmann (1846) recorded the frequency of alternating fixation between two pins throughout 30s. He was aware that the value derived confounded fixation time with the duration of eye movements and so he presented a range of separations between the pins. Some years later, a student of Helmholtz (Lamansky, 1869) estimated the angular velocity of eye movements using an afterimage technique; he delivered light flashes in a fixed location at intervals of 5 ms and counted the number of afterimages visible when the eye passed over them. Values of between 720 and $1500°s^{-1}$ were reported, but the task was said to be very difficult to perform.

Helmholtz did describe a discontinuity of eye movements (jerks) in the context of visual vertigo:

> "For example, when a person travelling on a train has been looking for some time at objects close to the track outside, and then turns to look at the floor of the carriage, although the latter is at rest relative to his body, it seems to be moving from under him in the same direction as the train. The reason of this is because there is an apparent motion of the objects on the track in the direction opposite to that of the motion of the train. Wherever the traveller tries to focus one of them, he has to jerk his eyes quickly in the direction opposite to that of the motion of the train.... But if the passenger gazing out of the coach should happen to fix his attention constantly on a speck on the window, the aforesaid giddiness will not be developed." (1925/2000, pp. 247–248)

This account occurs in the section on 'The direction of vision' rather than that on 'Movements of the eyes'. The term 'jerk' was added by the translator (James Southall); an exact translation of Helmholtz's text would be that 'the eyes moved quickly' in the opposite direction. Helmholtz then addressed visual vertigo from body rotation. When he whirled round with his eyes closed, he did not experience any visual motion afterward if he opened his eyes when the sense of body rotation had ceased (as would be expected). However, if he opened his eyes beforehand, he experienced visual motion but attributed this "to an illusion about the time when the body itself comes to rest" (p. 248). He did not make the distinction between saccadic and other types of movement and rather appears to hold the view that eye movements are continuous, but with varying velocities. One must look slightly later than Helmholtz to find reports in which the discontinuity of eye movement is recognized outside the context of nystagmus.

SACCADES

It appears that while Mach, Brown, and Breuer appreciated the distinction between fast and slow eye rotations and the discontinuity of movement within nystagmus, this was not immediately or widely associated with normal viewing conditions. In this respect, Louis-Émile Javal (1839–1909) is generally credited as being one of the first researchers to report discontinuity of eye movements outside the context of nystagmus (see Wade, Tatler, and Heller, 2003). Javal used the term *saccade* in his papers on the physiology of reading, published between 1878 and 1879. In the last of these papers, Javal mentioned that saccades occur at a frequency of one every 15 to 18 letters during reading, although this is a reference to work by his colleague Lamare, rather than by Javal himself (see Javal, 1905; Lamare, 1892). Javal (1878) did try to use afterimages to examine eye movements during reading, but found that the technique was difficult to apply because of the contrast between the letters and the paper. Moreover, his principal concern was to determine whether the eyes moved vertically between lines during reading. He also considered attaching a feather to the eye so that movements could be recorded on a smoked drum, and he attempted (unsuccessfully) to measure the deflections of light from a mirror attached to his eye.

In the late 1860s Hering worked with Breuer in Vienna on the regulation of respiration, although this was not the major interest of either physiologist. Hering had studied medicine at Leipzig, was engrossed in his studies of binocular visual direction, and his disputes with Helmholtz over their interpretation (see Turner, 1994). Hering had been appointed professor of physiology at Joseph's Academy, Vienna in 1865; his tenure at Vienna was fraught because Ernst Brücke (1819–1892), who occupied the chair in physiology at the university, was a close friend of Helmholtz's. Hering moved to Prague, to succeed Purkinje, in 1870, and finally returned to Leipzig in 1895; he was a colleague of Mach while at Prague. Despite his teaching commitments, Hering was a very productive and ingenious researcher, and he turned his skills to recording the characteristics of eye movements. He offered a description of the discontinuity of eye movements and recognition of the class of rotations that we now refer to as saccadic, concurrent with Javal's reports of Lamare's experiments. Hering (1879b) used a miniature hearing device, like a stethoscope, placed on the eyelids to listen to the sounds of the ocular muscles. Using this technique he noted: "Throughout one's observations, one hears quite short, dull clapping sounds, which follow each other at irregular intervals" (Hering, 1879b, p. 145). Hering found that these transient clapping sounds—which he described as 'momentary sounds' (Momentangeräusche)—were evident when observers read lines of text but disappeared if they were instructed to fixate a stationary target. He attributed these sounds to contractions of the oculomotor muscles:

> "The momentary sounds are demonstrably the consequence of unintentional, jerky movements of the eyeballs. When attending to the continuous sounds, one is not at all conscious that the eyes are constantly engaged in this restless activity, and especially not that their movements occur jerkily. If one fixates a point quite steadily, then the momentary sounds disappear, only reappearing as soon as fatigue or temporary inattention results in further movements of the eyeballs." (Hering 1879b, p. 145)

In his report *Über die Muskelgeräusche des Auges*, Hering was amongst the first to offer a description of the discontinuity of eye movements outside the context of vestibulo-ocular reflexes, describing the 'jerky movements of the eyeballs'.

Crum Brown, in the Robert Boyle Lecture of 1895, gave a graphic description of eye movements in general:

> "We fancy that we can move our eyes uniformly, that by a continuous motion like that of a telescope we can move our eyes along the sky-line in the landscape or the cornice of a room, but we are wrong in this. However determinedly we try to do so, what actually happens is, that our eyes move like the seconds hand of a watch, a jerk and a little pause, another jerk and so on; only our eyes are not so regular, the jerks are sometimes of greater, sometimes of less, angular amount, and the pauses vary in duration, although, unless we make an effort, they are always short. During the jerks we practically do not see at all, so that we have before us not a moving panorama, but a series of fixed pictures of the same fixed things, which succeed one another rapidly." (Brown 1895, pp. 4–5)

The evidence that we do not see during the jerks was derived from a simple experiment: moving the eyes over a scene containing a bright light results in a series of bright afterimages rather than the visibility of a continuous path. Brown (1895) went on to describe an afterimage method for demonstrating these discontinuous eye movements.

Javal is correctly regarded as the first to have used the term saccade in the context of eye movements. It is likely that he used this term in its literal French sense to describe the eyes as moving in 'jerks' or 'twitches'. The word saccade derives from the old French *saquer* or *sachier* meaning 'to pull' and, after first being used by Rabelais in the sixteenth century, it referred to certain rapid movements of a horse during dressage. The term has only relatively recently been associated with eye movements. However, while Javal's descriptions may be the origin of the term saccade in its oculomotor sense, it was not immediately adopted into descriptions of eye movements throughout the scientific community.

The adoption of the term into the English language in its present sense appears to originate some years later, from Raymond Dodge (1871–1942): "German and Scandinavian writers are commonly using the descriptive class term 'saccadic' to denote the rapid eye movements for which we have only the arbitrary name of 'type I'. I am not sure with whom the term originated, but it seems worth adopting" (Dodge, 1916, pp. 422–423). To which writers Dodge refers is somewhat unclear. However, Marius Hans Erik Tscherning (1854–1939) was a Danish ophthalmologist. Tscherning was the adjunct director at the ophthalmology laboratory of the Sorbonne; he became director when Javal retired because of the onset of his blindness due to glaucoma. Whereas Javal had translated Helmholtz's *Handbuch*, Tscherning translated and annotated Thomas Young's papers on optics and the eye (Young, 1894). This could have been the spur to Tscherning's interests in the movements of the eyes. In his *Optique physiologique*, Tscherning included a section on "Les mouvements saccadés des yeux" (translated as "Jerking Movements of the Eyes") in which he observed:

> "It seems as if the eye should be kept motionless in order to obtain an impression, at least an impression which can be perceived with some distinctness. If, in a railroad train which is going quite fast, we fix a point on the window, the landscape appears confused, the images of its different parts succeeding one another too quickly on the retina to be perceived distinctly. Observing the eyes of any one who is looking at the landscape, we see that they move by jerks. The eyes of the person observed make alternately a rapid movement in the direction of the train to catch the object, and a slower movement in the opposite direction to keep the image of the object on the *fovea*. Then they again make a rapid movement with the train to catch a new object, and so forth." (Tscherning 1900, p. 299, original italics)

While the origins of the term "saccade" appear to be accountable, there is some uncertainty about the origins of the term "nystagmus" in its application to eye movements. Wells (1792) described the characteristics of nystagmus for the first time, but it was not given that name. Boissier de Sauvages (1772) did describe a disease he called nystagmus which "consists of a spasmodic and alternate movement of the eye" (p. 6), but the term did not come into common currency until the nineteenth century. Ruete (1846) referred to the involuntary movements of the eyes in post-rotational vertigo as nystagmus. Wells (1792) restricted his description to the involuntary, slow drift of the eyes in one direction and their ballistic return. The term nystagmus is an old one, but it referred to the nodding of the head in a drowsy state, before being associated with discontinuous movements of the eyes.

FIXATIONS

A key development in the understanding of oculomotor behavior came from the recognition of the importance of the periods that lie between saccades. While slow movements of the eyes may occur during these periods, closer observation of the eye reveals that during these periods the fovea remains fixated on a single point in space. The observed slow phase movements operate to stabilize the retinal image in spite of ego-motion or motion within the environment. Since saccades typically last a few tens of milliseconds and occur at a frequency of approximately 3 Hz, it can be seen that the eye spends much of its time fixating, maintaining a stable retinal image of a target in the visual scene. Understanding the importance of fixations requires both the recognition that slow phase movements operate to maintain stationary fixation in space and that it is within these periods of fixation that intake of information for visual perception proceeds. Such an appreciation of eye movements reveals that the fundamental principle that drives the movements of the eyes is in fact to keep the image on the retina stationary for as much of the time as possible, while moving the fovea to locations in the world where it is needed. This principle was recognized by Walls (1962), who wrote: "Their origin [eye movements] lies in the need to keep an image fixed on the retina, not in the need to scan the surroundings." (Walls 1962, p. 69)

That the eyes can be used to maintain regard of a particular, stationary visual target has been noted throughout the history of eye movement research. Helmholtz (1867) offers detailed geometrical descriptions of binocular fixation, but does not appear to recognize the necessity to maintain stable fixation. The prevalence and importance of fixation in oculomotor behavior was not explicitly described in the literature until the work of Breuer and Brown in the context of vestibular influences, and in the context of reading, Dodge and his mentor Benno Erdmann (1851–1921).

READING

Dodge became fascinated with the problem of designing apparatus that would improve the study of reading, a task that Erdmann considered to be impossible. Hence Dodge's initiation into psychology was in the form of addressing this technical problem, which he solved in the development of the Erdmann-Dodge tachistoscope. Dodge's prowess as an engineer of experimental apparatus was echoed throughout his academic career. Indeed, he is probably best known as a key figure in the development of photographic eye movement recording devices, paving the way for instruments that serve as key components of eye movement research to the present day and have been of fundamental importance to the progress and direction of eye movement research. However, Dodge's abilities extended far beyond the construction of ingenious experimental devices. It was in the employment of such equipment and of simple observational approaches that he excelled. Prior to Dodge's research, studies that attempted to relate the detailed metrics of eye movements (such as those conducted by Helmholtz and his contemporaries) to the perception of visual stimuli were rarely undertaken.

Dodge's explorations of the relationship between eye movements and perception arose primarily from a chance observation when conducting experiments, with Erdmann, on vision during reading (Erdmann and Dodge, 1898). They had been using mirrors to observe subjects' eye movements while reading text. When looking into the mirrors themselves Erdmann and Dodge noted that they:

"chanced on the observation that when the head was held perfectly still we could never catch our own eye moving in a mirror. One may watch one's eyes as closely as possible, even with the aid of a concave reflector, whether one looks from one eye to the other, or from some more distant object to one's own eyes, the eyes may be seen now in one position and now in another, but never in motion." (Dodge, 1900, p. 456)

Until these reports by Erdmann and Dodge, it seems that the general consensus in the field was that eye movements were themselves an integral part of the processes of visual perception. It was believed that perception continued during eye movements and that the continuous movement of gaze over an object would be sufficient for its perception. Erdmann and Dodge, however, recognized that this was not the case. Critically, they appreciated the errors and pitfalls of self-observation when describing eye movements and perception, in the same way that Wells had distrusted Porterfield's recourse to subjective experience over 100 years earlier (Wells, 1792). Consequently, they employed an assistant to observe their eye movements, or to be observed.

It was this understanding of the problems of self-examination that led Dodge to make some crucial observations about the true nature of the saccade-and-fixate oculomotor strategy and its relation to perception. Dodge realized that in many situations where we feel that our eyes are moving continuously, at slow speeds, the reality is that we are making a series of small rapid eye movements separated by fixation pauses. Moreover, two observations led Dodge to propose that visual perception was suspended during the eye movements themselves. The first was the simple but elegant self-observation while looking at one's own eye in a mirror, described in the quotation given above. The second piece of evidence derives from experiments in reading whereby if a subject looks directly from one end of a line of text to the other, without any intervening fixations pauses (verified by an observer watching the reader's eyes) then the subject cannot perceive the text in the middle of the line. This inability to read the middle of the line occurs in spite of the fact that the eye traveled over this region of text during its movement from one end to the other. Using these two pieces of evidence, Dodge proposed that there was no visual perception during eye movements, only during fixation pauses and that the impression that we have of visual perception during eye movements is merely an illusion.

While Dodge's observations and studies of visual perception during and between eye movements (e.g. Erdmann and Dodge, 1898; Dodge, 1900, 1905) are of seminal importance to the development of current approaches to and understanding of vision, attention should be drawn to those of his predecessors who harbored similar feelings about oculomotor behavior. Wells offers a very early report of the possible lack of visual perception during eye movements in the context of post-rotational vision. In a letter to *The Gentleman's Magazine*, in response to Erasmus Darwin's (1794) criticism of his theory linking eye movements to visual vertigo, Wells wrote:

> "For I mentioned that, if, while giddy, and in possession of the spectrum [after-image] of a small luminous body, I direct my eyes to a sheet of white paper, fixed to a wall, a spot immediately appears upon the paper; that the spot and paper afterwards separate from each other to a certain distance, the latter seemingly moving from left to right, if I had turned from right to left; but from right to left if I had turned the contrary way; and that they suddenly come together again. My conclusion from this experiment is, that, although the eye during it moves forwards and backwards, still the two motions are not exactly similar, but that in one the picture travels slowly enough over the retina to allow me to attend to the progression of the paper; while in the latter the passage of the picture is so rapid, that no succession of the paper's apparent places can be observed."
> (Wells, 1794b, pp. 905–906)

Breuer (1874) also suggested that there was no visual awareness during rapid rotations of the eye in post-rotational nystagmus. Similarly, Brown (1895), when describing the 'jerky' movements of the eyes, suggested that "During the jerks we practically do not see at all" (p. 5). Hence these earlier authors must take their share of the credit in unraveling the relationship between saccadic eye movements and visual perception.

Recognition that we only receive useful information for visual perception during fixations or slow pursuit has served to highlight the importance and characteristics of the oculomotor strategy for sampling the visual surroundings and to give rise to new questions in the approach to the study of visual perception. Two key issues were raised by the work of Dodge and his predecessors that have been of great importance to the progress of vision research over the past century.

Dodge's writings on the suspension of visual perception during rapid eye movements can be found to have been posited in earlier works by Breuer, Brown and even Wells. Descriptions of saccadic eye movements during reading by Javal and Lamare were crucial precursors for the psychological explorations of Dodge. Despite Javal's popular plaudit as the discoverer of saccades, several researchers had already reported the existence of fast eye rotations. Hering offered a concurrent description of the strategy using a miniature stethoscope to listen to the oculomotor muscles, attributing his observed muscular sounds to the jerky movements of the eyes. Prior to both of these accounts, reports of the distinction between fast and slow phases of eye movement in the context of nystagmus during and after body rotation can be found in the work Wells, Purkinje, Brown, Breuer, and Mach. The importance of this work in the development of our understanding of eye movements is often overlooked, but should not be underestimated. That the study of nystagmus is valuable can be seen in Dodge's (1923) rediscovery of the problem and investigation of post-rotational eye movements after his early work in reading. The insight and competence of early eye movement researchers is revealed by the fact that the technique of using afterimages was employed in studies of eye movements and reading in the late nineteenth century; it was the same technique that had been used by Wells in his studies of vision nearly a century earlier.

When scanning a scene or text the eyes engage in periods of relative stability (fixations) interspersed with ballistic rotations (saccades). The saccade-and-fixate strategy, associated with voluntary eye movements, was first uncovered in the context of involuntary eye movements following body rotation. This pattern of eye movements is now referred to as nystagmus and involves periods of slow eye movements, during which objects are visible, and rapid returns, when they are not; it is based on a vestibular reflex which attempts to achieve image stabilization. Post-rotational nystagmus was reported in the late eighteenth century (by Wells), using afterimages as a means of retinal stabilization to distinguish between movement of the eyes and of the environment. Nystagmus was linked to vestibular stimulation in the nineteenth century, and Mach, Breuer, and Crum Brown all described its fast and slow phases. Wells and Breuer proposed that there was no visual awareness during the ballistic phase (saccadic suppression). The saccade-and-fixate strategy highlighted by studies of nystagmus was shown to apply to tasks like reading by Dodge, who used more sophisticated photographic techniques to examine oculomotor kinematics. The relationship between eye movements and perception, following earlier intuitions by Wells and Breuer, was explored by Dodge and has been of fundamental importance in the direction of vision research over the last century.

SUMMARY

The time-honored methods of phenomenology ushered in the nineteenth century, but they played a less vital role at its close. Descriptions of perceptual experience seemed suitable for naturally occurring pheneomena, and even for the novelties of philosophical toys. However, the growing awareness of individual differences in perception, not to mention the changes which occur within the same individual, led some to question the value of such verbal descriptions. At around the same time, vast strides were being made in the biological sciences: species similarities as well as differences were commented upon, and the continuity of sense organs was evident for all to see. How could creatures with similar sense organs but lacking language be studied? Goethe, who championed the use of phenomenology, did much to foster understanding of homologies between species.

Responses to stimulation were given serious consideration some time after the explosion of novel instruments for delivering the stimulus. From the mid-nineteenth century, attempts to quantify responses were introduced which led to the potent methods of psychophysics. Fechner (1860) not only described psychophysical methods which placed less reliance on language but he also introduced a lawful relationship between stimulus intensity and the magnitude of sensation. The term psychophysics suitably summarized his search for a bond between the physical domain of the stimulus and the psychological domain of the response.

Responses could be simplified and counted; they could also be timed. Helmholtz's measurement of the speed of nerve impulses in humans used reaction time, and Donders saw the utility of this technique for inferring decision times for cognitive tasks. The age of mental chronometry was born. Both psychophysics and reaction time played their parts in the emergence of psychology as an independent discipline, as did geometrical illusions. Wundt embraced them all in his new psychological institute.

Responses could be simplified and quantified using psychophysics, but they could be measured, too. One response that received intense examination towards the end of the nineteenth century was that of the eye, and how it moved following rotation of the body. The discontinuous nature of eye movements discerned in vertigo (nystagmus) was not an oddity but provided the pattern for scanning in reading, too. The eyes moved by rapid jerks (saccades) separated by relatively short intervals of stability (fixations). It was during fixations that information was extracted, and characteristic patterns of eye movements occurred during reading. Throughout the nineteenth century, the technique that had proved most fruitful in determining both eye position and eye movement was the comparison of the location of an afterimage and some real reference. Wells (1792) had used this technique with great success, but his work was woefully neglected. Mach, Breuer, and Crum Brown applied it with similar skill almost a century later. However, the use of afterimages is not the best method for determining where the eye is and how it moves. More sophisticated methods were introduced in the twentieth century.

Another technique that was applied to move the eyes was galvanic (electrical) stimulation. This proved to be a potent source of stimulation. It was applied by Helmholtz to measure the transmission rate of nerve impulses, and it was the method by which all the senses could be stimulated. Galvanic stimulation proved to be the force which extended the senses, as will be described in the next chapter.

7

The Fragmentation of the Senses in the Nineteenth Century

Prior to the nineteenth century, the senses were studied principally by naturalistic observation. Naturally occurring events, like rainbows and afterimages, were the source of speculation, as were the perceptual distortions that accompanied many diseases. It could be said that from nineteenth century perception became an experimental science, and its study was displaced from the natural environment to the laboratory. In the context of vision, this argument can be more readily sustained for spatial than for color vision. As was argued in Chapter 5, experimental advances in both departments were made when spatial and color phenomena could be studied independently of their object base. In the case of color, the prismatic spectrum enabled different components of white light to be isolated and combined with others, without reference to colored objects. From the seventeenth century onwards these methods of manipulating colored light have provided the foundations for color science. The case was somewhat more complicated for spatial vision, because it deals with the three-dimensional nature of objects. From the late 1830s, the stereoscope enabled depth perception to be studied independently of viewing solid objects. This opened avenues of experimental enquiry that had not been possible previously, and it can be taken as a turning point in the history of vision.

Similar arguments can be made for the other senses, too. Indeed, the number of senses themselves increased with more systematic studies of their function, and with increasing anatomical knowledge of their microscopic structure. Two factors were of particular importance in examining the senses and perception. One relates to the techniques that could be used to stimulate the senses. Scientists were not restricted to the natural sources of stimulation like light and sound. Similar sensations could derive from quite different modes of stimulation; mechanical or electrical stimulation could be applied to any sensory system. This relates to the second important factor: how can similar sensations follow from such disparate stimulation? Contemplating this problem led to the doctrine of specific nerve energies, which fuelled the investigations of the senses throughout the nineteenth century.

METHODS OF STIMULATING THE SENSES

Electricity provided the key to understanding not only nerve transmission, but also how the senses functioned. It provided a novel means for stimulating the senses, and it led to questions about their number. Aristotle's five senses had reigned supreme over two millennia, but were about to be challenged. The classical situation seemed secure at the end of the eighteenth century, at least from an anatomical viewpoint. John Hunter (1786) voiced this confidence:

> "There are some nerves which have a peculiarity in their course, as the recurrent and chorda tympani; and others which are appropriated to particular sensations, as those which go to four of the organs of sense, seeing, hearing smelling, and tasting; and some parts of the body having peculiar sensations, (as the stomach and penis) we may, without impropriety, include the fifth, or sense of feeling. This general uniformity, in course, connection and distribution, will lead us to suppose that there may be some other purpose to be answered more than mere mechanical convenience." (Hunter, 1786, p. 213)

The received wisdom was not questioned by anatomy but by physiology. The manner in which the nerves themselves worked was hinted at by Luigi Galvani (1737–1798; 1791) when he made a case for 'animal electricity'. He applied a discharge from a Leyden jar to the exposed crural nerve or muscle of an isolated frog's leg and it twitched. Galvani suggested that this was due to a special type of electrical fluid that accumulates in the muscles of animals (see Bresadola, 1998; Piccolino, 1997). Volta maintained that animal tissue was not necessary for a current to pass, and that Galvani's experiments were flawed. Volta had interests in the effects of electrical discharges on the senses; he carried out studies of galvanic light figures in the 1790s, and also found that intermittent stimulation produced longer lasting effects than constant stimulation. In his letter describing the pile or battery, Volta (1800) described how he applied electrical stimulation to the eyes, ears, nose, and tongue. He connected the wires from a battery between the mouth and conjunctiva of the eye, which resulted in the experience of light, even in a dark room. Moreover, he noted that the visual sensation was associated with the onset and offset of the current, and a continuous impression of light could be produced by rapid alternation of polarity (see Piccolino, 2000). When he applied a current to the two ears he reported: "At the moment the circuit was completed I felt a shaking in the head" (Volta, 1800, p. 427). This shaking did not last long; when the current was continued he experienced sound and then noise. The sensations were so disagreeable that he thought them potentially dangerous, and he did not wish to repeat them.

A few years earlier, Volta had applied a current to his tongue and noted an acidic taste. Volta's pile did much to hasten experimental studies of the senses. Electricity was a common stimulus that could be applied to different sensory organs, inducing different sensations. Müller used the effects to support his doctrine of specific nerve energies: "The stimulus of electricity may serve as a second example, of a uniform cause giving rise in different nerves of sense to different sensations" (1843/2003, p. 1063). The first example was mechanical stimulation.

The action of nerves on muscles led first Carlo Matteucci (1811–1862) and later Emil du Bois Reymond (1818–1896) to propose the ways in which nerves propagate impulses (Brazier, 1959, 1988). Experimental evidence of action potentials was to await technological advances in recording and amplifying small electrical signals; this was provided by Adrian (1928) who was able to record action potentials. When recordings of nerve impulses could be made from individual cells in the visual pathway their adequate stimuli could be determined. Adrian coined the term 'receptive field' to refer to this, and it was applied to other senses, too.

SPECIFYING THE SENSES

The senses were initially classified on the basis of phenomenal experience and gross anatomy. These were the sources used by Aristotle and those who followed. The situation regarding the senses was radically revised in the nineteenth century, with developments in physics, anatomy, and physiology. Sources of stimulation could be specified and controlled more precisely. With the addition of galvanic stimulation, the development of microscopy, and an appreciation of cortical localization, the criteria for specifying the senses were extended. Those that have been applied to separating the senses are the quality of the experience, the nature of the stimulus, the gross and microanatomy of the receptor system, and the pathways to and representation on the cortex. The psychological dimension is the oldest of these, and yet less attention has been paid to behavioral evidence for distinguishing and adding to the senses than to that derived from anatomy and physiology.

Muscle Sense

Appeals to muscular sensitivity have been commonplace in philosophy, particularly among the empiricists (see Chapter 4). It proved central to the later common-sense philosophers, too. For example, Thomas Brown (1778–1820) suggested it was a separate sense, and asked:

"To what organ, then, are we to ascribe the external influences, which give occasion to these feelings of resistance and extension? It is not touch, as I conceive, that either of these be traced. Our feeling of resistance, in all its varieties of hardness, softness, roughness, smoothness, solidity, liquidity, &c. I consider as the result of organic affections, not tactual, but muscular; our muscular frame being truly an organ of sense, that is affected in various ways, by various modifications of external resistance to the effort of contraction." (Brown, 1820, pp. 78–79)

This statement appeared in Brown's book *Physiology of the mind*, although there was little physiology in it. It was the physiological dimension of Bell's paper that led Boring to nominate him as the founder of this new sense. Bell (1826) argued that the anterior spinal nerve roots, which are involved in muscular contraction, also carry sensory signals. Moreover, a nerve circuit was proposed, which passes from the voluntary muscles to the brain. Muscle spindles were not isolated until four decades later by Kühne (1863). In fact, Bell (1823) had provided behavioral evidence for the muscular sense three years earlier, in the context of determining the visual direction of afterimages:

"There is an inseparable connection between the exercise of the sense of vision and the exercise of the voluntary muscles of the eye. When an object is seen, we enjoy two senses; there is an impression upon the retina; but we receive also the idea of position or relation which it is not the office of the retina to give. It is by the consciousness of the degree of effort put upon the voluntary muscles, that we know the relative position of an object to ourselves.... If we move the eye by the voluntary muscles, while the impression [of an afterimage] continues on

> the retina, we shall have the notion of place or relation raised in the mind; but if the motion of the eye-ball be produced by any other cause, by the involuntary muscles, or by pressure from without, we shall have no corresponding change of sensation." (Bell, 1823, pp. 178 and 179)

That is, the visual direction of an object is not determined by visual stimulation alone, but also involves information about the position of the eyes—otherwise objects would appear to move with every movement of the eyes. Helmholtz (1867) made a distinction between what have become called outflow and inflow theories. The former refers to deriving the eye movement information from efferent (centrally generated) impulses to the eye muscles, whereas the latter reflects use of afferent (sensory) signals from the eye muscles themselves.

It is surprising that Bell did not refer to the earlier experiments by Wells (1792) on this topic, because his monograph was referred to by Bell (1803/2000) in the context of vertigo. Wells had performed the same experiment and reached a similar conclusion:

> "When we have looked steadily for some time at the flame of a candle, or any other luminous body, a coloured spot [afterimage] will appear upon every object, to which we shortly after direct our eyes, accompanying them in all their motions, and exactly covering the point, which we desire to see the most accurately.... The apparent situation of the spot being... at the same time affected by the *voluntary* motions of the eye, it must, I think, be necessarily owing to the *action* of the muscles by which these motions are performed.... the apparent direction of an object, which sends its picture to any given point of the retina, depends upon the state of action existing at the same time in the muscles of the eye, and consequently that it cannot be altered, except by a change in the state of that action." (1792, pp. 65 and 70–71)

Bell also followed Wells (again without acknowledgement) in suggesting that the muscle sense is involved in the maintenance of balance: "Let us consider how minute and delicate the sense of muscular motion is by which we balance the body, and by which we judge of the position of the limbs, whether during activity or rest" (Bell, 1823, p. 181). Both Wells and Bell provided evidence for a muscle sense based on perceptual experiments, but these were not considered to carry the same weight as Bell's anatomical dissections and physiological speculations:

> "The muscles have no connection with each other, they are combined by the nerves; but these nerves, instead of passing betwixt the muscles, interchange their fibres before their distribution to them, and by this means combine the muscles into classes. The question therefore may thus be stated: why are nerves, whose office is to convey sensation, profusely given to muscles in addition to those motor nerves which are given to excite their motions? and why do both classes of muscular nerves form plexus? To solve this question, we must determine whether muscles have any other purpose to serve than merely to

contract under the impulse of the motor nerves.... That we have a sense of the condition of the muscles, appears from this: that we feel the effects of over exertion and weariness, and are excruciated by spasms, and feel the irksomeness of continued position. We posses a power of weighing in the hand:- what is this but estimating the muscular force? We are sensible of the most minute changes of muscular exertion, by which we know the position of the body and limbs, when there is no other means of knowledge open to us." (Bell, 1826, pp. 166–167)

Bell provided phenomenological support for his physiological hypothesis. In addition, he drew attention to the ability to discriminate between small differences in weight when they are handled. This technique of comparing lifted weights was at the heart of Weber's psychophysics (see Chapter 6). In his first monograph devoted to the sense of touch, Weber (1834) distinguished between judging weights by touch alone or by the additional action of the muscle sense:

"The weight of an object is perceived in two ways: first by the touch-sense in the skin, and then by the special sense of the voluntary muscles. The latter sense tells us the degree of tension of the muscle when lifting weights and other objects. These two methods of discovering the weights of objects are very different: the former method depends upon the objective sense of touch, while the latter depends on the subjective sense of muscular kinaesthesis. This assumes, of course, that we call a sense 'objective' when we use it to perceive objects that have a certain pressure on our organs and produces some effect; and that we call it 'subjective' when we seem to perceive only the effect of the objects and not the objects themselves." (Ross and Murray, 1978, p. 55)

In making this distinction between objective and subjective, Weber displayed his reliance on the philosophy of Aristotle, rather than the contemporary physiology (Ross, 1999). Müller's doctrine of specific nerve energies was based on all sensation being subjective, that is, not in perfect accord with the stimulus giving rise to it.

The combination of Bell's tentative hypothesis of a nervous circle, the specific nerve energies doctrine, and psychophysical studies of lifted weights confirmed for many the force of the muscle sense as the sixth sense. By the end of the century, Sherrington was able to devote a chapter of a textbook to the muscular sense; he defined it as including "all reactions on sense rising in motor organs and their accessories" (1900, p. 1002). Six years later, he introduced a novel classification of the senses into extero-ceptors, proprio-ceptors, and intero-ceptors:

"The excitation of the receptors of the *proprio-ceptive* field in contradistinction from those of the *extero-ceptive* is related only secondarily to the agencies of the environment. The proprio-ceptive receive their stimulation by some action, *e.g.* a muscular contraction, which was itself a primary reaction to excitation of a surface receptor by the environment." (Sherrington, 1906/2000, p. 130)

Thus, the contention that the muscle sense is the sixth sense was reasonably well supported by phenomenology, physiology, and psychophysics in the nineteenth century.

TEMPERATURE SENSE

As was noted in Chapter 4, observational evidence had been proposed for a temperature sense. Erasmus Darwin (1794) distinguished not only between touch and temperature sensitivity, but also accorded the muscle sense its independence. A few years later, Bell (1803/2000) stated:

> "By the sense of touch we perceive several qualities, and of very different kinds: hardness, softness, figure, solidity, motion, extension, and heat and cold. Now, although heat be a quality, and cold be the privation of that quality, yet in relation to the body, heat and cold are distinct sensations. But in a more precise acceptance of the term, the sense of touch is said to be the change arising in the mind from external bodies applied to the skin." (p. 472)

Two years earlier, in 1801, further experimental support for warmth and cold as sensory qualities had been obtained by Johann Wilhelm Ritter (1776–1810) using galvanic stimulation of the tongue. Ritter was an ardent student of galvanism and its general application. His interpretations of galvanic phenomena in the context of German Romantic philosophy has led to some neglect of his experimental work, but he did follow Volta in applying electrical discharges to the areas around his sense organs. Ritter's first reports regarding warm and cold were in 1801: "Another contrast in sensation is that between warm and cold . . . if one brings into contact a zinc pole on the tongue and silver on the gums, that on the tongue feels very clearly warm, but it feels cold with silver in the same arrangement" (Ritter, 1801, p. 458). Thus, stimulation by the positive pole produced the sensation of warmth, whereas the negative pole resulted in experiencing cold. Slightly earlier in the same year, Pfaff (1801) had described the sensation of coldness when he applied a current to his finger. Ritter (1805) extended the studies on temperature sensitivity on the tongue as well as the finger; he found that the sensation could vary according to the intensity and duration of the current. His general conclusion was that: "one must consider the sense of temperature (for warmth and cold) as essentially different from the common sense, and as a special sense" (Ritter, 1805, p.10). Galvanic stimulation resulted in a short shock as well as the particular sensation. In the case of temperature sensitivity, Ritter reported that the shock remained constant even when the sensation changed from warm to cold. Rather than merely speculating that warmth and cold are separate sensory qualities, Ritter afforded experimental evidence for this via his studies of galvanic stimulation.

Weber (1846) also followed Volta's lead in applying electric currents to the sense organs, although he was disparaging of Ritter's work. Weber added little to what was known at that time about galvanic stimulation, but he did conduct experiments that supported the existence of a temperature sense: "The sensations of warmth and cold are not like the sensations of brightness and darkness, for the former are positive and negative quantities between which lies a null point determined by the source of heat within us" (Ross and Murray, 1978, p. 210). Weber's great contribution was the introduction of experimental methods, like determining two-point thresholds, which enabled quantification of sensitivity over the skin surface (Weber, 1834). These could then be applied to establish acuity differences over the skin surface, and interpreted in terms of regions of receptiveness (Weber 1846). Furthermore, Weber suggested that the sensory circles could be related to the underlying nerve supply:

> "But no matter how the elementary nerves do extend to cover the skin, the suggestion may be put forward that the skin is divided into small *sensory circles*, i.e., into small subdivisions each of which owes its sensitivity to a single elementary nerve-fibre. Now my investigations have shown that two stimulations of similar kind applied to separate sites within a single sensory circle on the skin are felt as if they were made at one and the same site; and moreover, that the sensory circles of the skin are smaller in regions provided with an accurate touch-sense and larger in areas provided with a less accurate touch-sense." (Ross and Murray, 1978, p. 187, original italics)

Cutaneous sensory "spots" specifically responsive to touch (pressure) and pain, as well as warmth and cold, were isolated later in the century, using more sensitive and specific apparatus (see Norrsell, Finger, and Lajonchere, 1999). A division of the skin senses into three separate systems (one to register temperature, a second for pressure, and a third for touch) was proposed by Ludwig Natanson (1822–1871; 1844). He supported the contention of peripheral independence by describing how these systems succumb in sequence when a limb "falls asleep". Three sets of independent studies were reported in the 1880s by Magnus Blix (1849–1904), Alfred Goldscheider (1858–1935) and Henry Donaldson (1857–1938), and they are jointly credited with the discovery. All were principally concerned with establishing cold and warm spots. Blix (1884) continued in the tradition of applying low intensity electric currents to the skin; he found separate warm and cold spots. Goldscheider (1884) stimulated the skin with a range of devices, like needles, heated brass cylinders, cooled capillary tubes, and brushes coated with ether to isolate the cutaneous spots. Donaldson (1885) discovered the warm and cold sensory spots independently in the course of moving metal points slowly over the skin.

The sensory spots could be mapped and attempts were made to match them to receptors revealed by histological sections of excised skin. Towards the end of the century Max von Frey (1852–1932; 1895) advanced the theory that the sensations of warmth, cold, pressure, and pain are subserved by specific end organs in the skin. His theory was based on meager evidence, and was soon under attack on empirical as well as theoretical grounds (see Sinclair, 1967).

Ritter's observations faded into oblivion with the discovery of specific receptors in the skin. This provided the platform for Blix and others to relate structure to function. Perhaps it was the equation of cutaneous sensations with the underlying nerves that has given authority to Blix; he stated: "The different sensations of cold and warmth are produced by stimulation of separate specific nerve end-organs in the skin" (1882, translated in Zotterman, 1959, p. 431). In the context of sensory physiology Blix had clearly defined a path that would be followed by others. For example, Zotterman (1959) opened his survey of thermal sensations thus: "Since the discovery by Blix of cold and warm spots from which adequate or electrical stimuli elicited cold and warm sensations, respectively, numerous authors have described the distribution of cold and warm spots in the skin" (p. 431).

The phenomenological distinctions between the dimensions of touch, voiced since antiquity, were given some empirical support from the late-eighteenth century and integrated with cutaneous anatomy and physiology in the late-nineteenth century.

Movement Sense

At the beginning of the nineteenth century, the movement sense was a term applied to experiences deriving from both muscular and vestibular stimulation, although this distinction was not then made. Galvanic stimulation was applied to the regions around the ears, and provided some indication that more than hearing was involved in the structures of the inner ear. As was noted above, Volta (1800) reported that his head seemed to be shaking when current was applied to his ears. Ritter (1801) described the dizziness generated by experiments on applying galvanic stimulation to the head. A similar account was given by Augustin (1803): "If one surrounds the ears with wire . . . one becomes dizzy and sees electrical lights" (p. 129).

Purkinje (1820) carried out further studies on galvanic stimulation of the ear and the subsequent vertigo that it induced. He constructed a voltaic pile from twenty zinc and copper pairs and applied the current to the ear. The immediate sensations were of light flashes and a metallic taste, and then he reported feeling dizzy. It was like a motion from ear to ear, and its direction depended on the polarity of stimulation. He felt nauseous following ten minutes continuous stimulation, and experienced aftereffects for the following two hours. These effects could only be produced when the current was applied to the ears; similar application elsewhere on the head did not produce vertigo. Purkinje extended his observation in a later article:

> "The direction of the rotary motion from vertigo goes from right to left if the copper pole is in the right ear, and the zinc pole is in the left, and in the opposite direction from left to right, if the copper pole is applied to the left and the zinc pole to the right ear. As often as the galvanic current is alternated, the vertigo is experienced in the opposite direction and lasts for a longer or shorter time according to the longer or shorter application." (Purkinje, 1827, p. 297)

More systematic investigations were conducted by Hitzig (1871). In examining the effects of vestibular stimulation, one year after co-discovering the motor cortex, Hitzig applied electrical currents between the mastoid bones and recorded not only the direction of apparent visual motion but of actual body and eye movements. When the head moved in one direction the eyes moved in the opposite direction. The actual and apparent movements of the body were in the same direction. Hitzig found that the effects of galvanic stimulation were more pronounced when they were applied with the head tilted, and that it was difficult to maintain balance under these conditions. Two blind subjects felt that their bodies were rotating when the current was applied, as did sighted subjects with their eyes closed.

The effects of body rotation, both on apparent body movement and on apparent visual movement provided a ready means of studying the movement sense. Purkinje (1820) unknowingly repeated many of Wells' (1792) experiments on body rotation, although he was able to add a mechanically rotating device to study vertigo. In one study he described the effects of being rotated for one hour in such a contrivance. Initially, Purkinje examined the introspective aspects of post-rotational vertigo and made many experimental manipulations of it. He described the pattern of eye movements during and after body rotation and suggested that "visual vertigo is a consequence of the conflict between unconscious involuntary muscular actions and voluntary conscious ones in the opposite direction" (Purkinje, 1820, p. 95). Among the few sources of earlier research he cited were a translation into German of Erasmus Darwin's *Zoonomia* (Darwin, 1795) and Herz's (1786) medical text on dizziness and its treatment.

Purkinje deduced a general principle from his experiments: "that the midpoint of the head (considered as a sphere), around which the initial rotation was performed, invariably determined the direction of apparent motion regardless of the subsequent position of the head" (1820, p. 86). Kruta (1964) referred to this as "Purkinje's law of vertigo". There was no clear indication of how such motions in the head could be detected, and his initial interpretation was that motion of the brain itself lagged behind that of the head, with particular influence exerted by the cerebellum. Purkinje concluded his first article with a statement that was soon to be realized: "It remains for a future work to establish the possible movements in the brain which measure its structure and organization" (1820, p. 125). Purkinje later wrote several briefer articles on vertigo, but his interpretation of it did not change substantially. The dimension that Purkinje added to Wells' studies was the application of galvanic stimulation to the ears.

The significance of the vestibular system to the maintenance of posture and balance slowly emerged after Flourens (1824, 1830, 1842) conducted his lesion studies, initially on the cerebellum and later on the semicircular canals. In the year that his first book was published he sectioned the semicircular canals of pigeons: "On 15 November 1824, I cut the two horizontal semicircular canals of a pigeon. This lesion was immediately followed by two habitual phenomena: the horizontal oscillation of the head, and the turning of the animal in the same direction" (Flourens, 1842, p. 452). In later experiments, he was able to demonstrate that sectioning a particular semicircular canal elicited nystagmus in the same plane, as well as disturbances of posture and equilibrium: the bodies of the experimental animals always turned in the direction of the severed canal. Similar results were obtained with rabbits.

Despite providing this experimental evidence, Flourens did not make the link between semicircular canal function and the movement sense. This was to wait another fifty years, when Mach, Breuer, and Brown independently formulated the hydrodynamic theory: during head rotation the endolymph in the canals displaces receptors in the ampulla, signaling angular accelerations and exerting control over posture and eye movements.

Mach (1873, 1875) constructed a rotating chair that was mounted in a frame that could also rotate, and he examined the perception of the visual vertical during static tilt and also visual aftereffects of body rotation. From experiments using this apparatus he concluded that it was not angular velocity that was sensed, but angular acceleration. Brown (1874) based his analysis on thresholds for detecting body rotation on a revolving stool; the thresholds were lowest when the head was positioned so that one of the semicircular canals was in the plane of rotation. Breuer (1874) made systematic lesions of the semicircular canals of pigeons and dogs; he also distinguished between the canal receptors and the otolith organs of the vestibular system, which detected orientation with respect to gravity.

Mach (1910) placed these observations in the context of Aristotle's strictures about the senses:

"But at times some extremely artless animadversions are heard that almost nonplus us. 'If a sixth sense existed it could not fail to have been discovered thousands of years ago.' Indeed, there was a time, then, when only seven planets could have existed! But I do not believe that any one will lay any weight on the philological question whether the set of phenomena which we have been considering should be called a sense. The phenomena will not disappear when the name disappears. It was further said to me that animals exist which have no labyrinth, but which can yet orientate themselves, and that consequently the labyrinth has nothing to do with orientation. We do not walk forsooth with our legs, because snakes can propel themselves without them! But if the promulgator of a new idea cannot hope for any great pleasure from its publication, yet the critical process which his views undergo is extremely helpful to the subject-matter of them." (Mach, 1910, p. 297)

Mach, Breuer, and Brown continued to investigate the consequences of the hydrodynamic theory of semicircular canal function, but Brown, in 1878, made a particularly astute prediction: if deaf-mutes have defects in all the parts of the inner ear, then they will not be able to experience vertigo:

"A great deal of valuable information might be obtained by carefully testing the delicacy and accuracy of the sense of rotation in deaf-mutes. Many deaf-mutes have not only the cochlea, but the whole internal ear, destroyed; if, then, the inmates of deaf and dumb establishments were systematically tested by means of such experiments as Mach and Brown made upon themselves, experiments which would, no doubt, greatly interest and amuse them, and if the condition of the internal ear were, in each case of *post-mortem* examination of a deaf-mute, accurately noted, we should soon obtain a mass of information which would do more to clear up the relation between the sense of rotation and the semicircular canals than any number of experiments on animals unable to describe to us their sensations." (Brown, 1878b, p. 658)

William James (1842–1910; 1882) put this to the test with a specially constructed devise for rotating the body. Almost all normal observers experienced vertigo. However, of over 500 deaf-mutes tested, almost 200 experienced no dizziness. The results were confirmed by Kreidl (1891), who found that over 80% of congenitally deaf individuals experienced no vertigo following rotation. Moreover, there were no nystagmic eye movements in those who did not experience vertigo. As Brown described in a lecture some years later: "Just as there are blind men and deaf men, so there are men who have lost or never had the sense of rotation. Such persons are always deaf-mutes" (1895, p. 27).

Mach extended his own research to examine visual orientation during body tilt, as well as visual motion following body rotation. He was able to use his rotating chair and to exclude the visibility of the surround. His research on orientation was stimulated by an experience of visual disorientation when traveling in a vehicle:

"Thus my attention was drawn to this point by the sensation of falling and subsequently by another singular occurrence. I was rounding a sharp railway curve once when I suddenly saw all the trees, houses, and factory chimneys along the track swerve from the vertical and assume a strikingly inclined position. What had hitherto appeared to me perfectly natural, namely, the fact that we distinguish the vertical so perfectly and sharply from every other direction, now struck me as enigmatical. Why is it that the same direction can now appear vertical to me and now cannot? By what is the vertical distinguished for us?" (Mach, 1910, pp. 286–287)

Mach appreciated that judgments of orientation are made with respect to frames of reference. Normally those available from the senses correspond with the cardinal directions defined by gravity, but occasionally this accord is disrupted. Mach did have recourse to the structures within the inner ear—what Wells (1792, p. 85) had referred to as "some secret reference to the position of our bodies"—and Mach conducted experiments with his tilting chair to confirm it.

The receptors that mediate vestibular sensitivity are closely linked to those for hearing. Hair cells in the cochlea were first observed in the 1850s, and they were later identified in the vestibular system. In the twentieth century, the fine detail of the hair cell receptors could be observed with electron microscopes and a cortical projection from the vestibular nuclei was demonstrated.

The vestibular sense is unusual in various respects. First, the sensory experiences following stimulation are not localized as they are with the other senses; we feel giddy or see the world spin rather than have a single sensation like sight or hearing. Secondly, the gross anatomy of the vestibular system was known long before its function was appreciated. Thirdly, systematic experiments indicating the action of the semicircular canals (in vertigo) was available from the late-eighteenth century. Nonetheless, behavioral studies which provided support for a new sense were not accorded the status given to isolating specific receptors or establishing projections to the brain. It was the behavioral dimension that encouraged Brown (1895) to state: "I am not sure whether in this account of the sense of rotation, of its organ, and of the use of it, I have carried all my hearers with me, and convinced you of the real existence and the real practical use of this sense" (p. 28).

Specific Nerve Energies

The doctrine of specific nerve energies is associated closely with Johannes Müller: in 1826 he first presented the idea that the sensations experienced are dependent on the nerves excited, no matter how those nerves are stimulated. What he maintained at that time, and later in various editions of his *Elements of physiology*, was that no matter how the auditory nerve is stimulated, we hear sounds; we do not see lights, smell things, and so forth. Similarly, no matter how the optic nerve is stimulated, whether by light, electricity, or pressure, the phenomenological experience will be visual. This seminal contention, backed by a myriad of observations on each of the sensory systems, has come to be known as the 'doctrine of specific nerve energies.'

This was not a novel insight, but Müller was able to bolster it with an impressive armory of observations and experiments. Hunter (1786) had voiced similar ideas when discussing the pathways between sensory nerves and the brain:

> "For it is more than probable, that what may be called organs of sense, have particular nerves, whose mode of action is different from that of nerves producing common sensation; and also different from one another; and that the nerves on which the particular functions of each of the organs of sense depend, are not supplied from different parts of the brain. . . . it is more probable, that every nerve so affected as to communicate sensation, in whatever part of the nerve the impression is made, always gives the same sensation as if affected at the common seat of the sensation of that particular nerve." (1786, pp. 215–216)

Young (1802a) had proposed essentially the same concept within the confines of a single sense when he proposed that there was a limited set of retinal mechanisms for responding to color. However, the clearest formulation prior to Müller was given by Charles Bell in 1811: "In this inquiry it is most essential to observe, that while each organ of sense is provided with a capacity for receiving certain changes to be played upon it, as it were, yet each is utterly incapable of receiving the impression destined for another organ of sensation" (1811/2000, pp. 8–9). Bell supported the concept with observations similar to those that would later be described by Müller:

> "If light, pressure, galvanism, or electricity produce vision, we must conclude that the idea in the mind is the result of an action excited in the eye or in the brain, not any thing received, though caused by an impression from without. The operations of the mind are confined not by the limited nature of things created, but by the limited number of our organs of sense." (1811/2000, p. 12)

Müller presented the same general idea with considerably more force, in much greater detail, with more examples, and in more widely-read publications. He first presented the ideas in one of his books on vision, published in 1826: "The eye does not radiate, the ear does not sound, the tongue is not salty, sour, etc. Only external objects radiate, sound, and so forth. The sense organs experience the external light, sound, etc with difficulty; the different sense organs only have a so-called specific receptivity for particular stimuli" (1826a, pp. XII–XIII). It was restated in greater detail in Müller's *Elements* (1843/2003, pp. 1059–1086), where ten consequences of the doctrine are described.

Müller used the doctrine to speculate upon the number of senses that might exist. He stated: "The essential attribute of a new sense is, not the perception of external objects or influences which ordinarily do not act upon the senses, but that external causes should excite in it a new and peculiar kind of sensation different from all the sensations of our five senses" (1843/2003, p. 1087). He was questioning whether the Aristotelian limit of the senses to five was justified, and what evidence would be required to extend them. Despite the debate concerning the multiple dimensions of touch, Müller did not consider that an increment was justified, and his analysis was in terms of the classical senses of vision, hearing, smell, taste and touch. As with all books on the senses, then as now, vision commanded the lion's share of treatment in the *Elements*.

The doctrine of specific nerve energies effectively gave scientists a new way of looking at sensory systems, although its importance was much greater than this. On the one hand, it showed how unreliable sensory impressions could be, forcing scientists and philosophers to ponder what can be known about the outside world. And on the other, it stimulated several scientists, like Helmholtz, to consider the possibility of specificity within the confines of a single sensory system (e.g., vision).

It has been argued that the doctrine of specific nerve energies was misnamed from the outset (Riese and Arrington, 1964). Because it does not deal with the finer aspects of sensation within a sensory system, but only with sensations across the five classical sensory systems, it might have been more appropriate to call it "the doctrine of specific 'sense' energies." Helmholtz ranked the doctrine alongside Newton's physical law of gravitation, and he applied it extensively to his analysis of color.

SUBJECTIVE PHENOMENA

Helmholtz represents the shift from the subjective to the objective in German research on the senses. That is, he turned his back on the subjectivism championed by Goethe and the movement of Naturphilosophie, placing perception in the Newtonian mold. The struggle was a difficult one because Goethe was in the German rationalist philosophical tradition whereas Helmholtz sought support from British empiricist philosophy. However, the methods of phenomenology were placed on firmer ground by Purkinje (1819, 1823, 1825), who argued that all subjective phenomena have objective correlates. Goethe saw in Purkinje an advocate of his phenomenology, through which Newton's approach to perception could be challenged. In a letter to Purkinje in 1826, Goethe wrote: "The Newtonian scarecrow prevails like devils and witches in the darkest centuries. I am the happier because of your clear, comprehensive course and I regard as fortunate those youths who are indebted to you for their teaching" (John, 1959, p. 20).

Goethe was drawn to Purkinje as a consequence of reading Purkinje's first book on subjective visual phenomena. Purkinje's doctoral dissertation, published in 1819, was entitled *Contributions to the understanding of vision in its subjective aspect*. When it was reprinted in 1823 the title was extended to *Observations and experiments on the physiology of the senses. Contributions to the understanding of vision in its subjective aspect*. There were 28 topic headings in the book, the principal ones being: light and shade figures; pressure figures; Galvanic light figures; wandering cloudy stripes; scintillating light points when viewing a white surface; the place of entry of the optic nerve; disappearance of objects outside the entry of the optic nerve; vascular patterns of the eye; afterimages; cloudy streaks while viewing parallel lines; zigzag scintillations following observation of parallel lines; changes of parallel straight lines into wavy lines; voluntary movement of the pupil; visibility of blood circulation in the eye; flying gnats; eye movements; and persisting images, imagination, and visual memory.

Subjective visual phenomena had a long history before Purkinje gave them that title, but he added greatly to the detail of their classification, description, and interpretation. The description of one's own sensations might seem the simplest of things to report upon, but this is not the case. Helmholtz appreciated this only too well and he commended Purkinje's special talent in this regard. He commenced his research on visual phenomena because he had little access to equipment which would have allowed him to conduct experimental enquiries into other aspects of physiology. The second volume of *New contributions*, which was dedicated to Goethe, appeared in 1825. Goethe was both disappointed that Purkinje did not cite his own color research sufficiently and hopeful that Purkinje would advance phenomenological theory in an otherwise hostile climate among sensory physiologists. Their correspondence indicates the esteem in which Goethe was held by Purkinje, but also the independence of mind that the latter retained (see Kruta, 1969).

Goethe (1824) wrote an extensive review of Purkinje's first book. He reprinted particular short passages from it, and then added his own comments in parentheses. These were either of a general nature or related to Goethe's own observations. He was clearly impressed by the subtlety of Purkinje's vision because he wrote "we are grateful to the author for undertaking this task and for raising it to a new level" (1824, p. 103). Goethe was not alone in his admiration of Purkinje's powers of observation. In 1826, Müller extended the work in two books entitled *On fantastic visual appearances*, and *On the comparative physiology of vision in humans and animals*. Later, in his influential text, *Elements of physiology*, he remarked "of these phenomena... knowledge of which we are principally indebted to Purkinje" (1843/2003, p. 1210) before summarizing his own observations. In the 1830s, Purkinje and Müller were to found the two most influential laboratories of physiology—in Breslau and Berlin, respectively.

One of the few reviews in English of Purkinje's first book was under the initials C.W. (Charles Wheatstone); it appeared in 1830 and it was confined to the 1823 reprint of Purkinje's first volume. Wheatstone commenced his review of Purkinje's book by noting that "this little volume has excited considerable interest in Germany" (C.W., 1830, p. 102), but he took issue with the use of the term 'subjective':

> "To distinguish these phenomena from those which arise on the presence of their appropriate external objects, the author employs the term subjective, which, as denoting this class of phenomena better than any other we are acquainted with, and, to avoid circumlocution, we have purposely retained; it will, however, on consideration, be perceived, that the term is not strictly proper, as, correctly speaking, all phenomena, *as such*, are subjective, *i.e.* in the mind; and were we, without qualification, to admit the classification of phenomena into objective and subjective, we should be unable to determine, with any degree of accuracy, where the objective ends or the subjective begins." (p. 102)

Wheatstone's strictures apply as much today as they did then. He not only gave a summary of selected sections from Purkinje's book, but he also added novel methods for observing some phenomena—particularly the visibility of retinal blood vessels. Wheatstone closed his review with a sentiment that was common to those that had appeared in German reviews: "The condition of Dr. Purkinje's sight might further raise some doubts whether some of his experiments be not the effects of a morbid state, rather than depending on the organization of the human eye" (C.W., 1830, p. 117).

Purkinje is perhaps best known for the brightness changes of colors at dawn or dusk: blue objects that appear brighter than red ones before sunrise reverse thereafter. This phenomenon is now called the Purkinje shift, and later in the century it was related to the different spectral sensitivities of rod and cone receptors in the retina. He described it thus:

> "The degree of objective illumination has a great influence on the intensity of colour quality. In order to prove this most vividly, take some colours before daybreak, when it begins slowly to get lighter. Initially one sees only black and grey. Then the brightest colours, red and green, appear darkest. Yellow cannot be distinguished from a rosy red. Blue looks to me the most noticeable. Nuances of red, which otherwise burn brightest in daylight, namely carmine, cinnabar

and orange show themselves as darkest, in contrast to their average brightness. Green appears more bluish, and its yellow tint develops with the increasing daylight." (1825, pp. 225–226)

The Purkinje shift was described in the second book on subjective vision, which bore a title very similar to that of the first book: *Observations and experiments on the physiology of the senses. New contributions to the understanding of vision in its subjective aspect*, and it was published in 1825. The content had been published as three long articles in three issues of Rust's *Magazin für die gesammte Heilkunde* in the same year. Eighteen topics were covered in the book; some extended descriptions of phenomena addressed in the first volume, whereas others were novel. The principal new contributions were: indirect vision; real and apparent movements; investigations of the interaction of colors; focal image inside the eye; visual flicker after the use of digitalis; some comments on distant and near vision; intentional squinting; and the effect of belladonna on vision. The description of the brightness changes of red and blue objects at dawn or dusk (the Purkinje shift) was given in the section on the interaction of colors. He also described a perimeter and color zones of the eye (under indirect vision), the motion aftereffect and visual vertigo (under real and apparent movement), the distortions visible in regular geometrical patterns, and the failure of accommodation following application of the mydriatic, belladonna. The color zones were charted with the aid of a perimeter. He found that colors could not be distinguished in the peripheral retina, that yellow and blue were recognizable at slightly greater peripheral angles than red and green, and that all colors were visible more peripherally in the temporal than the nasal fields. Prolonged observation of a pattern of concentric circles had the effect that "there appear in all directions bands of clearly distinguishable parallel lines, over which the multitude of lines slide and entwine as cloudy streaks and points; they all radiate from the centre to the periphery, and their number, width and direction differ with different individuals, but remain constant for any one" (Purkinje, 1825, p. 261).

Purkinje opened a new domain of enquiry in the long history of vision research—that of subjective visual phenomena. His remarkable observations were lauded by both phenomenologists and empiricists. With regard to Purkinje's first book, Goethe noted:

"One has to be born strong to be able to examine his own interior without fear. The ability to take a healthy glance back into one's own interior without being buried by it, coupled with talent for profound investigation into the unexplored problems with a clear insight but not with illusion and fantasy, are precious gifts; the results of this research indeed are rare good luck for both the world and science." (John, 1959, p. 18)

The summary by Helmholtz was similarly telling: "It might seem that nothing could be easier than to be conscious of one's own sensations; and yet experience shows that for the discovery of subjective sensations some special talent is needed, such as Purkinje manifested in the highest degree" (1925/2000, p. 6).

OBJECTIVE CORRELATES

Helmholtz's contributions to the study of perception were truly monumental. He adopted the methods of physics to study the physiology of the senses, which led him to the psychology of perception. He wrote treatises on vision and hearing and he adopted the same approach to analyzing the two senses. Each was examined progressively with regard to the physics of the stimulus, the physiology of the sense organs, and the psychology of perception. These divisions are represented in the three parts of the *Handbuch der physiologischen Optik*, which were published separately in volumes of Gustav Karsten's *Allgemeine Encyklopädie der Physik* in 1856, 1860, and 1866. In 1867 they were published together, with Supplements added by Helmholtz. Volume 1 treats the anatomy and optics of the eye, with consideration of image formation and optical aberrations. Volume 2 examines the sensations of vision, dealing principally with color and contrast phenomena. Volume 3 is entitled the theory of visual perception and it addresses eye movements, visual direction, and binocular vision.

In 1867, when the *Handbuch* was published in its entirety, Helmholtz virtually ceased his active involvement in sensory physiology. In 1869 he wrote: "For the time being I have laid physiological optics and psychology aside. I found that so much philosophizing led to a certain demoralization, and made one's thought lax and vague; I must discipline myself awhile by experiment and mathematics, and then come back later to the Theory of Perception" (Koenigsberger, 1906, p. 266). When he did eventually revise the *Handbuch* it took almost as long as its original production: the revisions for a second edition were published separately in nine parts between 1885 and 1895 (the final part, published after his death, was edited by Arthur König), and they were assembled as a single volume in 1896. Most of the revisions were confined to the physical and physiological parts, with few changes to the third part (on the theory of visual perception). Nagel, together with Gullstrand and von Kries, based the third edition (Helmholtz, 1909–1911) of the *Handbuch* on the text from the first edition of 1867, rather than its revision of 1896. There is more than an implied criticism in Nagel's Preface that the second edition was inferior to the first. It was the third edition of the *Handbuch* that was translated into English by James Southall as *Helmholtz's Treatise on physiological optics* (1924/5). It was commissioned by the Optical Society of America to mark the centenary of Helmholtz's birth. As Nagel noted in his Preface to volume 1 "The demand for the book has not ceased and will not cease for a long time to come, for no new treatise has superseded Helmholtz's work" (p. x).

Sensory physiology was not the primary concern of Helmholtz. He was trained in medicine but was at heart a physicist who made intellectual forays into mathematics. His initial research was concerned with the conservation of energy. Helmholtz's advocacy of the principle was well received by his contemporaries but was treated less rapturously by his seniors. On the other hand, the invention of the ophthalmoscope in 1850 met with instant acclaim. It revealed a new world to ophthalmologists, and assisted greatly in the diagnosis and treatment of eye ailments. Helmholtz would take the instrument on his travels and delight his scientific acquaintances by demonstrating its use: "The ophthalmoscope is, perhaps, the most popular of my scientific performances" (Helmholtz, 1895, p. 278).

The instrument sparked his interests in physiological optics and it ushered in almost two decades of research on the senses. The ophthalmoscope was also part of an instrumental revolution that had engulfed the study of vision during the previous two decades (see Chapter 5), and Helmholtz was able to capitalize on it. The invention of instruments like the stereoscope, chronoscope, and stroboscope rendered many aspects of spatial vision open to experiment in a way that had been deemed impossible by Kant. In 1855, shortly before leaving Königsberg, Helmholtz delivered the Kant memorial lecture on the nature of human perception. In the lecture he outlined, in embryonic form, the principle that was to guide his subsequent empiricist theory of perception—unconscious inference (see Hatfield, 1990). Thereafter, the importance of experience in determining the perception of spatial attributes became a cornerstone of his vision.

Helmholtz's initial experimental studies, published in 1852, involved the nature of the stimulus to vision; he assessed and repudiated Brewster's (1830) analysis of sunlight into three spectral components. Helmholtz repeated Brewster's experiments adding more precise controls and found that the results did not diverge from Newtonian predictions. Nonetheless, it could well have been an illustration of 'the triple spectrum' by Brewster that led to Helmholtz's speculative spectral sensitivity curves. These are taken as the basis for what has been called the Young-Helmholtz, or trichromatic, theory of color vision, although Helmholtz did not initially embrace Young's (1802a) suggestion that there were three detectors for primary colors. Helmholtz became a more ardent proponent of Young's theory following publication of more detailed support for it by Maxwell (1855) using his color disc (see Turner, 1994). Helmholtz differentiated between additive and subtractive color mixing in volume 2 of the *Treatise*.

The next major problem Helmholtz tackled was the perplexing one of accommodation. In order to measure the curvatures of the optical surfaces in the living eye Helmholtz invented the ophthalmometer; he confirmed the speculations of Descartes (1664/1909) and Young (1793, 1801) that the lens changes curvature during accommodation, and Helmholtz proposed the mechanism by which this is achieved (see Chapter 4). The material on accommodation was incorporated and enlarged in the first volume of the *Treatise*, but the analysis of color vision was presented in the second volume. By that time, Helmholtz had examined several color blind individuals and had conducted experiments using Maxwell's color wheel. He had also initiated research on binocular vision, which assumed a pivotal importance in visual science following publication of Wheatstone's (1838) experiments on stereoscopic depth perception. Helmholtz invented the telestereoscope in 1857, although the large body of experiments concerned with binocular eye movements, the horopter, and stereoscopic vision were undertaken in the early 1860s. Wundt was his assistant between 1858 and 1862, and he too addressed the problem of space perception (Wundt, 1862), carrying Helmholtz's empiricism towards the realm of an independent discipline of psychology.

Helmholtz's knowledge of physics informed his studies in mathematics and physiology. Thus, his systematic treatment of light and sound provided a new rigor to understanding the early stages of vision and hearing. His experimental procedures were precise (although the results were based almost entirely on his own observations) as was his analysis of the ensuing results. Despite his close contact with Fechner, Helmholtz continued to place greater reliance on his own qualitative and quantitative observations than on any generalizations of them to other observers. In common with his contemporaries, the processes of perception were considered to be universal so that general principles could be derived from particular observations. Much of the polemic surrounding the heated debates in nineteenth century visual science was based on the conviction that personal perception was pervasive; individual differences were only taken seriously in areas like color blindness. Novel observations were accepted as fact when they were seen by another investigator. Helmholtz was at his most vulnerable when his observational skills were impugned (see Howard, 1999). However, his lasting influence in perception has related to neither this physical rigor nor his observational precision, rather to his epistemology as it was enunciated in volume 3 of the *Treatise* (see Hatfield, 1990; Turner, 1994). The final section of the volume, reviewing theories of vision, posed him the greatest problems and required the most protracted preparation. He acknowledged that little he wrote on the issue was novel, but he marshaled the arguments over a wider range of phenomena than others had done before. He summarized his position succinctly: "The sensations of the senses are tokens for our consciousness, it being left to our intelligence to learn how to comprehend their meaning" (1925/2000, p. 533). By adopting a starkly empiricist interpretation of perception, and by contrasting it so sharply with nativism, he reopened a debate that has reverberated throughout perception ever since. Indeed, Turner (1994) has argued that Helmholtz essentially redefined nativism and its historical lineage, so that he could place Hering squarely in that line and to contrast nativism with his own empiricist position.

SUMMARY

The senses were electrified in the nineteenth century. Initially, they were stimulated by galvanism and later the mode of nerve transmission was shown to be electrochemical. Galvanic or electrical stimulation provided a novel means of stimulating all the senses with the same source. Prior to that, mechanical stimulation (for example, by pressure applied to the eye) provided the common source of sensory stimulation. Electrical current produced more clearly defined experiences than pressure had done, and the characteristic experiences of light, sound, taste, touch, and smell could be elicited. An additional, and unexpected, consequence was that electrical stimulation around the ear led to feelings of postural instability and dizziness. The specific experiences that followed common (galvanic) stimulation resulted in a growing awareness that no matter how the senses were stimulated they yielded the same experience—light for the eye, sound for the ear, etc. Although this was voiced by several writers, it is associated most with Müller's enunciation of 'the doctrine of specific nerve energies'. This proved to be a catalyst for sensory physiologists to probe the characteristics of sensory systems in greater detail. Helmholtz applied it with acumen to vision and hearing, as well as to sensory qualities within those senses. He adapted Young's theory of three distinct color detectors to suggest that there were three types of fiber in the optic nerve with energies specific to the red, green and blue parts of the visible spectrum.

Specific energies were associated with nerves rather than regions in the brain because so little was known about the brain itself. Bell (1811/2000) had suggested a principle of specific nerve energies and tried to trace the course of the nerves from the senses to specific areas of the brain. Because this remained technically difficult wilder conjectures were entertained. Franz Joseph Gall (1758–1828) speculated about 'functions of the brain' and this was the title for his six volumes of 'observations on the possibility of determining the instincts, propensities and talents, and the moral and intellectual dispositions of men and animals by the configuration of the brain and head' (see Gall, 1835). It was also the title of Ferrier's (1876) more systematic approach to cortical localization. Indeed, localization of function provided one of the dominant themes of theory and research throughout the century. As Sherrington noted: 'Progress of knowledge in regard to the nervous system has been indissolubly linked with determination of localization of function in it' (1906, p. 270). By the end of the century, localized regions of the brain were associated with specific senses rather than energies specific to sensory nerves. The electrochemical manner in which neurons communicated was also better understood, the neuron doctrine had been accepted, and Sherrington introduced the concept of the synapse across which nerve impulses could be transmitted.

The specific senses themselves expanded during the century. Galvanism not only provided a clue to exposing the functions of the vestibular system but it also broke the sense of touch into several domains. Warm and cold spots were isolated, as were sensory circles on the skin. The many qualities associated with touch that had been voiced since antiquity were given anatomical and physiological support. The achromatic microscopes, introduced from the 1820s, exposed a vast array of cellular structures, some of which were specialized for particular senses. These became called receptors and the adequate stimuli for their excitation were also sought.

The growth of knowledge about the anatomy of the senses, and the dawning of their physiology, led writers to relate structure to function—to link characteristics of anatomy (and later physiology) with the experience that derived from their stimulation. Phenomena, like color vision could be interpreted in terms of cone receptors. From this time onwards, greater weight was assigned to structure than to function, and the desire to seek interpretations in terms of structure was firmly founded. Some sought to swim against this tide. Phenomenologists like Goethe, Purkinje, and Hering, examined subjective phenomena and queried the value of reductionism. Purkinje and Hering both added considerably to our knowledge of anatomy and physiology, but they did not consider that they provided the ultimate reference relative to which perceptual experience should be compared. Their tradition was continued in the twentieth century by Gestalt psychologists.

8

The Twentieth Century—The Multiplication of Illusion

Perception provides not only the roots to the tree of knowledge but also to the sapling of psychology. As was argued in Chapters 6 and 7, it was a dominant factor in the development of psychology and it remains one of the domains in which progress can be charted. The empiricist philosophers, from Locke onwards, routed the acquisition of knowledge through the senses, and subsequent empirical psychologists have sought to sign the way in greater detail. The first stage involved developing experimental procedures that would bring some precision in stimulus control akin to that adopted successfully in the physical sciences (Chapter 5). The second stage invested a similar concern with measurement of responses to stimulation (Chapter 6).

Natural philosophers in the nineteenth century devised the principles on which the perception of color, motion, and depth could be rendered experimentally tractable. Helmholtz (1867) was particularly attracted to the experimental approach and his students developed the methods further (see Cahan, 1993). The dominance of nineteenth-century German research in perception is clearly, though indirectly, reflected in what is perhaps the most thorough review of vision at the turn of the century: in Rivers' (1900) survey more than 75% of references were to German sources.

Boring (1942) remarked that Helmholtz carried the torch for philosophical empiricism in a hostile Kantian climate, as did his erstwhile assistant Wundt. However, their brands of empiricism were quite different. Helmholtz borrowed the notion of unconscious inference from Berkeley to account for characteristics of color and space perception, and the concept is still active in some theories. Wundt was more ambitious and applied empiricist and associationist ideas to account for consciousness itself. His ideas were carried to America by the likes of Edward Bradford Titchener (1867–1927; 1910), but his structuralist theory was not widely followed and faced the theories of both Gestalt and behaviorism (see Chapter 2).

The pursuit of perception in the twentieth century has followed many paths: it became even more interdisciplinary than it was in the nineteenth century. The strides made in physiology and computer science impacted critically on observation, experiment, and theory. The discovery by Hubel and Wiesel (1962) of single cells in the visual cortex that respond to oriented edges fuelled a fury of research. Similarly, the development of high speed digital computing changed the ways in which human information processing was conceived (see Gardner, 1985). Thus, many of the paths have been determined by advances in technology, which have rendered new aspects of perception experimentally tractable. Others have explored features of perception that were neglected in the nineteenth century.

One of these is the developmental dimension. Charles Darwin (1877) had earlier made a detailed record of his firstborn's development from a few days to over two years of age, and these were published in the journal *Mind*; they implicitly suggest that the development of the individual mirrors the evolution of species. Evolutionary theory transformed biology and it was the motive force in defining a distinct brand of American psychology. Uncovering the details of infant perception has been one of the achievements of twentieth century psychology.

THE DEVELOPMENTAL DIMENSION

Experiments on perception involve communicating the experimenter's requirements to an observer, and the discussion so far has been in terms of studying perception in someone who can communicate with language; but what about cases where this cannot be done? How is it possible to investigate perception in infants, in animals, or perhaps in people whose linguistic abilities are impaired? For these, the requirements of the experimenter must be communicated by some other means, and the response cannot be verbal. Clearly, it must be some action which is within the behavioral repertoire of the observer. Thus, for example, it may be possible to use the methods of conditioned learning to study discrimination between stimuli. If one response, like turning the head or raising a paw, can be conditioned to a red stimulus, and another to a green one, then we may be justified in concluding something about the ability to perceive color; provided of course that the discrimination is not based on some other characteristic like the brightness of the stimulus. If an infant spends more time looking at a picture of a face than at a random collection of lines, then this preference might demonstrate an ability to recognize faces as a special class of object. Clearly it would also be necessary to establish that these measurements did not simply reflect a preference for symmetrical patterns, or even for looking left rather than right. Such behavioral measures are not intrinsically different from verbal ones, and similar sorts of inference may be made from them. However they are less subject to biases, and the inferences are therefore likely to be more secure.

Infant Vision

William James remarked, from his armchair, that "The baby, assailed by eyes, ears, nose, skin, and entrails at once feels it all as one great blooming, buzzing confusion" (1890, p. 488). The conclusion concerning infantile confusion was based on the observation of their seemingly random and chaotic movements. More detailed scrutiny indicated that some aspects of behavior were systematic and could be used to determine what interests infants. Many novel methods were devised to study infant vision in the 1960s. For example, it was noted that infants spent different amounts of time fixating on visual patterns and so infant perceptual discrimination was inferred from the patterns of preferential fixation. Recordings of eye movements in infants only a few days old showed that they were concentrated on contours or corners of simple patterns. When a stimulus is presented many times the response to it typically declines or habituates. Habituation to repeated presentations of patterns provided another source of inference regarding discrimination, particularly when novel patterns were presented; if the infants dishabituated then it was assumed that the novel pattern was discriminated from the habituated pattern. Operant conditioning techniques were applied to demonstrate the emergence of perceptual constancies. These methods were refined and the course of perceptual development began to be charted.

In order to extract the spatial detail from an object it needs to be focused on the retina, and the state of focus will need to change for objects at different distances. This process of accommodation is poorly developed at birth and newborns can only focus on objects within their reach. Indeed, the receptors in the retina are not fully developed at birth nor are the nerve cells in the visual cortex, and so their development is likely to have a profound effect on what can be seen. It is not surprising, therefore, that the visual acuity of the newborn is more than ten times poorer than that of adults, but it improves rapidly in the first months of life until it reaches almost adult level at age six months. Similarly, infants in the first few months of life are not able to detect low contrast patterns (where the differences between the lightest and darkest parts are small) that are readily detectable by adults. The contributors to the books by Vital-Durand et al (1996) and Slater (1998) describe the capabilities of infants on a wide range of visual tasks.

VISUAL DEVELOPMENT

The cortical mapping of visual receptive fields had an unexpected influence on the age-old nativist/empiricist debate, providing fuel for both sides. Hubel and Wiesel (1963) demonstrated that receptive fields were present prior to visual experience but that they could be modified by it. This applied to both binocularity and orientation selectivity. For example, the responsiveness of cortical cells to stimulation by either eye, present at birth, could be modified by monocular deprivation from birth. The timing of such modification was critical; the sensitive period was in the first few months for kittens and monkeys. A similar approach was taken for examining human development. Naturally occurring conditions, like astigmatism or strabismus, can be corrected at different stages of development. Corrections made in the first few years of life proved beneficial, but those made thereafter had relatively little effect (see Blakemore, 1978, for a review of the early research).

Contour extraction was also considered to be one of the first tasks tackled by the visual systems of newborns, and many novel methods were devised to study them. For example, Fantz (1961) inferred infant perceptual discrimination from the patterns of differential fixation, and Bower (1966) used operant conditioning techniques for investigating the emergence of perceptual constancies. Fantz even suggested that there was an innate preference for viewing human faces, although the outline figures he used as stimuli had very little ecological validity, but his suggestions have been supported in subsequent research. Salapatek and Kessen (1966) recorded eye movements of infants only a few days old and found that they were concentrated on contours or corners. Habituation to repeated presentations of a stimulus provided another source of inference regarding discrimination. These methods were refined and the course of perceptual development began to be charted. From the late 1960s the principal stimulus for vision research became the sine-wave grating, and these were presented to infants, too.

THE NEW PHYSIOLOGY

Wundt's "New Psychology" was accompanied by a "New Physiology", which was actively pursued by Ferrier (1876, 1886), John Hughlings Jackson (1835–1911; 1863), Sherrington (1906) and others. The continuing research on color vision was driven by the physical control of the stimulus, and by increasing understanding of receptor function and color anomalies. Indeed, it was the concept of "schema", developed within this new physiology by Henry Head (1861–1940; 1920), that was applied by Bartlett to skilled tasks of memory and perception. According to Bartlett: "'Schema' refers to an active organization of past reactions, or of past experiences, which must always be supposed to be operating in the well-adapted organic response" (1932, p. 201). The constructive aspects of both memory and perception were emphasized at the expense of their holistic or sequential features. Perception was attached to a new type of theory linking perception to prediction and action.

Emphasis on the constructive and individual aspects of perception contradicted approaches that stressed perceptual constancy, and equations for quantifying this had been proposed by Brunswik (1928) and Thouless (1931). Both proposed ratios involving differences between perceived and projected values on the one hand and physical and projected on the other, although Thouless used logarithmic transformations in order to avoid anomalies that arose with the direct ratios. Thouless referred to perceptual constancy as "phenomenal regression to the real object", and provided plentiful evidence to support its operation for shape, size, orientation, brightness, and color perception.

The approach to perception adopted by Bartlett was applied to human operators of complex systems, like flight simulation (see Bartlett, 1946; Saito, 2000). The experimental research on perception in the 1940s harmonized with developments in cybernetics (Wiener, 1948), and Craik (1943) conflated the two by considering the human operator as a complex, self-organizing system. Craik's studies of visual adaptation had indicated that there was constant feedback from previous and concurrent stimulation, and that it could be modeled by physical processes. He wrote: "some of the flexibility of the perceptual process—for instance, the recognition of relational rather than absolute properties and of changes rather than constant stimulation, and a primitive type of abstraction—follows from the known properties of the physiological structure and can be imitated by physical mechanisms" (1940, reprinted in Craik, 1966, p. 6).

FEATURE DETECTORS

Research on patterned stimulation at the receptor level had proceeded throughout the first half of the century, but its pace quickened thereafter. The glimmerings of pattern processing beyond the receptors emerged in the 1950s, and were amplified in the 1960s. When recordings of nerve impulses could be made from individual cells in the visual pathway their adequate stimuli could be determined. Adrian (1928) coined the term 're-ceptive field' and Hartline (1938) applied it to describe the region of the receptor surface over which the action of light modified the activity of a neuron. It came as something of a surprise that retinal ganglion cells of frog responded to quite complex features of stimulation (like moving dark regions of a specific visual angle, resembling a bug), and stimulus properties that excited or inhibited neurons were generally called 'trigger features' (Barlow, 1953). Retinal ganglion cells of cat, on the other hand, were excited by rather simpler stimulus arrangements. Kuffler (1953) found that they were concentrically and antagonistically organized; if the center was excited by light the surround was inhibited, and vice versa. Such an arrangement served the detection of differences in luminance well, but steady states would have little effect, since excitation nullified inhibition. This pattern of neural activity was retained in the lateral geniculate body, but it underwent a radical change at the level of the visual cortex. Hubel and Wiesel (1962, 1968) found that single cells in primary visual cortex (V1), first of cat then of monkey, responded to specifically oriented edges. The receptive fields of visual cells could be classified hierachically accord-ing to the stimuli that excited them. Those orientation detectors that could be mapped using points of light were called simple; those with larger re-ceptive fields which would respond only to edges (preferably moving in a particular direction) were called complex; a class called hypercomplex responded to lines of a specific length or to a corner.

Physiologists refined the stimulus characteristics of trigger features thereafter, while psychologists sought their phenomenal counterparts. Al-most any experiment involving contours paid lip service to Hubel and Wiesel, despite the tenuousness of the links between particular phenom-ena and their underlying physiology. At least an appeal to trigger features was considered preferable to reliance on the speculative neurophysiology advanced by Köhler (1940). Spatial illusions, for example, attempted to rise above their enigmatic status by adopting this reductionist path. Despite the attractions of this approach the greatest success was found for contour repulsion (Blakemore et al, 1970). The alternative lure of illusions was to relate them to the traditional empiricist concept of constancy (Gregory, 1963). The links between perception and physiology were made explicit for the MAE resulting in an explosion of empirical studies examining their consequences. Barlow (1963) also investigated the link between visibility and retinal image motion using afterimages and optically stabilized retinal images.

The concept of channels or spatial filters emerged during the decade, and it was applied with particular rigor by Campbell and his colleagues to the detection of and adaptation to sine-wave gratings (see Campbell and Robson, 1968). The attraction of gratings was that they provided at one and the same time a definition of the stimulus and a theory of the response to it. Craik characteristically foresaw the principle behind these developments:

> "the action of various physical devices which 'recognize' or respond identically to certain simple objects can be treated in terms of such [mathematical] transformations. Thus the essential part of physical 'recognizing' instruments is usually a filter—whether it be a mechanical sieve, an optical filter, or a tuned electrical circuit—which 'passes' only quantities of the kind it is required to identify and rejects all others." (1966, pp. 44–45)

Two Visual Pathways

As the functional specialization of visual areas of the cortex became better understood, so there have also been suggestions that different regions of the visual brain are organized into two rather different kinds of processing pathway or stream. An early idea was that of "two visual systems" (Ungerleider and Mishkin, 1982) which developed the distinction drawn in the 1960's between the "what" and "where" systems of the cortex and superior colliculi, respectively. Ungerleider and Mishkin's proposal was that there were two distinct cortical streams of processing, the inferotemporal pathway or "ventral" route allowing the detailed perception and recognition of an object (its size, shape, orientation and color) with the posterior parietal or "dorsal" route allowing the perception of an object's location.

Milner and Goodale (1995) produced an important development of this theory by suggesting that these two parallel streams of visual processing are actually separately specialized for *action* (dorsal stream) and for visual *experience* of the world (ventral stream). The dorsal route is said to be the evolutionarily older visual system which enables a creature to navigate through the world and catch prey. The ventral route is developed particularly in primates to allow the detailed perception and interpretation of objects and, possibly, a conscious awareness of these. Amongst the evidence for their theory was the performance of a single patient who as a result of brain injury was almost completely unable to recognize or describe the shapes of objects, but was able to orient shapes appropriately in order to do things with them. For example, the patient could not match the orientations of a card with a slot placed in different orientations in front of her, but her performance was almost normal when the task was changed to reaching out and posting the card into the slot.

The distinction between conscious form perception and perception for action assists the interpretation of the puzzling phenomena of "blindsight" (Weiskrantz, 1986). Human patients who had damage to the visual cortex which left them apparently blind could nevertheless respond much better than chance when asked to make certain kinds of visual judgment—particularly about the locations of lights which moved or had abrupt onsets. It seemed that not only was there residual visual capacity in areas of the visual system outside visual cortex, but that this activity apparently did not reach consciousness. The blindsight patients were not aware of the lights they pointed to, but felt as though they were guessing, or using some "feeling" about the target.

THE INFORMATION REVOLUTION

Information theory was developed in the context of telecommunications, and the mathematical measurement of information was formalized by Shannon and Weaver (1949); its powerful impact on perception was felt in the 1950s. Miller (1957) linked the concept of limited information capacity to absolute perceptual judgments. Attneave (1954) devised procedures to determine the locations of highest information in simple patterns. They corresponded to boundaries of brightness (contours) and particularly to abrupt changes in contour direction (corners). Support for the significance of contours in perception derived from two other sources—single unit recordings from various levels in the visual pathway, and scanning eye movements. Indeed, early attempts to stabilize the retinal image by compensating for any involuntary eye movements resulted in disappearance of the target (Ditchburn and Ginsborg, 1952; Riggs and Ratliff, 1952).

However, it was the qualitative concept of information processing rather than quantitative information measures that was to have lasting appeal. The perceiver was conceived of as a limited capacity information processor, and the information could be filtered, filed, or reformulated on the basis of stored events. Broadbent's (1958) model was amongst the first to formalize and represent pictorially the putative processing stages. He stated that the "advantage of information theory terms is . . . that they emphasize the relationship between the stimulus now present and the others that might have been present but are not" (1958, pp. 306–307). Thus, Broadbent combined Bartlett's approach of examining skilled tasks with Craik's modeling metaphor.

Theoretical attention shifted towards pattern recognition by both humans and computers because they were both thought of as information processors or manipulators of symbolic information. The patterns were typically outline figures or alphanumeric symbols and rival theories, based on template matching and feature analysis (Uhr, 1966), vied for simulated supremacy at recognition and one result was pandemonium (Selfridge, 1959)! Sutherland sounded a cautionary note on this endeavor that was not generally heeded then nor has been subsequently:

> "Patterns are of importance to animals and man only in so far as they signify objects. It is the recognition of objects that is vital for survival and as a guide to action, and the patterned stimulation of our receptors is of use only because it is possible to construct from it the nature of the object from which it emanated." (Sutherland, 1973, p. 157)

While there were dangers in the oversimplification of the stimulus, the approach also allowed important tools to be developed to probe discrete visual achievements. One example was the random dot stereogram developed by Julesz (1960). Wheatstone (1838) had employed outline figures for his stereoscope in order to reduce any monocular cues to depth, but he was acutely aware that some remained. Julesz employed the dawning power of the computer to produce pairs of matrices of black and white dots, the central areas of which were displaced with respect to the common backgrounds, and hence disparate. The displays looked amorphous when viewed by each eye alone, but when viewed binocularly patterns gradually arose or descended from the background. This not only spawned a new area called cyclopean perception (Julesz, 1971), but the technique was adopted in the clinic as a test for stereoscopic depth perception. Analogous developments in the temporal domain produced random dot kinematograms which were used by Braddick (1974) and others to make distinguish between different types of motion processing for briefly presented patterns.

THE MACHINE METAPHOR

The machine metaphor was to prove particularly attractive to experimental psychologists, although only relatively simple machines were enlisted initially. For example, Craik worked with analogue devices as the digital computer was still embryonic. Nonetheless, he did formalize the input, processing, and output components of servo-systems in a manner that could be applied to digital computers:

"The essential feature of the sensory device is its ability to translate the change
it is to measure... into some form of energy which can be amplified and used to
drive the restoring cause... The next part is what may be called the computing
device and controller, which determines the amount and kind of energy to be
released from the effector unit to restore equilibrium... The final part is the
power unit or effector (equivalent to the muscles in men and animals) which
restores the state of equilibrium." (Craik, 1966, pp. 23–24)

When computing machines increased in speed and complexity the tasks
that they could simulate became more complex. Concepts from engineer-
ing, like information and self-organization, were also integrated with a
growing knowledge of neurophysiology resulting in the computer becoming a metaphor for the brain.

The computers mounted for this metaphorical odyssey were digital
and serial, but at around the same time the ground was being laid for principles of parallel processing. McCulloch and Pitts' (1943) model of the neuron
provided the foundation for later connectionist models of pattern recognition, and the networks connecting perception to its underlying physiology
were further woven by Hebb (1949) in his speculative synthesis of perception and learning. Hebb proposed that perceptual learning takes place
when assemblies of cells fire together; their reverberating activity resulted
in synaptic changes which further increased the probability of the nerves
firing together. The functions of cell-assemblies and phase sequences were
based on his neurophysiological postulate: "When an axon of cell A is near
enough to excite cell B and repeatedly or persistently takes part in firing it,
some growth process or metabolic change takes place in one or both cells
such that A's efficiency, as one of the cells firing B, is increased" (Hebb, 1949,
p. 62). Hebb's postulate is taken as providing the foundation for current
connectionist models of recognition and learning despite the fact that the
principle had been enunciated over 70 years earlier by Bain (see Chapter 6).
Hebb later applied the concepts to account for a wide range of phenomena,
from stabilized retinal images to sensory deprivation (see Hebb, 1980).

Bartlett's emphasis on the constructive nature of perception found an
echo in the 'New Look' experiments, like those reported by Bruner and
Postman (1947), where motivation was considered to interact with perception. Similar experimental investigations had been undertaken earlier
by Brunswik (1934, 1935) who examined the perceived sizes of postage
stamps of different value. Ames' many demonstrations of the ambiguities
of stimulation and their perceptual resolutions (see Ittelson, 1952) were
also accorded renewed attention in this cognitive climate. In these heady
postwar years personality flirted with perception, but their liaison was
not lasting. Certain subthreshold recognition phenomena were brought
to their perceptual defense (McGinnies, 1949), but the sober verdict was

not in their favour: "It would seem wise to regard with great caution the existence of limitations on speed and accuracy of perception imposed by personality factors, at least in normal observers" (Vernon, 1970, p. 237).

COMPUTERS AND VISION

Craik, as well as Turing (see Millican and Clark, 1996), anticipated that the computer would be a powerful tool to simulate theories of perception, as well as providing a metaphor for the processes of perception and cognition themselves. Since the late 1960s, the study of visual perception had been profoundly influenced by computers. As well as allowing scientists to collect or to analyze data more quickly, the digital computer provided a tool for the laboratory scientist to develop new ways of testing the visual system with novel kinds of visual displays. The move away from reliance on oscilloscopes to present sine wave and other simple patterns facilitated the increasing use of more naturalistic patterns, as well as those which can be constructed and manipulated in controlled ways. Computer developments also enabled the better recording of eye movements and the linkage of eye movements to changes in display features, allowing a number of groups to conduct ingenious experiments into the control of eye-movements in reading (see Rayner, 1978; Findley & Gilchrist, 2003).

Marr (1982) set out to develop a complete framework for vision, spanning the very lowest level processes within the retina up to the process of visual object recognition. The key feature of Marr's theory was that vision can be understood at different levels. The first 'computational' level is a theory of the task that the visual system is to solve, and an understanding of the constraints that can enable solution of that task. The second level, of 'representation and algorithm', is a means of achieving the task, and the final 'hardware implementation' level describes how the brain, or a computer, actually implements these algorithms in neural tissue or silicon. Marr argued that:

> "For the subject of vision, there *is* no single equation or view that explains everything. Each problem has to be addressed from several points of view—as a problem in representing information, as a computation capable of deriving that representation, and as a problem in the architecture of a computer capable of carrying out both things quickly and reliably." (Marr, 1982, p. 5, original italics)

In addition to presenting a unified approach to different topics within vision, Marr and his colleagues also presented a theory of the different stages of representation (called primal sketch, $2^1/_2$D sketch, 3D models) involved in the interpretation of an image on the retina. In so doing, Marr distinguished a stage which tried to make explicit the three-dimensional layout of the world with respect to the viewer (the $2^1/_2$D sketch), potentially useful for action in the world from the more abstract 3D models which allowed object recognition.

THE NEW IMAGE

The activity of the human brain has been studied using external measurements of electrical and/or magnetic activity from the early twentieth century. In 1929, Hans Berger (1873–1941) discovered that electrical activity could be measured by placing electrical conductors on the human scalp and amplifying and transcribing the resulting signals. This electroencephalogram (EEG) was an early and important tool for diagnosing brain damage, but also provided a research tool for examining electrical responses to events (event related potentials, or ERPs). Productive research using ERPs to map cognitive activity in the brain was conducted in the last decades of the twentieth century, but there have always been problems of interpretation due to limited information about the spatial origins of ERP components. Subsequent developments of dense-mapped ERP and the related technique of using a magnetometer to record the magnetoencephalogram (MEG) and detect magnetic event-related fields (ERFs) attracted much more attention. In part, this was because the precise temporal information gained by these techniques could complement the spatial precision achieved with newer techniques of brain imaging.

Another technique based on magnetic fields generated in the cortex is called transcranial magnetic stimulation (TMS). Following the lead of Thompson (1910), alternating magnetic fields can be applied to restricted regions of the head in order to stimulate or to disrupt neural activity in some way. In TMS a magnetic coil is positioned over a particular area of a subject's head and a current is briefly passed through the coil. The magnetic field so produced induces an electrical current in a specific part of the subject's brain (see Walsh and Cowey, 1998). The timing of such TMS is very precise and so it can be applied at known intervals after some visual stimulation has taken place. It is as if the technique produced virtual patients because the disruption is temporary.

Neuroimaging of visual function in normal human brains proceeded apace in the last decade of the twentieth century. Initially positron emission tomography (PET) scans were used to examine the regional cerebral blood flow when volunteers looked at different kinds of visual patterns. A colored pattern produced activation in regions corresponding to monkey V1, V2 and V4. When the same pattern was shown in shades of gray, the activation in V4 was much reduced, suggesting that V4 was an area for the analysis of color in humans. Similarly, a moving compared with a static pattern produced specific activation of "human V5", and illusory motion seen in static patterns has also been attributed to this area (see Zeki, 1993, 1999).

These are sophisticated ways of examining human brain activity during perceptual processing but all techniques have drawbacks, and experiments must be designed with great care if they are to be clearly interpretable. In comparison to PET scans, magnetic resonance imaging (MRI) yields more precise spatial resolution. Developments in functional MRI (fMRI) allow activity to be temporally as well as spatially mapped, and it will be work using fMRI combined with developments in other technologies with more temporal precision such as TMS and MEG which is likely to hold the key to understanding the neural processing of visual information by people.

The growth in visual neuroscience has revealed an increasingly complex, though elegant, picture, and diagrams of visual areas, their interconnections and their microstructure, are likely to get increasingly complicated. For example, the route map of primate visual systems charted by Van Essen et al (1992) would place great demands on a navigator. Evidence for the analytic separation of different aspects of the visual scene—motions, forms, colors, etc, raises the question of how these elements become associated, or "bound". In addition to the problem of binding within the visual domain, however, there is the problem of how, and when, different modalities (vision, touch, hearing) become integrated or otherwise influence each other.

NATURAL IMAGES

Much of the computational research in vision prior to Marr made use of simplified images, such as worlds comprised of blocks. Marr's work on early visual processing stressed the perception of, and constraints on, processing natural images. Psychophysics, however, has tended to continue studying the perception of simple dots, lines and gratings. Yet in the last decades of the century one particular class of visual pattern became of increasing interest to both perceptual and cognitive psychologists—the human face (see Bruce, 1986).

Face perception had been investigated earlier in the century, but the stimuli employed were typically schematic outlines manipulated in artificial ways. Experiments concerning recognition and identification of the human face assumed a novel significance, due in no small part to the advances in computer image manipulation. One enduring theme in the study of face processing has been the question of whether faces are processed by special mechanisms. In addition, there was widespread public concern about legal cases of mistaken identity, demonstrating the fallibility of the human eye-witness to a crime. During the same period research into the perceptual processing of face patterns was also growing, particularly emphasising how face processing seemed to be based upon some special sensitivity to the configuration or holistic pattern of the upright face, with particular importance to relatively coarse-scale information (Yin, 1969). Roman potters had made similar manipulations of facial inversion in the second century (Wade, Kovács, and Vidnyánzky, 2003).

Developments in computer graphics enabled manipulations of photographic quality images of the human face in ways that had only previously been available to cartoonists. For example, the technique of morphing allowed researchers to produce and transform characteristics of faces: they could be aged or given characteristics of the opposite sex (Benson and Perrett, 1991). Such developments have affected not only the understanding of how faces are perceived but also have allowed novel explorations of the basis of facial attractiveness.

THE NEW VERIDICALITY

Gibson (1966) sought to stem the cognitive current and developed a novel theory that owed more to Thomas Reid (1764) than to his own contemporaries:

> "When the senses are considered as perceptual systems, all theories of perception become at one stroke unnecessary. It is no longer a question of how the mind operates on the deliverances of sense, or how past experience can organize the data, or even how the brain can process the inputs of the nerves, but simply how information is picked up." (Gibson, 1966, p. 319)

Gibson abolished the senses when he replaced them by perceptual systems. That is, the distinction between sensation and perception was abandoned, and perceptual systems afforded useful information for interaction with the external world:

> "We shall have to conceive the external senses in a new way, as active rather than passive, as systems rather than channels, and as interrelated rather than mutually exclusive. If they function to pick up information, not simply to arouse sensations, this function should be denoted by a different term. They will here be called *perceptual systems*." (1966, p. 47, original italics)

Moreover, there was considered to be a perfect correlation between the stimulus and its perception; no stages of representation were involved in perception. The doctrine of specific nerve energies, that had informed almost all studies of the senses since the time of Müller, emphasized the indirectness of perception. The brain had access only to the nerve signals initiated by external objects, not to the objects themselves. Gibson cast aside this tradition in favor of direct perception. However, Gibson retained separate perceptual systems which he called orienting, auditory, haptic-somatic, tasting and smelling, and visual.

Despite Gibson's pejorative purview of conventional perceptual experiments, the strongest support for his position derived therefrom: simplified dynamic dot patterns could be recognized far more easily than static ones (Johannson, 1964). Gibson's ideas established a new field of "ecological" optics which has been tilled by many.

ILLUSIONS AND VERIDICALITY

As we have seen in earlier chapters, in order for an illusion to be so considered two measurements of the stimulus are required. The most common are the physical characteristics of the stimulus and some suitable index of its perception. Illusions were studied in the late nineteenth century because they were not amenable to the extant physiology—hence their place in psychology. They also fostered the use of two-dimensional stimuli in perceptual experiments, giving vision the aura of scientific respectability. Such stimulus manipulation is grist to the modern neuroscientists mill, and so that a common stimulus language binds vision and neuroscience—the language of single stimulus dimensions. However, this degree of common stimulus control has nurtured a new neuroreductionism, and illusions are often interpreted in terms of underlying signs of neural activity. The giant step to solid objects remains elusive both for illusions and for neuroscience.

Illusions can provide signs for the neuroscientists to pursue. It is doubtful whether neuroscientists can provide signs to direct research on illusions until there is an adequate neurophysiological theory of visual processing. At present, there are sets of sub-theories which are over-interpreted in terms of visual psychophysics. It might seem unreasonable to demand a theory of neuroscience before applying it to visual perception, but it is realistic. It will take a long time, but that might be shorter than making many false starts, as has happened in the last decades of the twentieth century. It would also have the positive effect of making us concentrate on perception rather than its putative underpinnings. The conundrum is that there is a demand to conduct theory-driven experiments, and most of the theories are based on inadequate neuroscience. The need for a good perceptual taxonomy becomes pressing under such circumstances.

Many attempts have been made throughout the century to classify illusions in a manner that will facilitate interpreting them. For example,

Gregory (1966, 2000, 2003) has presented a fascinating classification of illusions, in terms of ambiguities, distortions, paradoxes, and fictions. He has also pointed to the difficulty of defining what an illusion is. The interest in the physiological and cognitive categories of illusions is that interpretations at this level are no longer feasible. What is sought for these is an internal correlation with perception—either in terms of neurophysiological signals for the physiological or inferential processes for the cognitive. The point worth making again here is that we are only dealing with correlations, and the tenuous the link between correlation and causation is well known.

Illusions freed psychology from physiology at its birth, now it is in danger of being strangled by them. The virtue of Gregory's classification is that it is tied to perception rather than to neuroscience: it emphasizes the primacy of measurements of vision over measurements of intervening processes.

SUMMARY

In the context of the perceptual process, the twentieth century was the age of illusion. The technological advances that were introduced expanded the ways in which stimuli could be presented so that novel phenomena were discovered and old ones were given new twists. Moreover, the responses elicited by the stimuli could be analyzed with far greater sophistication: dynamic processes like eye movements could be fractionated and neural activity could be sampled in alert observers.

However, the illusion of the century has not been a specific phenomenon but a preoccupation with a particular type of stimulus—the two-dimensional display. Drawings can easily be made and manipulated to produce stimuli for experiments. The task becomes easier when computer graphics are enlisted. Visual science has been seduced by such stimulus simplicity. It is evident in the topics that have been described in this chapter. Infant vision has been investigated predominantly with the stimuli that infants would never naturally encounter—two-dimensional displays rather than three-dimensional objects. A great deal has been discovered about the limits of vision in infants using such procedures—what they can discriminate at different developmental stages. However, we know little about the objects that they can discriminate because equivalent experiments have not been conducted. Indeed, the same applies to all aspects of object recognition. We know a lot about recognizing pictures of objects but not very much about object recognition.

This enchantment with pictorial images has been enhanced with the introduction of computer graphics. More complicated pictures can be produced. They can even be paired and presented in head-mounted displays to simulate real scenes. The naturalistic images referred to in this chapter are typically captured by a camera and may be presented in sequence to appear to be moving. Here there is a dual simulation—of depth and of motion.

The seductive allure of the pictorial image has amplified the legacy of Kepler, the belief that the first stage of vision is a two-dimensional image in the eye. The task of the theorist is then seen as restoring the third-dimension. An impressive array of neurophysiological results can be brought to bear on this problem: single cells in the visual cortex are excited by particular stimulus features and different visual modules process those features further. Most of the information is derived from the ideal assay for Kepler's legacy—an anaesthetized animal with a nonmoving eye. Neuroimaging techniques for studying human perception have generally supported these conclusions. Of course, the stimuli used in the constrained confines of the devices are pictorial. Much has been learned from the use of two-dimensional stimuli but sight must not be lost of the goal of perceptual research—understanding our interactions with a world of solid structures.

9

Conclusions

The history of studies of the perceptual process is essentially a history of art and illusion. Art has been produced by humans for thousands of years and it involves distilling aspects of perception and re-presenting them in ways that can be recognized by others. Paintings on cave walls are highly sophisticated because they can be recognized by observers who have had no contact with the civilizations that produced them. Perhaps it is this universality of the pictorial image that has proved so attractive to both observers and theorists of vision. When it was combined by Kepler with the principles of image formation in the eye its appeal was overwhelming. The metaphor of the picture-in-the-eye drives contemporary visual science in much they same way it did students in the seventeenth century. We now know much more about the optics of the eye and the physiology of vision, but the conceptual problem posed remains essentially unchanged.

Perception has been a continuing concern of philosophers for many centuries. A common thread that has linked the approaches to perception over this time-span has been a concern with the unusual and atypical; that is with illusions. Illusions have been defined in many different ways, but all have involved comparison with some reference. The constancies of perception have not received the same concerted attention. Another way of viewing this is that the constant concerns of students of perception have been those of change. Adaptation occurs when there is change to new conditions. In the context of perception, it refers either to changes with constant stimulation or to adjustments with varying stimulation. An example of the former is the change in the apparent intensity of a light source when observed for some time. A common instance of the latter is dark and light adaptation. Such changes in perception have often been commented upon, but their detailed study has awaited the machinery and methods of modern science. The instrumental and response revolutions in the nineteenth century enlarged the scope of perception. Stroboscopes, thaumatropes, stereoscopes, tachistoscopes and chronoscopes were all employed to examine old phenomena in new ways and often add novel phenomena to the traditional armory.

All these instruments were enlisted in broadening the scope of experimental psychology from the latter half of the nineteenth century. They enabled a range of new phenomena to be demonstrated and quantified. The stereoscope represents the instrument par excellence that transformed visual science. By isolating and manipulating stimulus variables and examining them with the methods of physics, the vista of an experimental science was exposed to the purview of perception. The instrument in its many guises remains at the heart of research on binocular vision to this day. The development of moving pictures has its origins in the phenakistoscope and stroboscopic disc. The experimental study of motion aftereffects was initiated by Plateau (1849) with a variant of his phenakistoscope (see Wade and Verstraten, 1998). Wertheimer (1912) commenced his studies on the phi-phenomenon using a phenakistoscope, and completed them with a Schumann tachistoscope. The rapid growth of what Exner (1873) described as reaction time studies, following Donders' (1869) experiments, was assisted by the use of chronoscopes. The adoption of some of these instruments by Helmholtz (1867) accelerated their wider use. Different types of memory drum were developed from the kymograph Müller and Schumann (1894) had used for the experiments that they believed to be replications and improvements of Ebbinghaus's studies (Heller, 1986). Brief illumination by electric sparks, or exposure of patterns in the tachistoscope, became a standard method for avoiding the influence of eye movements in visual tasks, like reading (Erdmann and Dodge, 1898).

However, it is evident that the benefits of the devices were not universally accepted. The ease with which some aspects of the stimulus could be controlled tended to result in the neglect of other, less manipulable, dimensions of stimulation (see Wundt, 1900). In the case of the stereoscope, it was simple to manipulate retinal disparities. Despite the fact that Wheatstone (1852) had demonstrated an interaction between retinal disparity and convergence, almost all attention has been addressed to the former to such an

extent that stereoscopic depth perception tends to be equated with disparity (see Wade, 1987). The restricted dimensions of tachistoscopic displays
focused experimental attention on the processing of single words or short
phrases rather than sentences. It has been said of the tachistoscope that:

> "Methodologically, its purpose is the accurate measurement of exposure times.
> However, it led to an emphasis on to the unmoving eye and static objects ....
> Moreover, technical limitations of the apparatus, e.g. the so-called 'window
> size', the minimum exposure duration or the maximum rate of successive
> frames, determined specific ways in which questions were formulated." (Heller,
> 1988, p. 38)

Accordingly, the slicing of time into small segments by both stroboscopes
and tachistoscopes led to the view that normal vision involves such sequences of discrete images, processed by a briefly stationary eye. Perhaps
one of the most trenchant attacks on this approach was made by Neisser
(1976):

> "Subjects are shown isolated letters, words, occasionally line drawings or pic-
> tures, but almost never objects. These stimuli are not brought into view in any
> normal way. Usually they materialize in a previously blank field, and they often
> disappear again so soon that the viewer has no chance to look at them properly.
> They are drawn as if suspended magically in space, with no background, no
> depth, and no visible means of support." (p. 34)

Thus, removing the perception of space and time from its object base is not
without its problems.

At present the computer, using a display screen similar to the oscillo-
scope, has taken over practically all the experimental procedures used to
examine the perception of space and time. Stimuli can be presented briefly
and/or in succession, split fields can be used to produce stereopairs, and
the responses subjects make to the patterns can be accurately timed. Moreover, interactions are now possible, such that the stimuli displayed can be
contingent on a response or even an eye movement, and they can be dynamic. Experiments are now performed that formerly were either very difficult to conduct or even impossible to construct, but whether the computer-
generated stimulus manipulations are always an advantage is questionable
because of their tenuous relation to objects in three-dimensional space.

Kant (1786) maintained that psychology could not aspire to become
a science because its data consisted of thoughts about objects rather than
the objects themselves. Psychology, in contrast to other natural sciences,
could not be analyzed into its constituent parts, and this was most evident
to Kant in the context of space and time. The instruments developed in
the nineteenth and twentieth centuries did indeed demonstrate that the
perception of space could be analyzed into its constituent parts, and that

presentation time could be sectioned into short intervals; moreover, such investigations resulted in reliable phenomena. Psychology started to collect its specimens, as biology had done at an earlier period. The instruments achieved a feat that Kant had considered impossible: they removed space and time from their object base. Newton had established that color could be examined independently of objects. Wheatstone's stereoscope, similarly removed binocular depth perception from its object base. The conditions for experimental manipulations of space and time in the laboratory were in place, and they awaited the development of methods for the quantification of the ensuing perception. This was to arrive with Fechner's psychophysics. The instruments not only broadened the scope of perceptual psychology, but they also constrained the manner in which stimuli could be presented or manipulated. These constraints have both fashioned the nature of the questions that can be addressed, and they tend to be represented in the single instrument that has replaced them all.

The lure of light and its many effects continues. The dominance of research on vision should not blind us to the other senses and their manifold interactions. To return to the issue with which this book commenced, the senses serve to guide our actions in order to secure our survival. Perception and action are directed to objects in space, the principle we should not let fade from sight.

References

Addams, R. (1834). An account of a peculiar optical phænomenon seen after having looked at a moving body. *London and Edinburgh Philosophical Magazine and Journal of Science, 5,* 373–374.

Addams, R. (1835). Optische Täuschung nach Betrachtung eines in Bewegung begriffenen Körpers. *Annalen der Physik und Chemie, 34,* 348.

Adrian, E.D. (1928). *The basis of sensation.* London: Christophers.

Aguilonius, F. (1613). *Opticorum libri sex. Philosophis juxta ac mathematicis utiles.* Antwerp: Moretus.

Aitken, J. (1878). On a new variety of ocular spectrum. *Proceedings of the Royal Society of Edinburgh, 10,* 40–44.

Albert, D. M., & Edwards, D. D. (1996). *The history of ophthalmology.* Cambridge, MA: Blackwell Science.

Alberti, L. B. (1435/1966). *On painting.* Trans. J. R. Spencer. New Haven: Yale University Press.

Alhazen (1572). *Opticae thesaurus.* F. Risner (Ed.) Basel: Gallia.

d'Almeida, J.-C. (1858). Nouvel appareil stéréoscopique. *Comptes Rendus Hebdomadaires des Séances de l'Académie des Sciences, 47,* 61–63.

Aquapendente, F. H. ab (1600). *De visione de voce de auditu.* Venice: Bolzetta.

Arnold, H. J. P. (1977). *William Henry Fox Talbot. Pioneer of photography and man of science.* London: Hutchinson Benham.

Ash, M. G. (1995). *Gestalt psychology in German culture, 1890–1967. Holism and the quest for objectivity.* Cambridge: Cambridge University Press.

Attneave, F. (1954). Some informational aspects of visual perception. *Psychological Review, 61,* 183–193.

Augustin, F. L. (1803). *Versuch einer vollständigen systematischen Geschichte der galvanischen Elek-tricität und ihre medizinischen Anwendung.* Berlin: Felisch.

Averroes (Abu'l Walid ibn Rushd). (1961). *Averroes Epitome of Parva Naturalia.* Trans. H. Blumberg. Cambridge, MA: Mediaeval Academy of America.

Bacon, F. (1625/1857). *Sylva sylvarum: or a natural history.* In J. Spedding, R. L. Ellis, and D. D. Heath (Eds.) *The works of Francis Bacon,* Vol. 2. London: Longman, Simpkin, Hamilton, Wittaker, Bain, Hodgson, Wasbourne, Bohn, Richardson, Houlston, Bickers and Bush, Willis and Sotheran, Cornish, Booth, and Snow.

Bacon, R. (1614). *Perspectiva.* J. Combachii (Ed.) Frankfurt: Hummij.

Bain, A. (1855). *The senses and the intellect.* London: Parker.

Bain, A. (1873). *Mind and body. The theories of their relation.* London: Henry King.

Bain, A. (1904). *Autobiography.* London: Longmans, Green.

Baird, J.W. (1903). The influence of accommodation and convergence upon the perception of depth. *American Journal of Psychology, 14,* 150–200.

Baltrusaitis, J. (1976). *Anamorphic art.* Trans. W. J. Strachan. London: Chadwyck-Healey.

Bárány, R. (1913). Der Schwindel und seine Beziehungen zum Bogengangapparat des inneren Ohres. Bogengangapparat und Kleinhirn. (Historische Darstellung. Eigene Untersuchun-gen.) *Naturwissenschaften, 1,* 396–401.

Barbaro, D. (1569). *La pratica della perspettiva.* Venice: Borgominieri.

Barlow, H. B. (1953). Summation and inhibition in the frog's retina. *Journal of Physiology, 119,* 69–88.

Barlow, H. B. (1963). Slippage of contact lenses and other artifacts in relation to fading and regeneration of supposedly stable retinal images. *Quarterly Journal of Experimental Psy-chology, 15,* 36–51.

Bartlett, F. C. (1932). *Remembering: A study in experimental and social psychology.* Cambridge: University Press.

Bartlett, F. C. (1946). Obituary notice. Kenneth J. W. Craik, 1914–1945. *British Journal of Psy-chology, 36,* 109–116.

Baumann, C. (2002). *Der Physiologe Ewald Hering (1834–1918).* Frankfurt: Hänsel-Hohenhausen.

Beare, J. I. (1906). *Greek theories of elementary cognition from Alcmaeon to Aristotle.* Oxford: Clarendon.

Bell, C. (1803). *The anatomy of the human body.* Vol. 3. London: Longman, Rees, Cadell and Davies. (Reprinted in N. J. Wade (2000). (Ed.) *The emergence of neuroscience in the nineteenth century.* Vol. 1. London: Routledge/Thoemmes Press.)

Bell, C. (1811). *Idea of a new anatomy of the brain; Submitted for the observations of his friends,* London: Published by the author; printed by Strahan and Preston. (Reprinted in N. J. Wade (2000). (Ed.) *The emergence of neuroscience in the nineteenth century.* Vol. 1. London: Routledge/Thoemmes Press.)

Bell, C. (1823). On the motions of the eye, in illustration of the uses of the muscles and of the orbit. *Philosophical Transactions of the Royal Society, 113,* 166–186.

Bell, C. (1826). On the nervous circle which connects the voluntary muscles with the brain. *Philosophical Transactions of the Royal Society, 116,* 163–173.

Benson, P. J. & Perrett, D. I. (1991) Synthesising continuous-tone caricatures. *Image and Vision Computing, 9,* 123–129.

Berkeley, G. (1709). *An essay towards a new theory of vision.* Dublin: Pepyat.

Bidder, F. (1839). Zur Anatomie der Retina, insbesondere zur Würdigung der stabförmigen Körper in derselben. *Archiv für Anatomie und Physiologie und wissenschaftliche Medizin,* 371–385

Blakemore, C. (1978). Maturation and modification in the developing visual system. In R. Held, H. W. Leibowitz, & H.-L. Teuber (Eds.) *Handbook of sensory physiology*. Vol. VIII. *Perception*. (pp. 377–436). New York: Springer.

Blakemore, C., Carpenter, R. H. S. & Georgeson, M. A. (1970). Lateral inhibition between orientation detectors in the human visual system. *Nature, 228,* 37–39.

Blix, M. (1884). Experimentelle Beiträge zur Lösung der Frage über die specifische Energie der Hautnerven. *Zeitschrift für Biologie, 20,* 141–156.

Bodenheimer, F. S. (1958). *The history of biology: An introduction.* London: Dawson.

Boissier de Sauvages, F. (1772). *Nosologie méthodique, ou distribution des maladies en classes, en genres et en especes, suivant l'esprit de Sydenham, & la méthode des botanistes.* Lyon: Bruyset.

Boring, E. G. (1929). *A history of experimental psychology.* New York: Appleton- Century.

Boring, E. G. (1942). *Sensation and perception in the history of experimental psychology.* New York: Appleton-Century.

Boring, E. G. (1950). *A history of experimental psychology.* 2nd ed. New York: Appleton-Century.

Borschke, A., & Hescheles, L. (1902). Über Bewegungsnachbilder. *Zeitschrift für Psychologie und Physiologie der Sinnesorgane, 27,* 387–398.

Bouguer, P. (1729). *Essai d'optique, sur la gradation de la lumière.* Paris: Jombert.

Bouguer, P. (1760). *Traité d'optique sur la gradation de la lumière.* Paris: Guerin and Delatour.

Bouguer, P. (1961). *Optical treatise on the gradation of light.* Trans. W. E. Knowles Middleton. Toronto: University of Toronto Press.

Bowditch, H. P., & Hall, G. S. (1881). Optical illusions of motion. *Journal of Physiology, 3,* 297–307.

Bower, T. G. (1966). The visual world of infants. *Scientific American, 215 (12),* 80–92.

Bowman, W. (1849). *Lectures on the parts concerned in the operations on the eye, and on the structure of the retina, delivered at the Royal London Ophthalmic Hospital, Moorfields, June 1847.* London: Longmans, Brown, Green, and Longmans.

Braddick, O.J. (1974). A short-range process in apparent motion. *Vision Research, 14,* 519–527.

Brazier, M. A. B. (1959). The historical development of neurophysiology. In J. Field, H. W. Magoun, & V. E. Hall (Eds.). *Handbook of physiology. Neurophysiology.* Vol. 1. (pp. 1–58). Washington DC: Americal Physiological Society.

Brazier, M. A. B. (1988). *A history of neurophysiology in the 19th century.* New York Raven.

Bresadola, M. (1998). Medicine and science in the life of Luigi Galvani (1737–1798). *Brain Research Bulletin, 46,* 367–380.

Breuer, J. (1874). Über die Funktion der Bogengänge des Ohrlabyrinthes. *Wiener medizinisches Jahrbuch, 4,* 72–124.

Brewster, D. (1819). *A treatise on the kaleidoscope.* Edinburgh: Constable.

Brewster, D. (1830). Optics. *Edinburgh encyclopædia.* Vol. 15. (pp. 460–662). Edinburgh: Blackwoods.

Brewster, D. (1832). *Letters on natural magic addressed to Sir Walter Scott, Bart.* London: John Murray.

Brewster, D. (1845). Notice of two new properties of the retina. *Report of the British Association for the Advancement of Science. Transactions of the Sections.* 9–10.

Brewster, D. (1849). Account of a new stereoscope. *Report of the British Association. Transactions of the Sections,* 6–7.

Brewster, D. (1851). Description of several new and simple stereoscopes for exhibiting, as solids, one or more representations of them on a plane. *Transactions of the Royal Scottish Society of Arts, 3,* 247–259.

Brewster, D. (1855). *Memoires of the life, writings, and discoveries of Sir Isaac Newton.* Edinburgh: Constable.

Briggs, W. (1682). A new theory of vision. *Philosophical Transactions of the Royal Society*. 167–178.

Broadbent, D.E. (1958). *Perception and communication*. London: Pergamon Press.

Brown, A. Crum (1874). Preliminary note on the sense of rotation and the function of the semi-circular canals of the internal ear. *Proceedings of the Royal Society of Edinburgh, 8*, 255–257.

Brown, A. Crum (1875). On the sense of rotation and the anatomy and physiology of the semicircular canals of the internal ear. *Journal of Anatomy and Physiology, 8*, 327–331.

Brown, A. Crum (1878a). Cyon's researches on the ear. I. *Nature, 18*, 633–635.

Brown, A. Crum (1878b). Cyon's researches on the ear. II. *Nature, 18*, 657–659.

Brown, A. Crum (1895). *The relation between the movements of the eyes and the movements of the head*. London: Henry Frowde.

Brown, T. (1798). *Observations on the Zoonomia of Erasmus Darwin, M.D*. Edinburgh: Mundell.

Brožek, J., & Sibinga, M. S. (1970). *Origins of psychometry: Johan Jacob de Jaager on reaction time and mental processes*. Nieuwkoop, Holland: de Graff.

Bruce, V. (1988). *Recognising faces*. London: Erlbaum.

Bruner, J. S. & Postman, L. (1947). Emotional selectivity in perception and reaction. *Journal of Personality, 16*, 69–77.

Brunswik, E. (1928). Zur Entwicklung der Albedowahrnehmung. *Zeitschrift für Psychologie, 109*, 40–115.

Brunswik, E. (1934). *Wahrnehmumg und Gegenstandwelt. Grundlegung einer Psychologie vom Gegenstand her*. Leipzig: Deuticke.

Brunswik, E. (1935). *Experimentelle Psychologie in Demonstrationen*. Vienna: Springer.

Bryan, C. P. (1930). *The papyrus Ebers*. London: Bles.

Burke, R. B. (1928). *The Opus majus of Roger Bacon*. Philadelphia: University of Pennsylvania Press.

Burton, H. E. 1945. The Optics of Euclid. *Journal of the Optical Society of America, 35*, 357–372.

C. W. (1830). Contributions to the physiology of vision. No. I. *Journal of the Royal Institution of Great Britain, 1*, 101–117. (Charles Wheatstone.)

Cahan, D. (Ed.) (1993): *Hermann von Helmholtz and the foundations of nineteenth-century science*. Berkeley, CA: University of California Press.

Campbell, F. C. & Robson, J. G. (1968). Application of Fourier analysis to the visibility of gratings. *Journal of Physiology, 197*, 551–566.

Cantor, G. 1977. Berkeley, Reid, and the mathematization of mid-eighteenth-century optics. *Journal of the History of Ideas, 38*, 429–448.

Carr, T. H. (1986). Perceiving visual language. In K. R. Boff, L. Kaufman & J. P. Thomas (Eds.) *Handbook of perception and human performance*. Vol. 2. New York: Wiley.

Cheselden, W. (1728). An account of some observations made by a young gentleman, who was blind, or lost his sight so early, that he had no rememberance of ever having seen, and was couch'd between 13 and 14 years of age. *Philosophical Transactions of the Royal Society, 35*, 447–450.

Choulant, L. (1945). *History and bibliography of anatomic illustration*. Trans. M. Frank. New York: Schuman.

Cohen, M. R., & I. E. Drabkin. (1958). *A source book in Greek science*. Cambridge, MA: Harvard University Press.

Collen, H. (1854). Earliest stereoscopic portraits. *Journal of the Photographic Society, 1*, 200.

Condillac, Abbé de, (1754). *Traité des sensations*. Paris.

Condillac, Abbé de, (1982). *Philosophical writings of Etienne Bonnot, Abbé de Condillac*. Trans. F. Philip & H. Lans. Hillsdale, NJ: Erlbaum.

Craik, K. J. W. (1943). *The nature of explanation*. Cambridge: University Press.

Craik, K. J. W. (1966). *The nature of psychology. A selection of papers, essays and other writings by the late Kenneth J. W. Craik*. S. L. Sherwood (Ed.) Cambridge: University Press.

Cranefield, P. F. (1974). *The way in and the way out: François Magendie, Charles Bell and the roots of the spinal nerves*. Mount Kisco, NY: Futura.

Crew, H. (1940). *The Photismi de lumine of Maurolicus. A chapter in late medieval optics*. New York: Macmillan.

Crombie, A. C. (1952). *Augustine to Galileo. The history of science A.D. 400–1650*. London: Falcon.

Crombie, A. C. (1953). *Robert Grosseteste and the origins of experimental science. 1100–1700*. Oxford: Oxford University Press.

Crombie, A. C. (1964). Kepler: De Modo Visionis. In *Mélange Alexandre Koyré I. L'Aventure de la Science*. (pp. 135–172). Paris: Hermann.

Crombie, A. C. (1967). The mechanistic hypothesis and the scientific study of vision: Some optical ideas as a background to the invention of the microscope. In S. Bradbury & G. L'E. Turner. (Eds.) *Historical Aspects of Microscopy*. (pp. 3–112). Cambridge: Heffer.

Crone, R. A. (1992). The history of stereoscopy. *Documenta Ophthalmologica, 81*, 1–16.

D'Arcy, P. (1765). Mémoire sur la durée de la sensation de la vue. *Mémoire de l'Académie des Sciences de Paris*, 439–451.

Darwin, C. (1877). A biographical sketch of an infant. *Mind, 2*, 285–294.

Darwin, E. (1794). *Zoonomia; or, the laws of organic life*. Vol. 1. London: Johnson.

Darwin, E. (1795). *Zoonomia, oder, Gesetze des organischen Lebens*. Trans. J. D. von Brandis. Hannover: Hahn.

Darwin, E. (1801). *Zoonomia; or, the laws of organic life*. ed.3. London: Johnson.

Darwin, R. W. (1786). New experiments on the ocular spectra of light and colours. *Philosophical Transactions of the Royal Society, 76*, 313–348.

de Jaager, J.C. (1865/1970). *De physiologische tijd bij psychische processen*. Dissertation: Medical Faculty of the University of Utrecht, 1 July, 1865. (See Brožek & Sibinga, 1970, for the original and an English translation.)

Delambre, J. B. J. (1812). Die Optik des Ptolemäus, verglichen mit der Euclid's, Alhazen's und Vitellio's. *Annalen der Physik, 40*, 371–388.

Dember, W. N. (1964). *Visual perception: The nineteenth century*. New York: Wiley.

Desaguliers, J. T. (1716a). An account of some experiments of light and colours, formerly made by Sir Isaac Newton, and mention'd in his Opticks, lately repeated before the Royal Society. *Philosophical Transactions of the Royal Society, 29*, 433–447.

Desaguliers, J. T. (1716b). A plain and easy experiment to confirm Sir Isaac Newton's doctrine of the different refrangibility of the rays of light. *Philosophical Transactions of the Royal Society, 29*, 448–452.

Desaguliers, J. T. (1719). *Lectures of experimental philosophy*. London: Mears, Creake, and Sackfield.

Desaguliers, J. T. (1728). Optical experiments made in the beginning of August 1728, before the President and several members of the Royal Society, and other gentlemen of several nations, upon the occasion of Signor Rizzetti's Opticks, with an account of the said book. *Philosophical Transactions of the Royal Society, 35*, 596–629.

Desaguliers, J. T. (1736a). An attempt to explain the phœnomenon of the horizontal moon appearing bigger, than when elevated many degrees above the horizon: Supported by an experiment. *Philosophical Transactions of the Royal Society, 39*, 390–392.

Desaguliers, J. T. (1736b). An explication of an experiment made in May 1735, as a farther confirmation of what was said in the paper given in January 30, 1734–5, to account for the appearance of the horizontal moon seeming larger than when higher. *Philosophical Transactions of the Royal Society, 39*, 392–394.

Desaguliers, J. T. (1744). *A course of experimental philosophy*. Vol. 2. London: Innys, Longman, Shewell, Hitch, and Senex.

Desaguliers, J. T. (1745). *A course of experimental philosophy.* Vol. 1, ed. 2. London: Innys, Longman, Shewell, Hitch, and Senex.

Descartes, R. (1637/1902). *La dioptrique.* In C. Adam and P. Tannery (Eds.) *Oeuvres de Descartes,* Vol. 6. (pp. 81–228). Paris: Cerf.

Descartes, R. (1662). *De homine figuris et latinitate.* Trans. F. Schuyl. Leyden: Leffen & Moyardum.

Descartes, R. (1664/1909). *Traité de l'homme.* In C. Adam and P. Tannery (Eds.) *Oeuvres de Descartes,* Vol. 11. (pp. 119–215). Paris: Cerf.

Descartes, R. (1677). *Tractatus de homine et formatione foetus.* Amsterdam: Elsevier.

Descartes, R. (1965). *Discourse on method, optics, geometry, and meteorology.* Trans. P. J. Olscamp. Indianapolis: Bobbs-Merrill.

Descartes, R, (1984). *The philosophical writings of Descartes.* Vol. 2. Trans. J. Cottingham, R. Stoothoff, & D. Murdoch. Cambridge: Cambridge University Press.

Descartes, R. (1991). *The philosophical writings of Descartes.* Vol. 3. Trans. J. Cottingham, R. Stoothoff, D. Murdoch, & A. Kenny. Cambridge: Cambridge University Press.

Dewan, L. (1980). St. Albert, the sensibles, and spiritual being. In J. A. Weisheipl (Ed.). *Albertus Magnus and the sciences. Commemorative essays 1980.* (pp. 291–320). Toronto: Pontifical Institute of Mediaeval Studies.

Dewhurst, K. (1980). *Thomas Willis's Oxford lectures.* Oxford: Sandford.

Diamond, S. (Ed.) (1974). *The roots of psychology. A sourcebook in the history of ideas.* New York: Basic Books.

Diderot, D. (1749). *Lettre sur les aveugles.* London.

Diderot, D. 1750. *An essay on blindness, in a letter to a person of distinction.* Trans. from the French. London: Barker.

Diogenes Laertius. (1925). *Lives of eminent philosophers.* Trans. R. D. Hicks. London: Heinemann.

Ditchburn, R. W. & Ginsborg, B. L. (1952). Vision with a stabilized retinal image. *Nature, 170,* 36–37.

Dodge, R. (1900). Visual perception during eye movement. *Psychological Review, 7,* 454–465.

Dodge, R. (1905). The illusion of clear vision during eye movement. *Psychological Bulletin, 2,* 193–199.

Dodge, R. (1916). Visual motor functions. *Psychological Bulletin, 13,* 421–427.

Dodge, R. (1923). Habituation to rotation. *Journal of Experimental Psychology, 6,* 1–35.

Donaldson, H. H. (1885). On the temperature-sense. *Mind, 10,* 399–416.

Donders, F. C. (1864). *On the anomalies of accommodation and refraction of the eye.* Trans. W. D. Moore. Boston: Milford House.

Donders, F. C. (1865). Over de snelheid der gedachte en der wilsbepaling: Voorlopige mededeeling. *Nederlandsch Archief voor Genees- en Natuurkunde, 1,* 518–521.

Donders, F. C. (1869) Over de Snelheid van psychologische Processen. *Nederlandsch Archief voor Genees- en Natuurkunde, 4,* 117–145. (Trans. W. G. Koster, as "On the speed of mental processes," in *Acta Psychologica,* 1969, *30,* 412–431.)

Dove, H. W. (1835). *Ueber Maas und Messen,* ed. 2. Berlin: Sanderschen Buchhandlung.

Dove, H. W. (1841). Die Combination der Eindrücke beider Ohren und beider Augen zu einem Eindruck. *Monatsberichte der Berliner preussische Akademie der Wissenschaften, 41,* 251–252.

Dove, H. W. (1851). Beschreibung mehrerer Prismensterereoskope und eines einfachen Spiegelstereoskops. *Annalen der Physik und Chemie, 83,* 183–189.

Du Tour, E.-F. (1760). Discussion d'une question d'optique. *Académie des Sciences. Mémoires de Mathématique et de Physique Présentés pars Divers Savants, 3,* 514–530.

Duke-Elder, S. (Ed.) (1961). *System of ophthalmology.* Vol. 2. *The anatomy of the visual system.* London: Kimpton.

Dunbabin, K. M. D. (1999). *Mosaics of the Greek and Roman world*. Cambridge: Cambridge University Press.

Dvorak, V. (1870). Versuche über die Nachbilder von Reizveränderungen. *Sitzungsberichte der Wiener Akademie der Wissenschaften, 61,* 257–262.

Eder, J. M. (1945). *History of photography.* Trans. E. Epstean. New York: Columbia University Press.

Edgell, B., & Symes, W. L. (1906). The Wheatstone-Hipp chronoscope: Its adjustments, accuracy, and control. *British Journal of Psychology, 2,* 58–87.

Edgerton, S. Y. (1975). *The Renaissance rediscovery of linear perspective.* New York: Basic Books.

Ellis, W. D. (1938). *A source book of Gestalt psychology.* London: Routledge & Kegan Paul.

Erdmann, B., & Dodge, R. (1898). *Psychologische Untersuchungen über das Lesen auf experimenteller Grundlage.* Halle: Niemeyer.

Exner, S. (1887). Einige Beobachtungen über Bewegungsnachbilde. Centralblatt für Physiologie, 1, 135–140.

Exner, S. (1888). Über optische Bewegungsempfindungen. Biologisches Centralblatt, 8, 437–448.

Fantz, R. L. (1961). The origin of form perception, *Scientific American, 204 (5),* 66–72.

Faraday, M. (1831). On a peculiar class of optical deception. *Journal of the Royal Institution of Great Britain, 1,* 205–223.

Fechner, G. T. (1838). Ueber eine Scheibe zur Erzeugung subjectiver Farben. *Annalen der Physik und Chemie, 45,* 227–232.

Fechner, G. T. (1840). Ueber die subjectiven Nachbilder and Nebenbilder. *Annalen der Physik und Chemie, 50,* 193–221.

Fechner, G. T. (1860). *Elemente der Psychophysik.* Leipzig: Breitkopf and Härtel.

Fechner, G. T. (1966). *Elements of psychophysics.* Vol. 1. Trans. H. E. Adler. New York: Holt, Rinehart and Winston.

Ferrier, D. (1876). *The functions of the brain.* London: Smith, Elder.

Ferrier, D. (1886). *The functions of the brain.* ed. 2. London: Smith, Elder. (Reprinted in N. J. Wade (2000). (Ed.) *The emergence of neuroscience in the nineteenth century.* Vol. 7. London: Routledge/Thoemmes Press.)

Findley, J. M. & Gilchrist I. D. (2003). *Active vision: The psychology of looking and seeing.* Oxford: Oxford University Press.

Finger, S. (1994). *Origins of neuroscience.* New York: Oxford University Press.

Finger, S. (2000). *Minds behind the brain.* New York: Oxford University Press.

Finger, S., & Hustwit, M. P. (2003). Five early accounts of phantom limb in context: Paré, Descartes, Lomas, Bell and Mitchell. *Neurosurgery, 52,* 675–686.

Finger, S., & Wade, N. J. (2002a). The neuroscience of Helmholtz and the theories of Johannes Müller. Part 1. Nerve cell structure, vitalism, and the nerve impulse. *Journal of the History of the Neurosciences, 11,* 136–155.

Finger, S., & Wade, N. J. (2002b). The neuroscience of Helmholtz and the theories of Johannes Müller. Part 2. Sensation and perception. *Journal of the History of the Neurosciences, 11,* 234–254.

Flourens, M. P. J. (1824). *Recherches expérimentales sur les propriétés et les fonctions du système nerveux dans les animaux vertébrés.* Paris: Baillière.

Flourens, M. P. J. (1830). Expériences sur les canaux semi-circulaires de l'orielle. *Mémoires de l'Académie Royale des Sciences, 9,* 455–466.

Flourens, M. P. J. (1842). *Recherches expérimentales sur les propriétés et les fonctions du système nerveux dans les animaux vertebras.* ed. 2. Paris: Baillière.

Fordyce, G. (1771). *Elements of the practice of physic, in two parts.* ed. 3. London: Johnson.

Frey, M. von (1895). Beiträge zur Sinnesphysiologie der Haut. *Sächsische Akademie der Wissenschaft, Leipzig, 47*, 166–184.

Gall, F. J. (1835). *On the functions of the brain and each of its parts, with observations on the possibility of determining the instincts, propensities and talents, and the moral and intellectual dispositions of men and animals by the configuration of the brain and head*. 6 vols. Trans.W. Lewis. Boston: Marsh, Capen and Lyon.

Galvani, L. (1791). De viribus electricitatis in motu musculari. *De Bononiensi Scientiarum et Artium Instituto atque Academia Commentarii, 7*, 363–418.

Gardner, H. (1987). *The mind's new science. A history of the cognitive revolution*. New York: Basic Books.

Garrison, F. H. (1914). *An introduction to the history of medicine*. Philadelphia: Saunders.

Gaur, A. (1984). *A history of writing*. London: The British Library.

Gibson, J. J. 1966. *The senses considered as perceptual systems*. Boston: Houghton Mifflin.

Gibson, J. J. (1979) *The ecological approach to visual perception*, Boston: Houghton Mifflin.

Goethe, J. W. (1810). *Zur Farbenlehre*, Tübingen, Cotta.

Goethe, J. (1824). Das Sehen in subjectiven Hinsicht, von Purkinje, 1819. *Zur Naturwissenschaft überhaupt, besonders zur Morphologie*, (pp. 102–117). Stuttgart: Cotta.

Goethe, J. W. (1840). *Theory of colours*. Trans. C. L. Eastlake. London: Murray.

Goldscheider, A. (1884). Die specifische Energie der Temperaturenerven. Monatsschrift für praktische Dermatologie, 3, 198–208.

Gombrich, E. H. (1960) *Art and illusion. A study in the psychology of pictorial representation*. London: Phaidon.

Gordon, I. E. (1997). *Theories of visual perception*. ed. 2. London: Wiley.

Gregory, R. L. (1963). Distortion of space as inappropriate constancy scaling. *Nature, 199*, 678–680.

Gregory, R. L. (1966). *Eye and brain. The psychology of seeing*. London: Weidenfeld and Nicolson.

Gregory, R. L. (2000). Ambiguity of 'ambiguity'. *Perception, 29*, 1139–1142.

Gregory, R. L. (2003). Delusions. *Perception, 32*, 257–261.

Griffith, C. R. (1922). *An historical survey of vestibular equilibration*. Urbana: University of Illinois Press.

Grimaldi, F. M. (1665). *Physico-mathemis de lumine coloribis et iride*. Bononiae.

Gross, C. G. (1995). Aristotle on the brain. *The Neuroscientist, 1*, 245–250.

Gross, C. G. (1998). *Brain, vision, memory. Tales in the history of neuroscience*. Cambridge, MA: MIT Press.

Grüsser, O.-J., & Hagner, M. (1990). On the history of deformation phosphenes and the idea of internal light generated in the eye for the purpose of vision. *Documenta Ophthalmologica, 74*, 57–85.

Grüsser, O.-J., & Landis, T. (1991). *Vision and visual dysfunction*. Vol. 12. *Visual agnosias and other disturbances of visual perception and cognition*. London: Macmillan.

Gudden, B. von (1870) Experimentaluntersuchungen über das peripherische und centrale Nervensystem. *Archiv für Psychiatrie und Nervenkrankheiten, 2*, 693–724.

Hall, T. S. (1972). *Treatise of man. René Descartes*. Cambridge, MA: Harvard University Press.

Haller, A. (1786). *First lines of physiology*. Trans. W. Cullen. Edinburgh: Elliot.

Hamilton, W. (1846). *The works of Thomas Reid*, D.D. Edinburgh: MacLachlan, Stewart.

Hannover, A. (1844). *Recherches microscopiques sur la système nerveux*. Copenhagen: Philipsen.

Harris, H. (1999). *The birth of the cell*. New Haven, CT: Yale University Press.

Harris, J. (1775). *A treatise of optics: Containing elements of the science; in two books*. London: White.

Hartline, H. K. (1938). The response of single optic nerve fibres of the vertebrate eye to illumination of the retina. *American Journal of Physiology, 121*, 400–415.

Hatfield, G. (1990). *The natural and the normative: Theories of spatial perception from Kant to Helmholtz.* Cambridge, MA: MIT Press.

Head, H. (1920). *Studies in neurology.* London: Oxford University Press.

Hebb, D. O. (1949). *Organization of behavior. A neuropsychological theory.* New York: Wiley.

Hebb, D. O. (1980). *Essays on mind.* Hillsdale, NJ: Erlbaum.

Heller, D. (1986). On natural memory. In F. Klix & H. Hagendorf (Eds.) *Human memory and cognitive capabilities.* (pp. 161–169). Amsterdam: North Holland.

Heller, D. (1988). On the history of eye movement recording. In G. Lüer, U. Lass, & J. Shallo-Hoffmann (Eds.) *Eye movement research. Physiological and psychological aspects.* (pp. 37–51). Göttingen: Hogrefe.

Helmholtz, H. (1852). On the theory of compound colours. *Philosophical Magazine and Journal of Science, 41,* 519–534.

Helmholtz, H. (1855). Ueber die Accommodation des Auges. *Archiv für Ophthalmologie, 1,* 1–74.

Helmholtz, H. (1857). Das Telestereoskop. *Annalen der Physik und Chemie, 101,* 494–496.

Helmholtz, H. (1867). *Handbuch der physiologischen Optik.* In G. Karsten (Ed.) *Allgemeine Encyklopädie der Physik.* Vol. 9. Leipzig: Voss.

Helmholtz, H. (1870). Neue Versuche über die Fortpflanzungsgeschwindigkeit der Reizung in den motorischen Nerven des Menschen, ausgeführt von Herr N. Baxt aus Petersburg. *Monatsbericht der Akademie der Wissenschaften, Berlin, März 23,* 184–191.

Helmholtz, H. (1871). Ueber die Zeit, welche nöthig ist damit ein Gesichtseindruck zum Bewusstsein kommt: Resultate einer von Herrn N. Baxt im Heidelberger Laboratorium ausgeführten Untersuchung. *Monatsbericht der Akademie der Wissenschaften, Berlin, Juni 8,* 333–337.

Helmholtz, H. (1873). *Popular lectures on scientific subjects.* Trans. E. Atkinson. London: Longmans, Green.

Helmholtz, H. (1895). *Popular lectures on scientific subjects,* First Series, New Impression. Trans. E. Atkinson. London: Longmans, Green.

Helmholtz, H. (1896). *Handbuch der physiologischen Optik,* ed. 2. Leipzig: Voss.

Helmholtz, H. (1909). *Handbuch der physiologischen Optik,* vol. 1. ed. 3. A. Gullstrand, J. von Kries & W. Nagel (Eds.) Hamburg: Voss.

Helmholtz, H. (1910). *Handbuch der physiologischen Optik,* vol. 3. ed. 3. A. Gullstrand, J. von Kries & W. Nagel (Eds.) Hamburg: Voss.

Helmholtz, H. (1911). *Handbuch der physiologischen Optik,* Vol. 2. ed. 3. A. Gullstrand, J. von Kries & W. Nagel (Eds.) Hamburg: Voss.

Helmholtz, H. (1924a). *Helmholtz's Treatise on physiological optics.* Vol. 1. Trans. J. P. C. Southall. New York: Optical Society of America.

Helmholtz, H. (1924b). *Helmholtz's Treatise on physiological optics.* Vol. 2. Trans. J. P. C. Southall. New York: Optical Society of America.

Helmholtz, H. (1925). *Helmholtz's Treatise on physiological optics.* Vol. 3. Trans. J. P. C. Southall. New York: Optical Society of America.

Helmholtz, H. (2000). *Helmholtz's Treatise on physiological optics.* 3 Vols. Trans. J. P. C. Southall. Bristol: Thoemmes.

Hering, E. (1879a). Der Raumsinn und die Bewegungen des Auges. In L. Hermann, (Ed.) *Handbuch der Physiologie.* Vol. 3. (pp. 341–601). Leipzig: Vogel.

Hering, E. (1879b). Über Muskelgeräusche des Auges. *Sitzungsberichte der Wiener Akademie der Wissenschaften. Abteilung 3, 79,* 137–154.

Hering, E. (1942). *Spatial sense and movements of the eye.* Trans. A. Radde, Baltimore: American Academy of Optometry.

Herz, M. (1786). *Versuch über den Schwindel.* Berlin: Voss.

Hill, E. (1915). History of eyeglasses and spectacles. In C. A. Wood (Ed.) *The American encyclopedia and dictionary of ophthalmology.* Vol. 7. (pp. 4894–4953). Chicago: Cleveland Press.

Hirsch, A. (1862). Expériences chronoscopiques sur la vitesse des différentes sensations et de la transmission nerveuse. *Bulletin de la Société Scientifique Naturelle de Neuchâtel, 6,* 100–114.

Hirschberg, J. (1899). Geschichte der Augenheilkunde. In Graefe-Saemisch (Eds.) *Handbuch der gesamten Augenheilkunde,* Vol. 12. Leipzig: Engelmann.

Hitzig, E. (1871). Ueber die bei Galvanisiren des Kopfes entstehenden Störungen des Muskelinnervation und der Vorstellungen vom Verhalten im Raume. *Archiv für Anatomie, Physiologie und wissenschaftliche Medicin,* 716–770.

Home, E. (1794). Some facts relating to the late Mr. John Hunter's preparation for the Croonian lecture. *Philosophical Transactions of the Royal Society, 84,* 21–27.

Hooke, R. (1665). *Micrographia: or some physiological descriptions of minute bodies made by magnifying glasses with observations and inquiries thereupon.* London: Martyn and Allestry.

Hoorn, W. van (1972). *As images unwind. Ancient and modern theories of visual perception.* Amsterdam: University Press.

Horner, W. G. (1834). On the properties of the dœdaleum, a new instrument of optical illusion. *London and Edinburgh Philosophical Magazine and Journal of Science, 4,* 36–41.

Howard, I. P. (1999). The Helmholtz-Hering debate in retrospect, *Perception, 28,* 543–549.

Howard, I. P., & Wade, N. J. (1996). Ptolemy's contributions to the geometry of binocular vision. *Perception, 25,* 1189–1202.

Hubel, D. H. & Wiesel, T. N. (1962). Receptive fields, binocular interaction and functional architecture in the cat's visual cortex. *Journal of Physiology, 166,* 106–154.

Hubel, D. H. & Wiesel, T. N. (1963). Receptive fields of cells in striate cortex of very young, visually inexperienced kittens. *Journal of Neurophysiology, 26,* 994–1002.

Hubel, D. H. & Wiesel, T. N. (1968). Receptive fields and functional architecture of the monkey visual cortex. *Journal of Physiology, 195,* 215–243.

Hunter, J. (1786). *Observations on certain parts of the animal œconomy.* London: Published by the author.

Hunter, J. (1861). *Essays and observations on natural history.* 2 vols. London: Voorst.

Huygens, C. (1653). *Dioptrique.* La Haye: Nijhoff.

Huygens, C. (1690). *Traité de la lumiere.* Leiden: vander Aa.

Huygens, C. (1912). *Treatise on light.* Trans. S. P. Thompson. London: Macmillan.

Ilardi, V. (2001). The role of Florence in the development and commerce of spectacles. *Atti della Fondazione Giorgio Ronchi, 56,* 163–176.

Ittelson, W. H. (1952). *The Ames demonstrations in perception.* Princeton. NJ: Princeton University Press.

J. M. (1821). Account of an optical deception. *Quarterly Journal of Science, Literature, and Art, 10,* 282–283.

Jackson, J. H. (1863). *Suggestions for studying diseases of the nervous system on Professor Owen's vertebral theory.* London: Lewis.

James, W. (1882). The sense of dizziness in deaf-mutes. *American Journal of Otololgy, 4,* 239–254.

James, W. (1890). *Principles of psychology.* Vol. 2. London: Macmillan.

Javal, L. É. (1878). Essai sur la physiologie de la lecture. *Annales d'Oculistique, 79,* 97–117.

Javal, L. É. (1905). *Physiologie de la lecture et de l'écriture.* Paris: Alcan.

Johannson, G. (1964). Perception of motion and changing form. *Scandanavian Journal of Psychology, 5,* 181–208.

John, H. J. (1959). *Jan Evangelista Purkyne. Czech scientist and patriot. 1787–1869.* Philadelphia: American Philosophical Society.

Julesz, B. (1960). Binocular depth perception of computer-generated patterns. *Bell System Technical Journal, 39,* 1125–1162.

REFERENCES

Julesz, B. (1971). *Foundations of cyclopean perception*. Chicago: University of Chicago Press.

Jurin, J. (1738). An essay on distinct and indistinct vision. In R. Smith *A compleat system of opticks in four books*. (pp. 115–171). Cambridge: Published by the author.

Kant, I. (1781). *Critik der reinen Vernunft*. Riga: Hartknoch.

Kant, I. (1786). *Metaphysische Anfangsgründe der Naturwissenschaft*. Riga: Hartknoch.

Keele, K. D. (1955). Leonardo da Vinci on vision. *Proceedings of the Royal Society of Medicine, 48*, 384–390.

Kemp, M. (1990). *The science of art. Optical themes in western art from Brunelleschi to Seurat*. New Haven: Yale University Press.

Kemp, S. (1990). *Medieval psychology*. New York: Greenwood.

Kepler, J. (1604). *Ad Vitellionem paralipomena*. Frankfurt: Marinium and Aubrii.

Kepler, J. (1611). *Dioptrice*. Augsburg: Franci.

Kircher, A. (1646). *Ars magna lucis et umbrae*. Rome: Scheus.

Kleiner, A. (1878). Physiologisch-optische Beobachtungen. *Archiv für die gesammte Physiologie des Menschen und der Thiere, 18*, 542–573.

Klooswijk, A. I. J. (1991). The first stereo photo. *Stereo World, May/June*: 6–11.

Koelbing, H. M. (1967). *Renaissance der Augenheilkunde. 1540–1630*. Bern: Huber.

Koenigsberger, L. (1906). *Hermann von Helmholtz*. Trans. F. A. Welby. Oxford: Clarendon Press.

Koffka, K. (1922). Perception: An introduction to Gestalt-theorie. *Psychological Bulletin, 19*, 531–585.

Köhler, W. (1930). *Gestalt psychology*. London: Bell.

Köhler, W. (1940). *Dynamics in psychology*. New York: Liveright.

Kölliker, A. (1852). *Mikroscopische Anatomie*. Leipzig: Engelmann.

Kornhuber, H. H. (1974). Introduction. In H. H. Kornhuber (Ed.) *Handbook of sensory physiology*. Vol. VI/1. *Vestibular system. Part 1: Basic mechanisms*. (pp. 3–14). New York: Springer.

Kreidl, A. (1891). Beiträge zur Physiologie des Ohrenlabyrinthes auf Grund von Versuchen an Taubstummen. *Archiv für gesamte Physiologie, 51*, 119–150.

Kruta, V. (1964). *M.-J.-P. Flourens, J.-E. Purkyne et les débuts de la physiologie de la posture et de l'équilibre*. Paris: Alençonnaise.

Kruta, V. (1969). *J. E. Purkyně [1787–1869] physiologist. A short account of his contributions to the progress of physiology with a bibliography of his works*. Prague: Czechoslovak Academy of Sciences.

Kruta, V. (Ed.) (1971). *Jan Evangelista Purkyne 1787–1869. Centenary symposium*. Brno: Universita Jana Evangelisty Purkyne.

Kuffler, S. W. (1953). Discharge pattern and functional organisation of mammalian retina. *Journal of Neurophysiology, 16*, 37–68.

Kühne, W. (1863). Die Muskelspindeln. *Archiv für pathalogische Anatomie, Physiologie und klinische Medizin, 28*, 528–538.

Kuntze, J. E. (1892) *Gustav Theodor Fechner (Dr. Mises). Ein deutsches Gelehrtenleben*. Leipzig: Breitkopf and Härtel.

La Hire, P. de. (1685). Dissertation sur la conformation de l'oeil. *Journal des Sçavans, 13*, 335–363.

Lamansky, S. (1869). Bestimmung der Winkelgeschwindigkeit der Blickbewegung. *Archiv für die gesamte Physiologie, 2*, 418–422.

Lamare, M. (1893). Des mouvements des yeux dans la lecture. *Comptes Rendus de la Société Français d'Ophthalmologique*, 354–364.

Lambert, J. H. 1760. *Photometria, sive de mensura et gradibus luminis colorum, et umbrae*. Augsburg.

Laurentius (1599/1938). *A discourse of the preservation of the sight: of melancholic diseases; of rheumes, and of old age*. Trans. R. Surphlet. London: The Shakespeare Association.

Le Clerc, S. (1712). *Système de la vision*. Paris: Delaulne.

Le Conte, J. (1881). *Sight: An exposition of the principles of monocular and binocular vision*. London: Kegan Paul.

Leeuwenhoek, A. van (1674). More observations from Mr. Leewenhook... *Philosophical Transactions of the Royal Society, 9*, 178–182.

Leeuwenhoek, A. van (1675). Microscopical observations from Mr. Leewenhoeck, concerning the optick nerve. *Philosophical Transactions of the Royal Society, 9*, 378–380.

Lejeune, A. (1948). *Euclide et Ptolémée. Deux stades de l'optique geométrique Grecque*. Louvain: Université de Louvain.

Lejeune, A. (Ed.) (1956). *L'Optique de Claude Ptolémée dans la version latine d'après l'arabe de l'Émir Eugène de Sicile*. Louvain: Université de Louvain.

Lejeune, A. (Ed. and Trans.) (1989). *L'Optique de Claude Ptolémée dans la version latine d'après l'arabe de l'Émir Eugène de Sicile*. Leiden: Brill.

Leonardo da Vinci (1721). *A treatise on painting*. London: Senex and Taylor.

Lindberg, D. C. (Ed. and trans.)(1970). *John Pecham and the science of optics*. Madison, Wisconsin: University of Wisconsin Press.

Lindberg, D. C. (1976). *Theories of vision from Al-Kindi to Kepler*. Chicago: University of Chicago Press.

Lindberg, D. C. (1978). The science of optics. In D. C. Lindberg (Ed.) *Science in the Middle Ages*. (pp. 338–368). Chicago: University of Chicago Press.

Lindberg, D. C. (1983). *Roger Bacon's philosophy of nature*. Oxford: Clarendon.

Locke, J. (1690). *An essay concerning humane understanding*. London: Basset.

Locke, J. (1694). *An essay concerning humane understanding*. ed. 2. London: Awnsham, Churchill and Manship.

Lucretius. (1975). *De rerum natura*. Trans. W. H. D. Rouse. Cambridge, MA: Harvard University Press.

MacCurdy, E. (1938). *The notebooks of Leonardo da Vinci*. Vol. 1. London: Cape.

Mach, E. (1873). Physiologische Versuche über den Gleichgewichtssinn des Menschen. *Sitzungsberichte der Wiener Akademie der Wissenschaften, 68*, 124–140.

Mach, E. (1875). *Grundlinien der Lehre von den Bewegungsempfindungen*. Leipzig: Engelmann.

Mach, E. (1910). *Popular scientific lectures*. ed. 4. Trans. T. J. McCormack. Chicago: Open Court.

Mach, E. (1926). *The principles of physical optics. An historical and philosophical treatment*. Trans. J. S. Anderson & A. F. A. Young. London: Methuen.

Magnus, H. (1901). *Die Augenheilkunde der Alten*. Breslau: Kern.

Marr, D. (1982). *Vision. A computational investigation into the human representation and processing of visual information*. New York: Freeman.

Marshal, A. (1815). *The morbid anatomy of the brain in mania and hydrophobia*. S. Sawrey (Ed.) London: Longman, Hurst, Rees, Orme, & Brown.

Massironi, M. (2002). *The psychology of graphic images*. Trans. N. Bruno. Mahwah, NJ: Lawrence Erlbaum Associates.

Matousek, O. (1961). J. E. Purkynes Leben und Tätigkeit im Lichte der Berliner und Prager Archive. *Nova Acta Leopoldina, 24*, 109–129.

Maurolico, F. (1611). *Photisme de lumine et umbrae*. Naples: Longus.

Maxwell, J. C. (1855). Experiments on colour, as perceived by the eye. *Transactions of the Royal Society of Edinburgh, 21*, 275–298.

May, M. T. (1968). *Galen. On the usefulness of the parts of the body*. Ithaca, NY: Cornell University Press.

Mayer, T. (1755). Experimenta circa visus aciem. *Commentarii Societatis Regiae Scientiarum Gottingensis, 4*, 97–112.

McCulloch, W. S. & Pitts, W. H. (1943). A logical calculus of the ideas immanent in nervous activity. *Bulletin of Mathematical Biophysics, 5*, 115–133.

McGinnies, E. (1949). Emotionality and perceptual defence. *Psychological Review, 56*, 244–251.

McMurrich, J. P. (1930). *Leonardo da Vinci the anatomist (1452–1519)*. Baltimore: Williams & Wilkins.

Meyerhof, M. (1928). *The book of the ten treatises on the eye, ascribed to Hunain ibn Is-Hâq (809–877 A.D.)*. Cairo: Government Press.

Meyering, T. C. (1989). *Historical roots of cognitive science*. Dordrecht: Kluwer.

Miller, G. A. (1957). The magical number seven, plus or minus two: some limits on our capacity for processing information. *Psychological Review, 63*, 81–97.

Millican, P. J. R. & Clark, A. (Eds.)(1996). *Machines and thought. The legacy of Alan Turing*. Vol. 1. Oxford: Clarendon Press.

Milner, A. D. & Goodale, M. A. (1995). *The visual brain in action*. Oxford: Oxford University Press.

Mitchell, S. W. (1871). Phantom limbs. *Lippincott's Magazine, 8*, 563–569.

Mollon, J. D., & Perkins, A. J. (1996). Errors of judgement at Greenwich in 1796. *Nature, 380*, 101–102.

Morgan, M. J. (1977). *Molyneux's question. Vision, touch and the philosophy of perception*. Cambridge: Cambridge University Press.

Müller, G. E., & Schumann, F. (1894). Experimentelle Beiträge zur Untersuchung des Gedächtnisses. *Zeitschift für Psychologie, 6*, 81–190, and 257–339.

Müller, J. (1826a). *Zur vergleichenden Physiologie des Gesichtssinnes des Menschen und der Thiere, nebst einen Versuch über die Bewegung der Augen und über den menschlichen Blick*. Leipzig: Cnobloch.

Müller, J. (1826b). *Über die phantastischen Gesichtserscheinungen*. Coblenz: Hölscher.

Müller, J. (1838). *Handbuch der Physiologie des Menschen*. Vol. 2. Coblenz: Hölscher.

Müller, J. (1843). *Elements of physiology*. Vol. 2, ed. 2. Trans. W. Baly. London: Taylor and Walton.

Müller, J. (2003). *Müller's Elements of physiology*. 4 vols. Trans. W. Baly. Bristol: Thoemmes.

Munk, H. (1879). Physiologie der Sehsphäre der Grosshirnrinde. *Centralblatt für praktische Augenheilkunde, 3*, 255–266.

Natanson, L. N. (1844). Analyse der Functionen des Nervensystems. *Archiv für Physiologie und Heilkunde, 3*, 515–535.

Neisser, U. (1976). *Cognition and reality. Principles and implications for cognitive psychology*. San Francisco: Freeman.

Neuberger, M. (1981). *The historical development of experimental brain and spinal cord physiology before Flourens*. Trans. E. Clarke. Baltimore: The Johns Hopkins University Press.

Newton, I. (1672). A Letter of Mr. Isaac Newton.... containing his New Theory about Light and Colours. *Philosophical Transactions of the Royal Society, 7*, 3075–3087.

Newton, I. (1704). *Opticks: Or, a treatise of the reflections, refractions, inflections and colours of light*. London: Smith and Walford.

Newton, I. (1730). *Opticks: Or, a treatise of the reflections, refractions, inflections and colours of light*. ed. 4. London: Innys.

Nicéron, J.-F. (1646). *Thaumaturgus opticus*. Leiden.

Norrsell, U., Finger, S., & Lajonchere, C. (1999). Cutaneous sensory spots and the 'law of specific nerve energies': History and development of ideas. *Brain Research Bulletin, 48*, 457–465.

O'Leary, De L. (1949). *How Greek science passed to the Arabs*. London: Routledge & Kegan Paul.

Oppel, J. J. (1856). Neue Beobachtungen und Versuche über eine eigentümliche, noch wenig bekannte Reaktionsthätigkeit des menschlichen Auges. *Annalen der Physik und Chemie, 99*, 540–561.

Osler, W. (1921). *The evolution of modern medicine*. New Haven, CT: Yale University Press.

Paré, A. (1649). *The workes of that famous chirurgion Ambrose Parey.* Trans. T. Johnson. London: Clarke.

Paris, J. A. (1827). *Philosophy in sport made science in earnest! Being an attempt to illustrate the first principles of natural philosophy by the aid of popular toys and sports.* Vol. 3. London: Longman, Rees, Orme, Brown, and Green.

Park, D. (1997). *The fire within the eye.* Princeton: Princeton University Press.

Pastore, N. (1971). *Selective history of theories of visual perception: 1650–1950.* New York: Oxford University Press.

Pendergrast, M. (2003). *Mirror mirror: A history of the human love affair with reflection.* New York: Basic Books.

Pfaff, C. W. (1801). Vorläufige Nachricht von seinen galvanischen Versuchen mit Voltaischen Batterie. *Annalen der Physik, 7,* 247–254.

Piccolino, M. (1997). Luigi Galvani and animal electricity: two centuries after the foundation of electrophysiology. *Trends in Neurosciences, 20,* 443–448.

Piccolino, M. (2000). The bicentennial of the Voltaic battery (1800–2000): the artificial electric organ. *Trends in Neurosciences, 23,* 147–151.

Pirenne, M. (1970). *Optics, painting and photography.* Cambridge: Cambridge University Press.

Plateau, J. (1829). *Dissertation sur quelques propriétés des impressions produites par la lumière sur l'organe de la vue.* Liége.

Plateau, J. (1833). Des illusions sur lesquelles se fonde le petit appareil appelé récemment Phénakisticope. *Annales de Chimie et de Physique de Paris, 53,* 304–308.

Plateau, J. (1836). Notice sur l'anorthoscope. *Bulletins de l'Académie Royale des Sciences et Belles-Lettres de Bruxelles, 3,* 7–10.

Plateau, J. (1849). Quatrième note sur de nouvelles applications curieurses de la persistance des impressions de la rétine. *Bulletins de l'AcadémieRoyale des Sciences, des Lettres et des Beaux-Arts de Bruxelles, 16,* 254–260.

Plateau, J. (1850). Vierte Notiz über neue, sonderbare Anwendungen des Verweilens der Eindrücke auf die Netzhaut. *Annalen der Physik und Chemie, 80,* 287–292.

Plateau, J. (1878). Bibliographie analytique des principaux phénomènes de la vision, depuis les temps anciens jusqu'a la fin du XVIIIe siècle. Première section. Persistance des impressions sur la rétine. *Mémoires de l'Académie Royale de Belgique, 42,* 1–59.

Plato (1946). *Timaeus.* Trans. R. G. Bury. London: Heinemann.

Platter, F. (1583). *De corporis humani structura et usu.* Basel: König.

Pliny (1940). *Natural history.* Trans. H. Rackham. London: Heinemann.

Plug, C., & H. Ross. (1989). Historical review. In M. Herschenson, (Ed.) *The Moon Illusion.* (pp. 5–27). Hillsdale, N.J.: Erlbaum.

Polyak, S. L. (1942). *The retina.* Chicago: University of Chicago Press.

Polyak, S. L. (1957). *The vertebrate visual system.* Chicago: University of Chicago Press.

Porta, G. B. (1589). *Magiae naturalis. Libri XX.* Naples: Salviani.

Porta, J. B. (1593). *De refractione. Optices parte. Libri novem.* Naples: Salviani.

Porta, J. B. (1669). *Natural magick.* Trans. J. Wright. London.

Porterfield, W. (1737). An essay concerning the motions of our eyes. Part I. Of their external motions. *Edinburgh Medical Essays and Observations, 3,* 160–263.

Porterfield, W. (1738). An essay concerning the motions of our eyes. Part II. Of their internal motions. *Edinburgh Medical Essays and Observations, 4,* 124–294.

Porterfield, W. (1759a). *A treatise on the eye, the manner and phænomena of vision.* Vol. 1. Edinburgh: Hamilton and Balfour.

Porterfield, W. (1759b). *A treatise on the eye, the manner and phænomena of vision.* Vol. 2. Edinburgh: Hamilton and Balfour.

Priestley, J. (1772). *The history and present state of discoveries relating to vision, light, and colours.* London: Johnson.

Purkinje, J. (1819). *Beiträge zur Kenntniss des Sehens in subjectiver Hinsicht.* Prague: Vetterl.

Purkinje, J. (1820). Beyträge zur näheren Kenntniss des Schwindels aus heautognostischen Daten. *Medicinische Jahrbücher des kaiserlich-königlichen öesterreichischen Staates, 6,* 79–125.

Purkinje, J. (1823). *Beobachtungen und Versuche zur Physiologie der Sinne. Beiträge zur Kenntniss des Sehens in subjectiver Hinsicht.* Prague: Calve.

Purkinje, J. (1825). *Beobachtungen und Versuche zur Physiologie der Sinne. Neue Beiträge zur Kenntniss des Sehens in subjectiver Hinsicht.* Berlin: Reimer.

Ramachandran, V. S., & Blakeslee. S. (1998). *Phantoms in the brain.* London: Fourth Estate.

Rayner, K. (1978). Eye movements in reading and information processing. *Psychological Bulletin, 85,* 618–660.

Reid, T. (1764). *An inquiry into the human mind, on the principles of common sense.* Edinburgh: Millar, Kincaid & Bell.

Reisch, G. (1503). *Margarita philosophica.* Freiburg: Schott.

Riese, W., & Arrington, G. E. Jr. (1964). The history of Johannes Müller's doctrine of the specific energies of the senses: Original and later versions. *Bulletin of the History of Medicine, 37,* 179–183.

Riggs, L. A. & Ratliff, F. (1952). The effects of counteracting the normal movements of the eye. *Journal of the Optical Society of America, 42,* 872–873.

Ritter, J. W. (1801). Versuche und Bemerkungen über den Galvanismus der Voltaischen Batterie. *Annalen der Physik, 7,* 431–484.

Ritter, J. W. (1805). Neue Versuche und Bemerkungen über den Galvanismus. *Annalen der Physik, 19,* 1–44.

Rivers, W. H. R. (1900). Vision. In E. A. Schäfer (Ed.). *Textbook of physiology.* Vol. 2. (pp. 1026–1148). Edinburgh: Pentland.

Robinson, J. D. (2001). *Mechanisms of synaptic transmission. Bridging the gaps (1890–1990).* New York: Oxford University Press.

Roget, P. M. (1825). Explanation of an optical deception in the appearance of the spokes of a wheel seen through vertical apertures. *Philosophical Transactions of the Royal Society, 115,* 131–140.

Roget, P. M. (1834). *Animal and vegetable physiology considered with reference to natural theology. Bridgewater Treatise V.* Vol. 2. London: Pickering.

Rohault, J. (1671). *Traité de physique,* Paris: Savreux.

Rohault, J. (1723). *Rohault's system of natural philosophy.* Trans. J. Clarke. London: Knapton.

Ronchi, V. (1970). *The nature of light. An historical survey.* Trans. V. Barocas. London: Heinemann.

Rosen, E. (1956). The invention of eyeglasses. *Journal of the History of Medicine, 11,* 13–46, and 183–218.

Ross, H. E. (1999). The prehistory of weight perception. In P. R. Killeen & W. R. Uttal (Eds.) *Fechner Day '99: The end of 20th century psychophysics.* (pp. 31– 36). Tempe, AR: The International Society for Psychophysics.

Ross, H. E., & Murray, D. J. (1978). *E. H. Weber: The sense of touch.* London: Academic Press.

Ross, H. E., & Plug, C. (2002). *The mystery of the moon illusion.* Oxford: Oxford University Press.

Ross, H. E., & Ross, G. W. (1976). Did Ptolemy understand the moon illusion? *Perception, 5,* 377–385.

Ross, W. D. (Ed.) (1913). *The works of Aristotle.* Vol. 6. Oxford: Clarendon.

Ross, W. D. (Ed.) (1927). *The works of Aristotle.* Vol. 7. Oxford: Clarendon.

Ross, W. D. (Ed.) (1931). *The works of Aristotle.* Vol. 3. Oxford: Clarendon.

Ruete, C. G. T. (1846). *Lehrbuch der Ophthalmologie*. Leipzig.

Ryff, W. H. (1541). *Das aller fürtrefflichsten...geschöpffs...wahrhafftige Beschreibung der Anatomie*. Strassburg: Beck.

Sabra, A. I. (1966). Ibn al-Haytham's criticisms of Ptolemy's *Optics*. *Journal of the History of Philosophy, 4*, 145–149.

Sabra, A. I. (1987). Psychology versus mathematics: Ptolemy and Alhazen on the moon illusion. In E. Grant & J. E. Murdoch, Eds. *Mathematics and its application to natural philosophy in the Middle Ages*. (pp. 217–247). Cambridge: Cambridge University Press.

Sabra, A. I. (Ed. and Trans.) (1989). *The Optics of Alhazen. Books I–III. On direct vision*. London: The Warburg Institute.

Saito, A. (Ed.) (2000). *Bartlett, culture and cognition*. Hove, East Sussex: Psychology Press.

Salapatek, P. & Kesson, W. (1966). Visual scanning of triangles by the human newborn. *Journal of Experimental Child Psychology, 3*, 155–167.

Saunders, J. B. de C. M., & O'Malley, C. D. (1950). *The illustrations from the works of Andreas Vesalius of Brussels*. New York: World Publishing.

Scaliger, J. C. (1557). *Exotericarum exercitationum liber quintus decimus, de subtilitate, ad Hieronymum Cardanum*. Paris: Vascosani.

Scarpa, A. (1789). *Anatomicae disquisitiones de auditu et olfactu*, Pavia: Galeati.

Scheiner, C. (1619). *Oculus, hoc est fundamentum opticum*. Innsbruck: Agricola.

Scheiner, C. (1630). *Rosa ursina*. Bracciani: Phaeum.

Schmitz, E.-H. (1982). *Handbuch zur Geschichte der Optik*. Vol. 2. Bonn: Wayerborgh.

Schmitz, E.-H. (1995). *Handbuch zur Geschichte der Optik*. Suppl. Vol. 3. *Die Brille*. Bonn: Wayerborgh.

Schultze, M. (1866). Zur Anatomie und Physiologie der Retina. *Archiv für mikroskopische Anatomie, 2*, 175–286.

Schwann, T. (1839). *Mikroskopische Untersuchungen über die Übereinstimmung in der Struktur und dem Wachsthum der Tiere und Pflanzen*. Berlin: Reimer.

Selfridge, O. G. (1959). Pandemonium: A paradigm for learning. In *The Mechanisation of Thought Processes*, London: HMSO.

Senden, M. von (1960). *Space and sight*. Trans. P. Heath. London: Methuen.

Shannon, C. E. & Weaver, W. (1949). *The mathematical theory of communication*. Urbana: University of Illinois Press.

Shapiro, A. E. (1980). The evolving structure of Newton's theory of white light and color. *Isis, 71*, 211–235.

Shastid, T. H. (1917). History of ophthalmology. In C. A. Wood (Ed.) *The American encyclopedia and dictionary of ophthalmology*, Vol. 11. (pp. 8524–8904). Chicago: Cleveland Press.

Shepherd, G. (1991). *Foundations of the neuron doctrine*. New York: Oxford University Press.

Sherrington, C. S. (1900). The muscular sense. In A. E. Schäfer (Ed.) *Text-book of Physiology*. Vol. 2. (pp. 1002–1025). Edinburgh, Pentland.

Sherrington, C. S. (1906/2000). *The integrative action of the nervous system*. New York: Scribner. (Reprinted in N. J. Wade (2000). (Ed.) *The emergence of neuroscience in the nineteenth century*. Vol. 8. London: Routledge/Thoemmes Press.)

Siegel, R. E. (1959). Theories of vision and color perception of Empedocles and Democritus: some similarities to the modern approach. *Bulletin of the History of Medicine, 33*, 145–159.

Siegel, R. E. (1970). *Galen on sense perception*. Basel: Karger.

Sinclair, D. (1967). *Cutaneous sensation*. London: Oxford University Press.

Singer, C. (1925). *The evolution of anatomy*. London: Kegan Paul, Trench, Trubner.

Slater, A. (Ed.) (1998) *Perceptual developments: Visual, auditory, and speech perception in infancy*. Hove, East Sussex: Psychology Press.

Smith, A. M. (1983). *Witelonis Perspectivae liber quintus. Book V of Witelo's Perspectiva. Studia Copernica XXII*. Warsaw: Polish Academy of Sciences Press.

Smith, A. M. (1996). *Ptolemy's theory of visual perception: An English translation of the Optics with introduction and commentary*. Philadelphia: The American Philosophical Society.

Smith, A. M. (1998). Ptolemy, Alhazen, and Kepler and the problem of optical images. *Arabic Sciences and Philosophy, 8*, 9–44.

Smith, A. M. (2001). *Alhacen's theory of visual perception: A critical edition, with English translation, introduction, and commentary, of Alhacen's De aspectibus, the medieval Latin version of Alhazen's* Kitab al-Manazir. Philadelphia: American Philosophical Society.

Smith, J. A., & Ross, W. D. (Eds.) (1910). *The works of Aristotle*. Vol. 4. Oxford: Clarendon.

Smith, R. (1738). *A compleat system of opticks in four books*. Cambridge: Published by the author.

Spillane, J. D. (1981). *The doctrine of the nerves*. Oxford: Oxford University Press.

Stampfer, S. (1833). *Die stroboskopischen Scheiben oder optische Zauberscheiben, deren Theorie und Wissenschaftliche Anwendung*. Vienna: Trentsensky & Vieweg.

Stevens, S. S. (1951). Mathematics, measurement, and psychophysics. In S. S. Stevens (Ed.) *Handbook of Experimental Psychology*. (pp. 1–49). New York: Wiley.

Stevens, S. S. (1975). *Psychophysics*. New York: Wiley.

Stratton, G. M. (1917). *Theophrastus and the Greek physiological psychology before Aristotle*. New York: Macmillan.

Strong, D. S. (1979). *Leonardo on the eye*. New York: Garland.

Sudhoff, K. (1907). *Tradition und Naturbeobachtung in der Illustrationen medizinischer Handschriften und Frühdrucke vornehmlich des 15. Jahrhunderts. Studien zur Geschichte der Medizin*. Leipzig: Barth.

Sutherland, N. S. (1973). Object recognition, In E.C. Carterette & M.P. Friedman (Eds.) *Handbook of perception*, Vol. 3. *Biology of perceptual systems*. (pp. 157–185). New York: Academic Press.

Swanston, M. T. & Wade, N. J. (1994). A peculiar Optical Phœnomenon. *Perception, 23*, 1107–1110.

Szily, A. von (1905). Bewegungsnachbild und Bewegungskontrast. *Zeitschrift für Psychologie und Physiologie der Sinnesorgane, 38*, 81–154.

Tatler, B. W. & Wade, N. J. (2003). On nystagmus, saccades, and fixations. *Perception, 32*, 167–184.

Taylor, J. (1738). *Le mechanisme ou le nouveau traité de l'anatomie du globe de l'oeil, avec l'usage de ses différentes parties, & de celles qui lui sont contigues*. Paris: David.

Taylor, J. (1750). *Mechanismus; oder, neue Abhandlung von künstlichen Zusammensetzung des menschlichen Auges*. Frankfurt: Stocks & Schilling,

Thompson, S. P. (1877). Some new optical illusions. *Report of the British Association for the Advancement of Science. Transactions of the Sections, 32*.

Thompson. S. P. (1880). Optical illusions of motion. *Brain, 3*, 289–298.

Thompson. S. P. (1910). A physiological effect of alternating magnetic field. *Proceedings of the Royal Society of London. Series B, 82*, 396–398.

Thomsen, E. (1919). Über Johannes Evangelista Purkinje und seine Werke. Purkinjes entoptische Phänomene. Auf Basis biographischer Daten und anderer Untersuchungen. *Skandanavisches Archiv für Physiologie, 37*, 1–116.

Thorwald, J. (1962). *Science and secrets of early medicine*. Trans. R. and C. Winston. London: Thames & Hudson.

Thouless, R. H. (1931). Phenomenal regression to the real object. I. *British Journal of Psychology, 21*, 339–359.

Titchener, E. B. (1901). Experimental psychology. *A manual of laboratory practice*. New York: Macmillan.

Treviranus, G. R. (1828). *Beiträge zur Anatomie und Physiologie der Sinneswerkzeuge des Menschen und der Thiere.* Bremen: Heyse.

Treviranus, G. R. (1835). *Beiträge zur Aufklärung der Erscheinungen und Gesetze des organischen Lebens.* Vol. 1, Issue 1. *Ueber die blättige Textur der Crystalllinse des Auges als Grund des Vermögens, einerlei Gegenstand in verschiedener Entfernung deutlich zu sehen, und über den innern Bau der Retina* (Bremen: Heyse)

Treviranus, G. R. (1837). *Beiträge zur Aufklärung der Erscheinungen und Gesetze des organischen Lebens.* Vol. 1, Issue 3. *Resultate neuer Untersuchungen über die Theorie des Sehens und über den innern Bau des Netzhaut des Auges.* Bremen: Heyse.

Tscherning, M. (1898). *Optique physiologique.* Paris: Carré and Naud.

Tscherning, M. (1900). *Physiologic optics.* Trans. C. Weiland. Philadelphia: Keystone.

Turnbull, H. W. (Ed.) (1960). *The correspondence of Isaac Newton. Vol. 2. 1676–1687.* Cambridge: Cambridge University Press.

Turner, G. L'E. (1998). *Scientific instruments 1500–1900. An introduction,* Berkeley, CA: University of California Press.

Turner, R. S. (1994). *In the eye's mind: Vision and the Helmholtz-Hering controversy.* Princeton, NJ: Princeton University Press.

Uhr, L. (Ed.)(1966). *Pattern recognition. Theory, experiment, computer simulations, and dynamic models of form perception and discovery.* New York: Wiley.

Ungerleider, L. G. & Mishkin, M. (1982). Two cortical visual systems. In D. J. Ingle, M. A. Goodale & R. J. W. Mansfield (Eds.), *Analysis of visual behaviour* (pp. 549–586). Cambridge, MA: MIT Press.

Van Essen, D. C., Anderson, C. H. & Felleman, D. J. (1992). Information processing in the primate visual system: An integrated systems perspective. *Science, 255,* 419–423.

Varioli, C. (1591). *Anatomiae, sive de resolutione corporis humani.* Frankfurt: Wechel & Fischer.

Vernon, M. D. (1970). *Perception through experience.* London: Methuen.

Verriest, G. (1990). Life, eye disease and work of Joseph Plateau. *Documenta Ophthalmologica, 74,* 9–20.

Vesalius, A. (1543). *De humani corporis fabrica.* Basel: Oporini.

Vieth, G. U. A. (1818). Ueber die Richtung der Augen. *Annalen der Physik, 28,* 233–253.

Vital-Durand, F., Atkinson, J. & Braddick, O. (Eds.) (1996). *Infant vision.* Oxford: Oxford University Press.

Vitellonis (Witelo) (1572). *Perspectiva. Thuringopoloni Opticae. Libri Decem.* F. Risner (Ed.). Basel: Gallia.

Volkmann, A. W. (1846). Sehen. In R. Wagner (Ed.) *Handwörterbuch der Physiologie.* Vol. 3. (pp. 265–351). Braunschweig: Vieweg.

Volkmann, A. W. (1859). Das Tachistoscop, ein Instrument, welches bei Untersuchung des momentanen Sehens den Gebrauch des elektischen Funkens ersetz. *Berichte über die Verhandlungen der königlichen sächsischen Akademie der Wissenschaften mathematische-naturwissenschaftliche Klasse, 2,* 90–98.

Volkmann, A. W. (1862). *Physiologische Untersuchungen im Gebiete der Optik.* Leipzig: Breitkopf and Härtel.

Vollgraff, J. A. (1936). Snellius' notes on the reflection and refraction of rays. *Osiris, 1,* 718–725.

Volpicelli, P. (1876). Scientific worthies. *Nature, 13,* 501–503.

Volta A. (1800). On the electricity excited by the mere contact of conducting substances of different species. *Philosophical Transactions of the Royal Society, 90,* 403–431.

Voltaire. (François Marie Arouet). (1738). *Elémens de la philosophi de Neuton.* Amsterdam: Desbordes.

Wade, N. J. (1983). *Brewster and Wheatstone on vision.* London: Academic Press.

Wade, N. J. (1987). On the late invention of the stereoscope. *Perception, 16,* 785–818.

Wade, N. (1990). *Visual allusions: Pictures of perception.* London: Erlbaum.

Wade, N. J. (1994). A selective history of the study of visual motion aftereffects. *Perception, 23,* 1111–1134.

Wade, N. J. (1998a). *A natural history of vision.* Cambridge, MA: MIT Press.

Wade, N. J. (1998b) Light and sight since antiquity. *Perception, 27,* 637–670.

Wade, N. J. (2003a). *Destined for distinguished oblivion: The scientific vision of William Charles Wells (1757–1817).* New York: Kluwer/Plenum.

Wade, N. J. (2003b). The search for a sixth sense: The cases for vestibular, muscle, and temperature senses. *Journal of the History of the Neurosciences, 12,* 175–202.

Wade, N. J. (2004a). Good figures. *Perception, 32,* 127–134.

Wade, N. J. (2004b). Philosophical instruments and toys: Optical devices extending the art of seeing. *Journal of the History of the Neurosciences, 13,* 102–124.

Wade, N. J. (2004c). Visual neuroscience before the neuron. *Perception, 33,* 869–889.

Wade, N. J. (2004d). Medical societies and insanity in late-eighteenth century London: The fight between Andrew Marshal and John Hunter. *Journal of the History of the Neurosciences,* in press.

Wade, N. J. (2005). The vertiginous philosophers: Erasmus Darwin and William Charles Wells on vertigo. In C. U. M. Smith & R. G. Arnott (Eds.) *The genius of Erasmus Darwin: Proceedings of a bicentenary conference.* London: Ashgate. In press.

Wade, N. J., & Brožek, J. (2001). *Purkinje's vision: The dawning of neuroscience.* Mahwah, NJ: Erlbaum.

Wade, N. J., Brožek, J., and Hoskovec, J. (2002). Images of Purkinje's vision. *History & Philosophy of Psychology, 4 (2),* 1–9.

Wade, N. J., & Finger, S. (2001). The eye as an optical instrument. From *camera obscura* to Helmholtz's perspective. *Perception, 30,* 1157–1177.

Wade, N. J., & Finger, S. (2003). William Porterfield (ca. 1696–1771) and his phantom limb: An overlooked first self-report by a man of medicine. *Neurosurgery, 52,* 1196–1199.

Wade, N. J., & Heller, D. (1997). Scopes of perception: The experimental manipulation of space and time. *Psychological Research, 60,* 227–237.

Wade, N. J., & Hughes, P. (1999). Fooling the eyes: *trompe l'oeil* and reverse perspective. *Perception, 28,* 1115–1119.

Wade, N. J., Kovács, G., and Vidnyánszky, Z. (2003). Inverted faces. *Perception, 32,* 1–6.

Wade, N. J., Ono, H., & Lillakas, L. (2001). Leonardo da Vinci's struggles with representations of reality. *Leonardo, 34,* 231–235.

Wade, N. J., Tatler, B. W. & Heller, D. (2003). Dodge-ing the issue: Dodge, Javal, Hering, and the measurement of saccades in eye movement research. *Perception, 32,* 793–804.

Wade, N. J., & Verstraten, F. A. J. (1998). Introduction and historical overview. In G. Mather, F. Verstraten, & S. Anstis (Eds.) *The motion after-effect: A modern perspective.* (pp 1–23). Cambridge, MA: MIT Press.

Wallin, J. E. W. (1905). *Optical illusions of reversible perspective: A volume of historical and experimental researches.* Princeton, NJ: Published by the author.

Walls, G. L. (1962). *The vertebrate eye and its adaptive relations.* New York: Hafner.

Walsh, V. & Cowey, A. (1998). Magnetic stimulation studies of visual cognition. *Trends in Cognitive Sciences, 2,* 103–110.

Watson, J. B. (1913). Psychology as the behaviorist views it. *Psychological Review, 20,* 158–177.

Watson, R. I. (1968). *The great psychologists. From Aristotle to Freud.* ed. 2. Philadelphia: Lippincott.

Watson, R. I. (1979). *Basic writings in the history of psychology.* New York: Oxford University Press.

Weber, E. H. (1834). *De pulsu, resorptione, auditu et tactu.* Leipzig: Koehler.

Weber, E. H. (1846). Der Tastsinn und das Gemeingefühl. In R. Wagner (Ed.) *Handwörterbuch der Physiologie*. Vol. 3. (pp. 481–588). Braunschweig: Vieweg.

Weiskrantz, L. (1986). *Blindsight: A case study and its implications*. Oxford: Oxford University Press.

Wells, W. C. (1792). *An essay upon single vision with two eyes: Together with experiments and observations on several other subjects in optics*. London: Cadell.

Wells, W. C. (1794a). Reply to Dr. Darwin on vision. *The Gentleman's Magazine and Historical Chronicle, 64*, 794–797.

Wells, W. C. (1794b). Reply to Dr. Darwin on vision. *The Gentleman's Magazine and Historical Chronicle, 64*, 905–907.

Wells, W. C. (1811). Observations and experiments on vision. *Philosophical Transactions of the Royal Society, 101*, 378–391.

Wendt, G. R. (1951). Vestibular functions. In S. S. Stevens (Ed.) *Handbook of experimental psychology*. (pp. 1191–1223). New York, Wiley.

Wertheimer, M. (1912). Experimentelle Studien über das Sehen von Bewegung. *Zeitschrift für Psychologie, 60*, 321–378.

Wertheimer, M. (1923). Untersuchungen zur Lehre von der Gestalt. II *Psychologische Forschung, 4*, 301–350.

Wertheimer, M. (1938). Gestalt theory. In W. D. Ellis (Ed.) *A source book of Gestalt psychology*. (pp. 1–11). New York: The Humanities Press.

Westfall, R. S. (1980). *Never at rest. A biography of Isaac Newton*. Cambridge: Cambridge University Press.

Wheatstone, C. (1827). Description of the kaleidophone, or phonic kaleidoscope: A new philosophical toy, for the illustration of several interesting and amusing acoustical and optical phenomena. *Quarterly Journal of Science, Literature and Art, 23*, 344–351.

Wheatstone, C. (1838). Contributions to the physiology of vision—Part the first. On some remarkable, and hitherto unobserved, phenomena of binocular vision. *Philosophical Transactions of the Royal Society, 128*, 371–394.

Wheatstone, C. (1845). Note on the electro-magnetic chronoscope. *Walker's Electrical Magazine, 2*, 86–93.

Wheatstone, C. (1852). Contributions to the physiology of vision—Part the second. On some remarkable, and hitherto unobserved, phenomena of binocular vision. *Philosophical Transactions of the Royal Society, 142*, 1–17.

Whytt, R. (1765). *Observations on the nature, causes, and cure of those disorders which have commonly been called nervous hypochondriac, or hysteric*. Edinburgh: Becket, Du Hondt, and Balfour.

Wiener, N. (1948). *Cybernetics: Control and communication in the animal and machine*. Cambridge, MA: MIT Press.

Wilkes, A. L. & Wade, N. J. (1997). Bain on neural networks. *Brain and Cognition, 33*, 295–305.

Willats, J. (1997). *Art and representation: New principles in the analysis of pictures*. Princeton, NJ: Princeton University Press.

Willis, T. (1664). *Cerebri anatome: cui accessit nervorum descriptio et usus*. London: Martyn and Allestry.

Willis, T. (1672). *De anima brutorum*. London: Wells & Scott.

Wohlgemuth, A. (1911). On the after-effect of seen movement. *British Journal of Psychology. Monograph Supplement, 1*, 1–117.

Wollaston, W. H. (1824). On the semi decussation of the optic nerves. *Philosophical Transactions of the Royal Society, 114*, 222–231.

Wundt, W. (1862). *Beiträge zur Theorie der Sinneswahrnehmung*. Leipzig: Winter.

Wundt, W. (1874). *Grundzüge der physiologischen Psychologie*. Leipzig: Engelmann.

Wundt, W. (1900). Zur Kritik tachistoscopische Versuche. *Philosophische Studien, 15*, 287–317.

Yin, R. K. (1969). Looking at upside-down faces. *Journal of Experimental Psychology, 81*, 141–145.

Young, L. R., Henn, V., & Scherberger, H. (2001). *Fundamentals of the theory of movement perception by Dr. Ernst Mach*. New York: Kluwer/Plenum.

Young, T. (1793). Observations on vision. *Philosophical Transactions of the Royal Society, 83*, 169–181.

Young, T. (1800). Outlines of experiments and enquiries respecting sound and light. *Philosophical Transactions of the Royal Society, 90*, 106–150.

Young T. (1801). On the mechanism of the eye. *Philosophical Transactions of the Royal Society, 91*, 23–88.

Young, T. (1802a). On the theory of lights and colours. *Philosophical Transactions of the Royal Society, 92*, 12–48.

Young, T. (1802b). An account of some cases of the production of colours, not hitherto described. *Philosophical Transactions of the Royal Society, 92*, 387–397.

Young, T. (1807). *A course of lectures on natural philosophy and the mechanical arts*. 2 Vols. London: Johnson .

Young, T. (1894). *Oevres Ophthalmologique de Thomas Young*. Trans. M. H. E. Tscherning. Copenhagen: Höst.

Young, T. (2002). *Thomas Young's lectures on natural philosophy and the mechanical arts*. 4 Vols. Bristol: Thoemmes.

Zeki, S. (1993). *A vision of the brain*. Oxford: Blackwell.

Zeki, S. (1999) *Inner vision. An exploration of art and the brain*. Oxford: Oxford University Press.

Zemplen, G. (2004). *The history of light, colour, and vision. Introduction, texts, problems*. Bern: Bern Studies.

Ziggelaar, A. (1983). *François de Aguilón S. J. (1567–1617) Scientist and architect*. Rome: Institutum Historicum S. I.

Ziggelaar, A. (1993). The early debate concerning wave-theory. In M. Petry (Ed.) *Hegel and Newtonianism*. (pp. 517–529). Amsterdam: Kluwer.

Zinn, J. G. (1755). *Descriptio anatomica oculi humani, iconibus illustrata*. Göttingen: Vandenhoeck.

Zöllner, F. (1862). Ueber eine neue Art anorthoscopische Zerrbilder. *Annalen der Physik und Chemie, 117*, 477–484.

Zotterman, Y. (1959). Thermal sensations. In J. Field, H. W. Magoun & V. E. Hall (Eds.). *Handbook of physiology. Neurophysiology*. Vol. 1. (pp. 431–458). Washington DC: American Physiological Society.

Name Index

Subject Index